AMERICAN INDUSTRY

and the

EUROPEAN IMMIGRANT

1860-1885

Studies in Economic History

Published in coöperation with the
Committee on Research in Economic History

American Industry and the European Immigrant 1860-1885

Charlotte Erickson

HARVARD UNIVERSITY PRESS
Cambridge, Massachusetts
1957

To My Parents

PREFACE

In 1864 Congress legalized the importation of contract labor. Twenty-one years later it declared the practice illegal. It has commonly been assumed that between these dates American industry imported great numbers of contract laborers from Europe to cut wages and break strikes. The Knights of Labor are thought to have obtained a victory in Congress when they succeeded in getting the Foran Act of 1885 passed, an Act which they claimed would remove the threat to union organization presumed to lie in industry's recruitment of hosts of unskilled Southern and Eastern European agriculturists contracted to work at low wages.

The thesis of this book is that contract labor was rare in America during the years after the Civil War, and never reached the proportions claimed by the advocates of a law against its importation. When, on rare occasions, American industrialists did resort to importations it was to bring in highly skilled workers for particular jobs. No mass importations of unskilled workers were made by mine operators and railroad contractors. The bulk of the immigration from Italy and Hungary in the eighties was as voluntary as the exodus from Sweden in the sixties and Ireland and Germany in the early fifties had been.

American industry, in fact, concerned itself very little with the process of immigration, although it was glad enough to employ those who found their way to American shores. Even the Act of 1864 to encourage immigration did not result from a general pressure from industrialists. Nor did American employers later, at the time of the anti-contract labor laws, the abortive literacy tests, or the eventual quota acts, speak with a united or intensely interested voice on the subject of immigration. Industry itself did not organize the immigrant labor market; nor did it provide constructive measures for dealing with abuses.

While industrialists ignored the issue, the labor movement, weak as it was in the post Civil War period, was constantly debating the immigration question. Various groups within the labor movement were feeling their way toward some kind of policy with regard to immigration, either labor or government sponsored, which would protect them from the sudden appearance of strangers in an area during a trade dispute.

The movement for legislation against contract labor, when taken up by the Knights of Labor in the eighties, was merely one of several ideas on the immigrant problem being discussed in the labor movement. The legislative success of the anti-contract labor movement, and the disappearance from the scene shortly thereafter of the Knights of Labor, frustrated the continuation and development of the more enlightened of those ideas. The American Federation of Labor became absorbed first in trying to strengthen by amendment the patently ineffective anti–contract labor laws, then in literacy tests, and finally put its weight behind demands for a quota system. Even today the quota system of restricting immigrants according to nationality rather than economic reality is regarded as a labor measure.

The contract labor laws put American labor on a track of prejudice and fear with regard to immigration which has become tradition and policy, unassailable and inviolate. Although Norman Ware stated the matter correctly, other labor historians have tended to misinterpret the origins of the contract labor laws. The contract labor laws were originally the program of a highly specialized, a-typical group of craft workers whose skills could be duplicated and whose strikes could be broken only by the importation on contract of skilled workers from England and Belgium. This group, the window glass workers, realizing that their case was a rather special one, sought support by playing on the prejudices against "new immigrants" which other Knights felt, and thus broadened their appeal.

Other groups in the Knights of Labor responded to the racialist appeal because in strike after strike they were being beaten with immigrant strikebreakers. But these strikebreakers were not contract laborers. They were immigrants and others supplied to manufacturers by private labor agencies in large cities. The prohibition of contract labor was unrelated to this more general problem of labor organization. Yet the American Federation of Labor when it emerged at the end of the eighties became wedded to a fruitless policy of trying to make those laws work through repeated amendment.

There is no convenient core of source materials for a study of this kind. Those which have been consulted are scattered among a large number of libraries in the United States, the British Isles, and the Scandinavian countries; and I have received assistance from many librarians. In nearly a score of United States libraries the most important sources used were corporation manuscript collections at the Baker Library, Harvard University, and the Newberry Library in Chicago, to which I have been guided in every case by someone who had worked on them for another purpose; corporation annual reports; labor, trade, and daily newspapers; the Powderly papers at Catholic University Library and the Henry Carey papers at the Historical Society of Pennsylvania; collections of trade-union materials at the University of Michigan, the Johns Hopkins University, Harvard University, and the University of Wisconsin; manuscripts of the old Federal Bureau of Immigration and United States consuls in Europe at the National Archives.

I have not been able to work on equally good sources in all the immigrant–yielding countries. British, Irish, and Scandinavian materials, including manuscript letters from consuls in the United States, government emigration reports, trade, labor, and immigrant journals, have been dealt with more thoroughly than either German or Italian sources. While I was doing research abroad on this subject in 1948 and 1949, travel restrictions and the disorganization of the libraries on account of the war limited my work on German sources. Fortunately, the British Museum and the Harvard libraries house reasonably good collections of German newspapers, immigrant journals, and the official publications of the various German states. I have not worked at all in Italy, but have relied heavily on the flood of investigations under the aegis of the United States government which began to concern itself with immigration at the time that Italian immigration to the United States became a significant movement.

My two years of study and research abroad were made possible by fellowships from the American Association of University Women, the Social Science Research Council, and the Fulbright Commission. I am indebted to Professor Paul Gates and Professor Maurice Neufeld for encouragement and advice during the period of seven years since I first began this study as a doctoral thesis at Cornell University, as well as for their careful reading of this manuscript in its early stages. I was able to spend several months revising the thesis with the assistance of the Gertrude A. Gillmore Fellowship of the Cornell Department of History.

Professor David Glass and Mr. H. L. Beales gave me many helpful suggestions during the hours which they generously spent with me discussing the problems of this study while I was a research student at the London School of Economics. I have received valuable guidance to the resources of the Baker Library from Professor Arthur H. Cole. Professor Oscar Handlin has given me the benefit of his advice on several occasions. Others who have pointed out to me sources which I have been able to use, or lent me material from their own files, are Harry James Brown, Irene Neu, Rev. Henry J. Browne, Albert Hess Leisinger, Sam Watson, James Bowman, F. L. Preston, John Wilson, the late Agnes Inglis, and Ingrid Gaustad Semmigsen. I should also like to express my gratitude to the busy men and women in the T.U.C., the British Labour Party, and the English Speaking Union in several of the industrial cities of England, Scotland, and Wales for all they did to make my visits to their cities both profitable and comfortable. My sister, Evangeline Erickson Hogue, and my husband, G. L. Watt, have helped with correcting the manuscript.

Charlotte Erickson

Dover, England, April 1955

CONTENTS

PART I

THE SEARCH FOR SKILL

Chapter 1

ORGANIZED EFFORTS
TO PROMOTE IMMIGRATION

When, in 1864, the Thirty-second Congress bestowed the official sanction of the federal government on the importation of immigrant contract labor, the legislators were not introducing, even on paper, any startling innovation in methods of recruitment of labor for American industry. Contract labor, the system of signing up workers for a period of service during which transportation advances were to be repaid, was a form of the old indenture system of colonial America, long ago decayed, which had been refurbished in order to get factory industry started in the United States. In time, and for reasons not based on fact, contract labor came to be associated in the popular mind with unskilled Oriental and Southern European workers for industry. But what the Republican sponsors of the contract labor law of 1864 had in mind was the encouragement of immigration of skilled industrial workers, chiefly from Great Britain.

Such a policy had precedents going back to the early days of the Republic. American industry had, in fact, for many years been following unofficially the course charted by Alexander Hamilton in his "Report on Manufactures" which was now merely revived and given official blessing by a Congress not unsympathetic with Hamilton's broader faith in a strong central government which might force the pace of industrialization. Hamilton, it will be remembered, had advocated attracting skilled artisans from Europe to set machinery in operation and to supervise native women and

3

children who were to provide the bulk of the industrial labor force.[1] Until Irish and German immigrants in the forties and fifties began replacing New England farm girls in mills in Lowell and elsewhere, this was what many would-be industrial capitalists did in recruiting a labor force.

In those branches of manufacture which had characterized the industrial revolution in Britain, America drew heavily on British experience via the immigrant. Even before Britain repealed the century–old prohibitions on the emigration of "artisans" in 1824, many a worker found his way out of the country and to the New World by one ruse or another at the inducement of American capitalists wanting to start a woolen or cotton mill, an iron mill, or a brass button factory.[2] The importance of men like Samuel Slater and the Schofield brothers, who introduced British machinery into the American textile industry, needs no elaboration. Students of the early stages of the industrial revolution in the United States have unearthed many examples of industry's importation of skilled workmen.[3] Nearly every new industry begun in America before 1840 was fertilized with British skills.

This is not to imply that American employers imported British workmen on a large scale. The cost of bringing out a single worker on contract, forwarding his transportation money and expenses, forced Americans to keep their direct importations to a minimum. These costs were particularly high in the days of illegal importation when the Waltham Company on one occasion paid $448.22 for the passage of a single English machinist.[4] Consequently, skilled workers were imported only in a limited number of circumstances: to nurse a new industry into life; to oversee or superintend a new factory or mill;[5] to operate or service complicated machinery; and to add a new process[6] or a finer make of goods to an existing industry.[7]

The terms of the contracts on which some of these immigrants came, in the years before 1840, suggest the importance which American manufacturers attached to their skills and knowledge of British machinery. Even when transportation advances were to be repaid by the immigrant, he was bound for a longer period of service than was necessary to clear the loan. Whereas after 1850, contracts were rarely drawn up for more than a year's duration, what information we have on early contracts indicates that the immigrant was generally bound for two or three, and sometimes as many as five or six, years.[8] Thus employers had to carry these key men through panics and depression and were in that sense as much committed as was the contract laborer. These long contracts probably measured the fear of the importer of losing his skilled men to rivals. Other immigrants brought to the United States on contracts were not required to repay transportation advances.[9] Some machinists were induced to come out on contracts containing profit–sharing clauses.[10]

To a great extent the workers trained in Britain's industries formed the aristocracy of the American labor force. In an already paternalist age they received favored treatment. Not left to fend for themselves, as were the unskilled Irish immigrants, these skilled contract laborers were often provided with specially built corporation houses.[11] A good example of the personal attention British immigrants received from their employers is to be found in the letters of John Wilson to his family in Yorkshire. Wilson worked in a Lowell carpet factory. Not only was he able to get assurances of jobs for his family and friends who were planning to emigrate, but when they arrived in July 1849, he was given the day off to go to Boston to meet them and bring all nine arrivals from his village in Yorkshire direct to the home of the principal of the carpet cloth-room whose wife nursed Wilson's sister-in-law back to health from an attack of cholera contracted on the journey.[12]

The English and Scottish workers as the "prima donnas" of the labor force were not entirely approved of by American manufacturers who very early sought to free themselves from reliance upon such independent and mobile workers. Textile manufacturers complained that although their immigrant workmen were skilled they were not "regular in their habits," a remark which referred to their taste for drink, and were not always reliable.[13] English workmen sometimes refused to instruct native apprentices and occasionally objected to having other workers near their benches or even working in the same building.[14] An employer might be forced to bargain with the trade-union of his English or Scottish workers.[15] Moreover they were difficult to retain as employees, for these immigrants frequently returned to England or set up mills of their own if they were dissatisfied.[16] One group of Sheffield cutlers at Waterbury, Connecticut, for example, old Chartists that they were, moved to Walden, New York, to establish a coöperative factory when their employers changed the terms of their employ in an effort to tighten factory discipline and standardize production methods.[17]

Thus until the Civil War produced something like a labor supply crisis, American industry was willing to recruit skill sporadically, for specific jobs, often at considerable expense, focusing its attention constantly upon such innovations as would enable it to rely less upon British workmen with their cherished independence and to employ more widely workers, whether native women or Irish immigrants, who had no such tradition. As to the recruitment of skill, each firm filled its requirements through its own agents and contacts in the British working population.

As the nation shifted to a wartime economy, many young men who might otherwise have entered the labor force were conscripted;[18] the expansion of war production called for an absolute increase in the labor force; and at the same time immigration, which had been since 1840 supplying workers at an increasing rate during prosperous years, fell off sharply. This situation led to two experiments in organizing the skilled immigrant labor market. Experiments in large-scale recruitment of skilled labor by centralized agencies, organized as private corporations, were inaugurated toward the end of the war to supply the needs of industry on a permanent basis and to supersede firm-by-firm recruitment. These experiments were encouraged by federal legislation. At the same time, through its Immigration Bureau, the central government made its sole attempt before 1907 to assist in the distribution of immigrant workers to jobs.

These two parallel schemes, the one private and the other public, both of which were abandoned by 1868, are of great importance in American immigration history and have not received the attention they deserve. No disinterested system for distributing immigrants to industry was developed to succeed these schemes. The great flood-tide of newcomers during the next fifty years could expect no help from federal officials in finding jobs. The failure of private agencies to establish themselves as distributors of skilled labor meant that industrialists had to fall back upon their own methods and resources in recruitment and that many a skilled worker during the following decades went to work digging ditches or laying railroad track after he landed in America.

Mine operators, railroad officials, and iron manufacturers began to complain of labor shortages and high wages in 1863 and 1864.[19] A few instances can be found of firms like the copper mine companies in the Calumet and Hecla region in Michigan or the

Chicago and Alton Railroad which took steps to import workers.[20] Illinois coal operators urged Lincoln to instruct State Department officials in Belgium to encourage the emigration of miners.[21] In spite of some uneasiness about the supply of labor, industrial spokesmen were not the leading promoters of the recruitment schemes of the Civil War period.

The main work of organizing agencies for recruitment, of providing the economic arguments for popularizing the movement, and of pressing for federal action was carried out by a relatively small group of men who were not primarily manufacturers and whose efforts on behalf of immigration did not succeed in obtaining the wholehearted support of American industrial capitalists. Henry Carey, whose economic writings since 1844 had raised the twin standards of protective tariff and immigration promotion as companion policies which he claimed would promote rapid industrialization, was the central figure in this group of immigration advocates.[22] Carey not only supplied the propaganda arguments which were repeated and simplified by his followers, but also, through his business and political friends, pressed for federal action to stimulate emigration from Europe.[23]

Some of Carey's business friends undertook to persuade industrialists to unite in recruiting immigrant labor. The president of the Wyandotte Mills in Detroit, Eber B. Ward, later president of the Iron and Steel Association, wrote to Carey late in 1862 to assure him that the mining companies of Lake Superior were taking steps to collect a pooled fund for the purpose of importing labor.[24] One of the leading promoters of the Boston Foreign Emigrant Society, another project envisaging a pooled employer fund, was Edward Atkinson, the textile manufacturer, who was known as a "disciple" of Carey. Associates of Carey in the wholesale branch of the Philadelphia iron industry initiated the move to organize the American Emigrant Company as a labor-recruiting agency.

At the same time as he agitated among manufacturers, Carey approached his friends in the Republican cabinet. As early as 1861 he obtained the approval of Secretary of the Treasury Chase to the principle of government encouragement of immigration.[25] While the Secretary of State, William H. Seward, probably needed little persuasion on the subject, he was undoubtedly encouraged to take some action by E. Peshine Smith, one of his constant supporters in New York politics and another "disciple" of Carey. At any rate, during the same month, September 1862, that Smith declined a suggestion from Carey that he go abroad to stir up emigration,[26] Seward circularized United States officials in Europe pointing out the high rates of wages paid in America and urged eastern Chambers of Commerce to try to find means of lowering emigrant fares.[27]

Seward's circulars were responsible, at least indirectly, for the birth of more than one of the agencies organized during the following year to supply immigrants to American industry. The publication of his note to consuls brought a rush of would-be immigrants to American legations in European cities to apply for financial aid to get to America.[28] United States consuls, eager to supplement their meager incomes, sent back to the State Department a flood of suggestions for government aid to emigration.[29] The Consul in Carlsruhe asked that the United States government employ a private firm of recruiting agents which "would guarantee to send twelve thousand emigrants in ten months," a firm in which his colleague in Mannheim was a partner.[30] One of the two most important such agencies to be started, the Boston Foreign Emigrant Society, appears to have been organized primarily in response to the appeal from the State Department.

During 1863 the United States Consul in London was paying from a "secret service fund" a certain Scottish agent, Peter Sinclair. Sinclair, who had spent several years in America prior to the war, returned to Britain at its outbreak, with five thousand Illinois Central posters, to work full time explaining the Northern cause to British workingmen, invariably linking his explanation with propaganda for emigration.[31] Early in 1863, Sinclair suggested to Seward that organizations of merchants such as the New York and Boston Boards of Trade might unite to raise passage money for emigrants whom he selected in England. Seward immediately forwarded Sinclair's suggestion to the Boston Board of Trade with the remark that in England, Ireland, Norway, Hamburg, and Bremen, "a feeling pervaded the very best classes of . . . workmen to emigrate to the United States," but that most of them lacked the small sum needed to pay the passage.[32]

The Boston Board of Trade found the problem which Seward handed them a nasty one "without public or private funds to induce emigration." As a beginning, they sent circulars to a large

number of manufacturing establishments requesting information
on rates of wages, prospective demand for labor, prices of board
and food, and kinds of dwellings for factory operatives. Answers
were received from about eighty cotton and woolen mills, machine
shops, and boot and shoe factories. These documents with photo-
graphs and engravings "of some of our best mills and workshops"
were sent to England for distribution by Sinclair.[33]

The work of the Boston men did not stop there. Late in 1863
a meeting was held in the Board of Trade rooms in Boston at
which a Foreign Emigrant Aid Society was established. This Society, in contrast to the American Emigrant Company, appears to
have been a bona fide organization of manufacturers. Textile
manufacturers were heavily represented in its thirty-two officers
among whom were Edward Atkinson, William Gray, George W.
Lyman, William Dwight, George Stark, James Lawrence, Thomas
J. Coolidge, Richard Borden, and J. Wiley Edmands. Machine
makers and iron manufacturers, such as William Amory and Israel
Whitney, were also on the board. Interestingly enough, however,
the board contained a strong sprinkling of men with transportation interests, who stood to gain from any increase in immigration,
with Chester William Chapin of the Boston and Albany and John
Murray Forbes of the Chicago, Burlington and Quincy in prominent positions, as were Edward S. Tobey and George B. Upton
whose investments were chiefly in shipping.[34]

Wishing to attract "artizans and laborers of more varied skill
and experience in those branches with which we are less familiar,"
the Society aimed to begin operations with a fund of $200,000 col-
lected from manufacturers for gifts or loans to emigrants. After
four months of collections, however, the $200,000 target was still
a long way off. Enough money had been raised by the first of May
to permit the appointment of an agent, but nothing was available
for emigrant passages. If manufacturers wanted Sinclair, as agent
of the Society, to advance fares, they had to supply the money for
each importation.[35] Clearly a government fund for passage loans
would relieve manufacturers of direct contributions and enable
the Society to function without asking them for donations.

During the early months of 1864 the American Emigrant Company was also being organized as a labor-recruiting agency. Although its aim, like that of the Boston Society, was to import
skilled labor for American industry, it differed from the latter or-

ganization in that it was a private business organized to procure labor for manufacturers, and its shareholders intended to derive profits from the undertaking.

The American Emigrant Company, as reorganized in March 1864, merged two previously unconnected firms. On 17 June 1863, the American Emigrant Company had been incorporated in Connecticut as a land agency with wide powers.[36] The Hartford members of this original company were a group of bankers, lawyers, and politicians closely associated both professionally and socially. Although their immediate interest was in selling the Company's Iowa lands, their connections with eastern business, their political influence in the Connecticut Republican Party, and their links with important eastern newspapers made them an ideal nucleus of men to coöperate with New York and Philadelphia iron warehousemen and hardware manufacturers interested in recruiting immigrants for industry.[37]

Meanwhile in New York, the editor of the *Hardware Reporter*, John Williams, was becoming interested in labor recruitment. The impetus probably came from Morris, Wheeler and Company, a Philadelphia firm of iron dealers, associates of Henry Carey, who in September 1863 asked Williams to prepare a paper for circulation in Britain.[38] Morris and Wheeler were active in trying to get support from iron manufacturers for the project. Some New England manufacturers were brought into the scheme through the efforts of Russell and Erwin Manufacturing Company, hardware manufacturers in New Britain, Connecticut, who had warehouses in New York.[39] Through them, Williams was, as he said, "thrown into contact with" the Hartford directors of the American Emigrant Company.[40] From December 1863 to March 1864, attempts were made to collect funds from iron manufacturers for stimulating emigration. By early March, Williams had formally joined forces with the American Emigrant Company under its Connecticut charter with an authorized capital of a million dollars.[41]

The first efforts to collect money from manufacturers were apparently no more promising than those of the Boston Society. Williams became, as a result, an ardent advocate of government financial aid to immigration. At first urging that the government appropriate three million dollars toward emigrant passages, he later modified the proposal in a letter to Seward to a single million.[42] The money should be placed under a board of trustees representing the recruiting industries to secure its "most effective and prudent use," for according to Williams, "judicious importation" could never be carried on by government officials. During May 1864, when bills to encourage immigration were being considered in Congress, the American Emigrant Company circulated petitions in favor of a revolving fund appropriated by the government, and obtained signatures from 185 manufacturers, merchants, bankers, and coal operators in Pennsylvania, New York, Connecticut, Massachusetts, and New Hampshire. Seventy-two of the signatures were from Hartford itself, the home of the American Emigrant Company.[43] What the Company really asked for was a kind of railroad land grant in money for immigration with the funds completely under its control.

By 1864 several interests were awaiting government action on the immigration question: would-be emigrants whose hopes had been raised by consuls and other government agents; consuls themselves who wanted commissions for selecting immigrants; steamship and railroad interests; manufacturers seeking to curb the rise in wages. Heading the movement, however, were the new recruitment agencies seeking government funds with which to run their businesses. When Lincoln, in his annual message to Congress in 1863, urged government action to stimulate immigration, even a labor journal agreed cautiously that if the President "can point out the manner of proceeding, so as to swell our population to one hundred millions of people without injury to the laboring masses now here, we will hail the movement as one of the best of the ages."[44]

The Act to Encourage Immigration, which was approved by the President on 4 July 1864, failed to fulfill the hopes of the emigrant agencies. During the debates Congress rejected all proposals, including Seward's, for assisted passages paid for by government funds. In the end the only gesture toward reviving the indenture system included in the Act was the provision that immigrant labor contracts which had been registered with the United States Commissioner of Immigration were to be valid in the courts. Unfulfilled contracts could serve as a lien upon future land acquired by the immigrant.[45] This seal of blessing on contract labor was not enough to revive the system on a large scale.

For the rest, Congress appropriated a mere $25,000 to be used for the administrative expenses of an office of Commissioner of Immigration in the State Department and a United States Immigrant Office in the port of New York. The duties of the federal superintendent at New York merely duplicated the functions state authorities were already performing with some measure of success to protect immigrants from fraud on their arrival. No federal officials were appointed in the other immigrant-receiving ports, none of which had facilities comparable to those available for immigrants at New York.[46] Federal protection of the immigrant was not implemented: the superintendent at New York did not even have offices in the immigrant-receiving depot at Castle Garden.

With the limited funds at their disposal the efforts of government officials to aid the distribution of immigrants to industry were indeed feeble. For the most part they had to work through existing channels—recruitment agencies, like the American Emigrant Company, state immigration boards, and consuls.

The successive commissioners of immigration in Washington and the superintendents at New York devoted most of their attention to the problem of distributing immigrants to jobs. This was the kernel of a very useful idea: public aid in finding employment for immigrants. After the Bureau of Immigration closed in 1868 no similar attempt to inform immigrants of wages and openings in the interior of the country was made by the federal government until 1907, virtually at the end of the great migration.

Hampered by inadequate funds the federal officials were not in a position to give the experiment an adequate test had they been so minded. While they encouraged United States consuls and diplomatic agents to publicize the terms of the Act to Encourage Immigration,[47] the more disinterested of the several men who served as commissioner during the Bureau's brief life found that they must constantly try to discourage the irresponsible and exaggerated statements consuls were inclined to make about wages in America.[48] The Bureau made an effort to obtain more accurate information on wages in various parts of the country by urging state officials and bureaus of immigration to cease their own recruiting activities and instead submit reports on local wages and the demand for labor to be tabulated in Washington and distributed among incoming immigrants.[49]

The Bureau was unable to undertake the more difficult task of supplying particular immigrants with jobs and particular employers with workers. Since the federal superintendent in New York City shared offices at No. 3 Bowling Green with the American Emigrant Company,[50] it is unlikely that he would have cared to infringe upon that agency's proposed scope of activity. The Commissioner of Immigration described the duty of federal officials at New York as one of "communicating all beneficial information to immigrants whether sought after or not" upon their arrival at the port and of refusing to give particulars about jobs.[51] On occasion the New York officials helped employers who were not willing to spend the money to bring workers out all the way from Europe by arranging for them to get access to Castle Garden to choose hands from among new arrivals.[52]

When the war ended it became abundantly clear that federal officials were unable to serve as distributors of labor largely because employers failed to make use of the Bureau. If for no other reason, the government agents could not give job particulars to immigrants because they themselves did not receive such information. The appointment of the Henry Carey enthusiast, E. Peshine Smith, as Commissioner of Immigration after the war heartened the American Emigrant Company officials[53] and provided a good test of whether or not employers could be induced to advance passage loans to obtain labor. Distressed by the "continued success of strikes by workmen of almost all kinds,"[54] Smith was eager to exploit his office to encourage immigration. Abandoning the caution of his predecessors, he offered more elaborate inducements in his letters to consuls and intending emigrants[55] and actually forwarded the American Emigrant Company's "Order to Import Workmen" to United States consuls[56] giving that Company a greater degree of official sanction than it had previously been able to obtain.

After a few months Smith was forced to admit that it was usually "only in the case of a need for skilled labor that employers resort to contracts abroad." Employers were not willing to incur all the risks of this mode of obtaining labor, that is, the dangers of "death, disability, and dishonesty."[57] Unable to find importers, Smith continued to assure applicants for jobs that they "would have no difficulty in finding employment immediately on [their] arrival, as labor is very much sought after by the various manufacturers at the present time, and the demand is likely to continue for years."[58] But this was a far cry from a government employment bureau.

For its part the American Emigrant Company, which advertised itself as the "handmaid of the new Immigration Bureau,'[59] provides an excellent case study in the problems met by the new recruitment agencies launched to supply American industry with skilled labor. While it never received official federal government endorsement,[60] its solicitations to employers for orders intimated as much and it did not want for what the British would call "guinea pig directors," prominent politicians, judges, bankers, railroad presidents, and clergymen who endorsed its work publicly.[61] The Company needed more than endorsements to fulfill its aims and the ranks of its paper supporters did not include many solid manufacturing interests.

When Congress failed to provide funds, the Company clearly had no intention of using its own capital to make loans to immigrants. Rather it turned to American industry for its working capital.

In soliciting the patronage of manufacturers the American Emigrant Company offered to supply labor in one of two ways. The employer could advance transportation money and fees to cover importation of the immigrant from Europe. This transaction was likely to require an advance by the employer of from $50 to $75 for a single skilled worker.[62] In the contract he signed with the Company's agent in Europe, the immigrant pledged twelve months' service to the employer who advanced his passage "according to all lawful and reasonable regulations prescribed" by the employer "for the observance of workmen. . . ." a provision probably intended to reduce trade unionism among imported workers.[63] The Company also offered a less expensive means of obtaining workers by which the employer need only advance enough money to cover transportation of the immigrant from New York City to the job plus the Company's fees. To effect this arrangement the Company secured permission from the authorities to make selections of workmen "who seem most suitable for the objects of its patrons," from newly arrived immigrants as they landed and also instructed its agents abroad to furnish skilled emigrants who paid their own way with letters of introduction to John Williams in New York.[64]

While the Company could expect a commission of 15 per cent from railroad and steamship firms for the tickets it sold to emigrants, its original plan was to gain its profits primarily from fees charged employers for skilled labor. Employers could later collect these fees from the wages of the immigrants, but if they did, the skilled worker was put in the position of refunding a considerably higher "fee" for securing his job than was the unskilled worker. The American Emigrant Company's fees for skilled workers ranged from $10 to $30 depending on the "quality" of the skill furnished, and it was believed by trade unionists that an extra charge was made for supplying strikebreakers.[65] To be a source of profit to the Company, the traffic in contract labor had to be financed by employers of skilled labor.

The funds which enabled the American Emigrant Company to send agents to Britain and Germany in the spring of 1864 appear to have come from the same group of hardware manufacturers and dealers in New York and Philadelphia who first approached John Williams on the subject of labor recruitment. Although it circularized capitalists all over the country in the interests of promoting the contract system and selling its publications for distribution abroad, the Company sought substantial financial support from the iron industry in particular. In seeking to enlist funds from iron manufacturers, John Williams obtained the assistance of Henry Carey whom he met for the first time personally in August 1864.[66]

In November 1864, Williams assured Carey that the latter's greatest service to the country could be in "bringing your influence to bear upon the Employers of labor in convincing them of the great importance of using the new law for promoting immigration." As a result, Carey began a series of articles for the *Iron Age* on the importance of importing labor. At Carey's suggestion, Williams called on the president of the Iron and Steel Association, Eber B. Ward, and other iron manufacturers to urge that pressure be brought on the ironmakers to supply funds for immigration.[67]

When the American Iron and Steel Association met in Pittsburgh in February 1865, Williams was there to try to get money for the American Emigrant Company. Speaking to the Convention, he commended their action in favor of duties on iron and proposed his supplementary method of strengthening the American iron industry, the system organized by the American Emigrant Company for importing contract labor.[68]

At this and subsequent meetings of the Association, the members would go no farther than to adopt a resolution: "That we favor, and that we welcome the unrestricted emigration from all the world of skilled and unskilled labor, and of manufacturing capital and experience."[69] Although the work of the American Emigrant Company was discussed by the iron and steel manufacturers, no specific authorization was granted and, what was more damaging from the Company's point of view, no funds were set aside to aid immigration. As the Company's recruitment activities tapered off through lack of orders in 1866 and 1867, Williams complained to Carey with increasing bitterness of his lack of success in getting money from the Association. "You *know* how hard it is to get the *iron men* to pay *anything*," he wrote in 1866.[70]

Although the American Emigrant Company later maintained in petitions to Congress that the chief reason for its inability to find importers of contract labor was the inadequate legal force of contracts, perhaps an even more important reason for the failure of American employers to utilize its services was the high cost of importing labor through the Company. George Harris, Land Commissioner for the Hannibal and St. Joseph Railroad, described the Company's prices as "exorbitant." For example, John Williams charged ten to fifteen cents for each copy of the *American Reporter* which he tried to induce manufacturers to buy for circulation abroad. "We can get up a sheet as good or better," wrote Harris, "and adapted especially to '*Northern Mo.*' for far less and distribute them as well or better than Mr. Williams' agents."[71]

The failure of the American Emigrant Company to obtain large numbers of orders for contract laborers which could have made its labor-recruitment activities pay is evident from the data we have on its financial position. Although Samuel Bowles, the editor of the Springfield *Republican,* who was one of the directors of the Company, claimed in 1864 that the Company was making money,[72] the account book of its president did not record a dividend on his preferred stock until 1872, five years after the Company had given up trying to recruit skilled labor for American industry.[73] In its annual statement, filed in 1869, the Company listed its assets, chiefly land in Iowa, as amounting to $117,000 and its liabilities as $204,000.[74]

While the financial obstacles to the American Emigrant Company plan were serious, they might have been overcome if conditions in the countries of recruitment had enabled the Company to maneuver itself into the position of handling the emigration of a significant proportion of skilled workers. The difficulties the Company encountered in Europe differed from country to country, depending on the attitudes of press and government, the level of trade union organization, and the state of trade in various industries.

England, Scotland, and Wales, the traditional sources of skilled labor for American industry, were regarded as the most promising areas from which to obtain skilled textile workers, puddlers, molders, and miners, and claimed the attention of both the American Emigrant Company and the Boston Foreign Emigrant Association at the outset.

Edward Williams, the first agent sent abroad by the American Emigrant Company, arrived in England in January 1864, armed with sixteen thousand copies of the *Hardware Reporter*. Since it had been chiefly iron manufacturers who furnished the money for his trip, he went directly to the iron country in Staffordshire. From Birmingham he made forays, during those first few months, into industrial cities of Staffordshire, to the cotton towns of Lancashire, to the iron-making and coal-mining areas of South Wales, and even over to Ireland, distributing the newspaper among workingmen "at their meeting places in the evening, at the blast furnaces, at the pits' mouths, at the railroad stations. . . ."[75] He also advertised in cheap penny newspapers such as the Birmingham *Daily Post* and the London *Star* and in labor papers like the London *Beehive*.[76]

The first successes of the American Emigrant Company took place among cotton textile workers of Lancashire rather than among the ironworkers of Staffordshire. When Edward Williams arrived in Manchester in March 1864, he was struck by the contrast between Lancashire and Staffordshire. "There [in Staffordshire] all was bustle, employment and comparative prosperity: here . . . groups of men walk about in listless idleness." The unemployment wrought by the "cotton famine" rendered the cotton cities a much more fruitful field for recruitment. Here he learned his first lesson in the recruitment of skilled industrial workers: seek out depressed areas and industries.

In the textile towns of Lancashire recruiting agents from American industry were welcomed by unemployed operatives. The appearance of an American agent, who, it was observed, came on a first-class railroad ticket accompanied by a "clerk," was a regular occurrence in the town of Oldham during 1864 and 1865. When he was expected, the railroad station would be crowded with op-

eratives seeking aid to emigrate to America.[77] Stories circulated
of men and women who were engaged on the spot and left immediately with the agent.

The chief obstacle to recruiting unemployed textile operatives lay not in persuading them to leave home but in providing
passage money. The emigration committees which were organized
by operatives in Manchester, Preston, Blackburn, and many other
cities of the cotton districts could get little money from the British
public to assist emigration to America. Operatives bereft of savings after two years of depression had to depend largely on funds
from America.[78] American agents had no trouble obtaining all the
operatives for whom they had money to advance passages.[79]

Edward Williams also found an audience in the mining valleys
of South Wales among ironworkers and miners faced with wage
reductions and unemployment. "Wales," he concluded, "is a more
likely field than Staffordshire in which to obtain a supply of men.
. . . The inducement to emigrate is stronger to them than to the
better paid and less ambitious men in Stafford and Shropshire."[80]
It is likely that the absence of an established trade-union tradition among the Welsh miners and ironworkers was behind Williams' inference as to their greater ambition.[81] Later he was to find
trade-unions, particularly at times of strikes or lockouts, convenient contacts with potential emigrants. In Wales at this time, he
had to appeal to workmen through personal approaches and in
the columns of local newspapers. As in Lancashire, his statements
in Wales suggest that he did not have many actual orders for workmen, for he continued to stress that those who could raise the
necessary three to five pounds for passages would be sure to better
their condition by emigrating.[82]

Elsewhere in Britain among skilled, unionized miners and
ironworkers, the policy of the American Emigrant Company and
other recruitment agencies developed into one of working through
trade-unions and of concentrating upon areas in which trade disputes broke out. Peter Sinclair of the Boston Society soon gave up
his original idea of recruiting workers through societies of "ladies
and gentlemen" and temperance organizations to concentrate his
efforts in the trade-unions.[83] One had the interesting spectacle, for
a short period during the mid-sixties, of British trade-union officers, particularly in the mining and iron industries, assisting the
agents of American industry to find recruits.

Many instances could be cited in which British trade-union

officers, in an effort to threaten employers with the loss of skilled workers, turned to the agents of American industry during strikes and lockouts.[84] One American mining firm whose agents did assist locked-out Scottish miners to emigrate under an arrangement with Alexander MacDonald, the president of their union, tried to get the trade-union officers to guarantee the repayment of passage loans.[85] While such efforts by individual American firms appear to have met success during trade disputes, the agencies were, even at such times, handicapped by their inability to provide "free" passages. In New York John Williams publicized the strikes of which his agents kept him informed as golden opportunities for American employers to reap a harvest of skilled workers through the American Emigration Company, but apparently to no avail.[86]

Moreover the liaisons between the British union officers and emigrant agents tended to be temporary and were terminated abruptly when disputes ended. This was the case, for example, during a lockout of puddlers in the North of England in March 1865. The emigration scheme organized by the North of England Puddlers Association under which the American Emigrant Company was to find jobs for the men on their arrival in New York fizzled out when, during a union meeting at Jarrow at which the men were reading and discussing the *American Reporter,* news arrived that they were called back to work the following day.[87]

Thus the emigrant agencies were not able to establish permanent working arrangements with British trade-unions to handle the emigration of their members. As time went on and opposition from American unions and warnings from British immigrants in America began to pour in, the unions refused to deal with the emigrant agency, even in times of strikes.

By mid-1866 the American Emigrant Company was no longer operating as a labor-recruiting agency in Britain, its activities having been concentrated in the short space of two and a half years. It would be interesting to know how many skilled textile operatives, miners, and ironworkers actually emigrated under its auspices. Although the Company claimed to have imported "thousands" of skilled operatives, the evidence of contracts registered with federal authorities under the 1864 act indicates that, at most, a few hundred workers were brought to the United States on prepaid passages by all the agencies combined. From the establishment of the federal Bureau in July 1864 until the end of the year, 165 contracts were registered; in 1865 the total was 119. After the war even these relatively insignificant figures declined to 27 in the first six months of 1866.[88]

More operatives came out during the early stages of its activities "under the guidance and protection" of the American Emigrant Company than came on contracts. Reports in Welsh newspapers suggest that in the spring of 1865 hundreds of miners who had enough money for their fares to America paid those fares to the Company's local agent who promised to find them jobs.[89] In the iron counties and the textile towns of Lancashire the representations of recruiting agents probably induced many who had enough money for the passage to leave for America. The meager success of the recruiting agencies in attracting Britain's skilled workers in large numbers is indicated by the fact that in May 1865, after its most intensive advertising campaign, the American Emigrant Company had applications for assistance from only 128 British workmen, and twenty of these were from ordinary "laborers" in whom the Company was not interested.[90]

If it did have temporary success in 1864 and 1865, the fact remains that the American Emigrant Company failed to capture a significant enough sector of the emigrant stream to enable it to continue operating in Britain as a labor agency. This outcome in the British Isles cannot be attributed to the opposition of the British government. In contrast to the position of continental governments, British emigration officials did not criticize the American Act to Encourage Immigration. The contract labor provisions were considered reasonable since they were "confined within moderate and to a certain extent defined limits—and the contract is to be subject to the control of a responsible Government officer."[91]

Nor was the American Emigrant Company criticized by British authorities, who for the most part allowed it to carry on its activities without interference. One incident occurred, in November 1864, which led British officials to suspect the American Emigrant Company of attempting to recruit soldiers for the Northern armies from among unemployed Lancashire operatives. An American-bound vessel, the *Great Western*, was detained in the Mersey for several weeks by order of the Foreign Secretary to investigate reports that large numbers of army recruits were among the passengers. Investigation revealed that while some four hundred men on board were probably army recruits going out to a fictitious glass factory in New York state, the cotton and linen weavers from Blackburn under the care of the American Emigrant Company's agent were really bound for mills in Fall River.[92] After authorities had persuaded about half the army recruits to turn back, and assisted some of them to return to their homes,[93] the vessel was permitted to sail because of "imperfect evidence" for detaining her any longer.[94] Although the American Emigrant Company was ostensibly cleared of charges of army recruitment, the British press continued to link the American Emigrant Company with army recruitment until the war ended.

The American Emigrant Company received an unfriendly reception from the daily press in most industrial areas until May 1865. It is important, however, that the chief objection raised was that the Company sought army recruits. A letter of the Mayor of New York City which accused the American Emigrant Company of recruiting soldiers was widely quoted in the British press.[95] Since this hostility of the press was temporary and not directed against contract labor as such, it could not have hindered the long-term aims of the skilled labor agency. The Company replied that it took only skilled men, refusing applications from men who asked to join the army as well as from unskilled workers who knew no trade.[96]

The only real opposition to the recruitment of skilled labor for American industry came from British manufacturing interests and appeared chiefly in the trade press. During the cotton famine in Lancashire employers objected strongly to the emigration of skilled workers. One manufacturer estimated that the industry lost eighty-one pounds annually for every workman who emigrated. "The emigration of one spinner," he wrote, "involves the stoppage of probably ten additional hands; and it is far more difficult to train a hand to the work of spinning, than to any other manipulation in a cotton mill."[97] It was better to support the unemployed with soup kitchens and clothing doles than to encourage emigration.[98] Unemployed operatives were advised to take jobs in domestic service or to go to other parts of the United Kingdom to await the time when the mills would again be supplying the world with cotton goods.[99]

Similarly employers in the Welsh iron and mining industries deplored the loss of skilled workmen through emigration. The large exodus of 1864 from South Wales produced many complaints of shortage of hands, particularly in the Aberdare Valley.[100] A spokesman of the Welsh iron industry declared that employers were not opposed to emigration as a general principle, but that when a skilled workman emigrated he could not be replaced by importing unskilled Irish workmen.[101]

The most vociferous denunciations of the work of the American Emigrant Company itself were to be found in *Ryland's Iron Trade Circular*. These began in earnest after the American Emigrant Company's attempt to profit from the iron trade lockout of March 1865. The editor of the industry's trade journal specified that he did not criticize the Company for recruiting soldiers, but for buying and selling men, "deluding them into taking contracts which made them virtual slaves."[102] *Ryland's* continued to try to counter the effectiveness of American Emigrant Company propaganda by labeling the company "kidnappers," by noting its lack of support from American iron manufacturers, by stressing wage reductions in America after the war, by printing letters from immigrants in America which discouraged emigration, and by calling attention to the opposition of American trade unions to immigration.[103]

This battle of the manufacturers against the recruitment of skilled workers does not explain the failure of the American Emigrant Company in Britain. It was undoubtedly more than counteracted by the early friendliness of labor journals and trade-union leaders. Probably few workers ever saw these criticisms of the recruitment agency in trade journals.

The explanation lies rather in the increasing avenues of information available to the skilled worker of England, Scotland, and Wales. The "American letter" has often been stressed as an important cause of emigration; in the case of British skilled workers, it often served as a deterrent. Many intending emigrants probably behaved as did one Welshman after he heard of the promises of the American Emigrant Company. Eager as he was to emigrate, he wrote first to his brother in Pennsylvania to verify the information on wages and cost-of-living contained in the *American Reporter*.[104] After the Civil War, trade-union and labor journals in Britain began to print letters from British immigrants in America as well as information from American trade-unions on the state of the labor market in their crafts.[105]

The American Emigrant Company left itself wide open for criticism and correction on the grounds of the unreliability of its published statements about wages and cost-of-living in America. As its errors were pointed out to them, British workers learned to distrust the statements of labor agencies. The tables of wages compiled by the Company took no account of constant fluctuations of wages, nor of differences in rates paid in the east and west. In 1866, it published its scale of wages for 1865 with no apologies for the fact that the list was almost a year old.[106] American trade-unions pointed out that the Company's "scales of wages" were "sufficiently indefinite to be of no purpose." How could anyone get a clear idea of the wages he might expect from vague statements such as these: boilermakers, $2.00 to $4.00 per day; carriage trimmers, $10.00 to $20.00 per week?[107] Moreover the wages advertised by the American Emigrant Company were frequently higher than the maximum reported in those states in which the iron, coal, mining, and textile industries were concentrated.[108] After the war, when the price of gold came down, the Company distorted the picture of American wages by translating them into sterling, by which technique wage reductions could even be made to look like increases.[109]

The statements in the *American Reporter* on the cost-of-living in America were no less misleading. Opponents of the Company pointed out that wholesale rather than retail prices of food were quoted in the Company's estimates. What is even more remarkable is that the Company took, as a norm, Chicago prices which were considerably lower than even the wholesale prices in the city of New York.[110] The most important oversight in its indexes was its failure to discuss the price of clothing and rent. One of the most typical requests of immigrants in letters to the old country at this time was for clothing. An Irish immigrant in Philadelphia, for example, wrote in 1866 that before the price of gold came down, "clothing was three times the price we used to have to pay for all kinds of woollen and cotton ware."[111]

The British skilled workers had at hand by the end of 1865 much information from trustworthy sources which showed the loopholes in the advertisements of the American Emigrant Company. The fact that he could keep himself informed on the state of trade in America through his trade union and through contacts with former emigrants was probably the most important factor in weakening the appeal of the emigrant agency among these men. The skilled British workman, as will be indicated later, could be secured much more readily for American industry by approaching him through a former immigrant or by offering him a specific contract, which the American Emigrant Company was rarely able to do.

The American Emigrant Company had less success in obtaining skilled labor for its clients in Ireland and on the continent of Europe than it had in Britain. One visit to Ireland convinced Edward Williams that it was not fruitful ground for his activities. The opinion of both American consuls and many Irish newspapers was that the unskilled Irish laborer would be only too willing to accept a free passage to America.[112] One or two railroad companies succeeded in importing Irish workers during the war in spite of the hostility of the press to recruiting agents.[113] Warnings of the Irish press against the American Emigrant Company proved misdirected because its agent, while recognizing that only the inadequate number of ships prevented a larger flow of emigration from that country, reported that most of the intending emigrants from Ireland were laborers. Since the "mechanics and miners" it sought were not to be found there, the Company made no effort to extend its work into Ireland.[114]

The French government put a quick stop to the attempts of the American Emigrant Company to recruit skilled French workmen. The agent at Le Havre had some difficulty in getting a license under the French law of 1860 regulating emigration agents. And even then, the French government drew a sharp distinction between contracts to carry passengers and labor contracts, the latter being "simply tolerated" by the government.[115] The government denied the American Consul at Marseilles permission to circulate copies of the Law to Encourage Immigration.[116] By December 1865, the American Emigrant Company's agent in Le Havre discontinued his operations.[117]

The American Emigrant Company began its work in Germany in May 1864, when John Knotte, a native of Prussia, arrived in his homeland as its agent. Funds for his work were probably supplied by the same few iron manufacturers who supported Edward Williams' trip to England. Knotte made straight for iron manufacturing districts in western Germany. He spent his first few months speaking to workmen's associations and reading societies in Solingen, the important cutlery city of the Ruhr, and mining and iron districts in Aachen, Siegen, Saarbrucken, and the Saar.[118]

In most of the German states the activities of emigration agents were regulated by licensing arrangements and were closely supervised.[119] The atmosphere contrasted sharply with that of free trade Britain. Labor recruiters appear to have encountered opposition from local police from the outset. Knotte of the American Emigrant Company came so near being arrested that he asked John Williams to avoid any statement which might resemble an invitation to emigration in his second German edition of the *American Reporter*.[120]

The German press turned almost unanimously against emigration to America.[121] The Act to Encourage Immigration was severely criticized by editors and government officials. Newspapers castigated it as making the government publicly responsible for "swindling" which previously had been characteristic of private parties only.[122] Only two of the important immigrant journals in the German states, *Der Ansiedler im Westen* and *Deutsche Auswanderer-Zeitung*, looked with favor upon the arrangements outlined in the federal law.[123]

The principle of prepaid passages and contract labor came in for general denunciation, even from emigrant journals which countenanced the "protective" features of the American law.

In an article which was widely reprinted, the editor of *Deutsche Auswanderer-Zeitung* wrote:

The craftiest of the proposed arrangements is the advance of passage money to needy emigrants—the repayment of which is to be made good by the labor of the emigrant brought over. This is just what the Brazilian Emigrant agents resorted to in order to cheat the German proletariat into slavery, much the same system as the infamous coolie trade . . ."[124]

Deutsche Gesellschaften in the United States sent frequent warnings to Germany that intending emigrants should under no circumstances sign labor contracts before they left Germany because they could get higher wages finding their own jobs.[125] During the Civil War, industrial recruiters ran a constant risk of being arrested as army agents,[126] while after the war editors and officials maintained that labor was no longer needed in America.[127] When the American Emigrant Company succeeded in placing an advertisement in a German journal, the editorial page, often as not, contained a warning against the Company.[128]

Because of these obstacles to its work in the German states, the American Emigrant Company adopted the policy of trying to enlist the aid of United States consuls in order to carry on their work quietly and discreetly. The dabbling of consuls in the immigration business was not unusual, and under Seward's administration it was extended. Consuls in the German states were more active in promoting emigration than were those in Britain, but less involved than were the officials in Scandinavia.

John Williams wrote to consuls asking them to coöperate in the work of the American Emigrant Company, phrasing his letters in such a way as to lead the consuls to believe that his activities were endorsed by the United States government.[129] When the Company appointed an agent for Hamburg, his instructions were sent direct to the Consul's office.[130] As late as 1866 the Consul at Hamburg was still under the impression that Williams' circular was actually endorsed by the Federal Commissioner of Immigration, and for that reason he distributed all that he received "in the most advantageous way."[131] The Consul at Altona, near Hamburg, posted the "Circular of the Commissioners of Immigration" reprinted by the American Emigrant Company in its attempt to ride on the government's prestige, on boats in Altona harbor, in emigrant boardinghouses, and also sent some to interior cities.[132] In 1865 the firm of Rabus and Stall, in which the Consul at Mannheim had an interest, became "general agents for Germany" of the American Emigrant Company.

In spite of its efforts in the German states, the American Emigrant Company did not receive applications for assistance from the type of worker manufacturers were willing to import on contracts. Of 130 applications in the Company's hands in May 1865, 101 were from common laborers.[133] After a year and a half of recruiting in Germany, the American Emigrant Company ceased advertising free passages and concentrated on promising to procure "paying wages for all classes of craftsmen, farmers and servants of both sexes" immediately after their arrival in New York City.[134]

The American Emigrant Company began work in the Scandinavian countries in 1865 with the appointment of Frederick Nelson as agent in Gothenberg, and the Consul at Porrsgrund as Norwegian agent.[135] Nelson announced his intention of drawing people from the factory and ironworking districts of Sweden in accordance with the American Emigrant Company's aim to import diversified skilled labor.[136] In Sweden the Company obtained more applications from miners and ironworkers for contracts than it had in the German states although almost half the 281 applications in hand in May 1865 were from common laborers.[137]

The Company encountered government opposition almost immediately. In reports to his government the Swedish minister in Washington charged that the Act to Encourage Immigration made the government responsible for recruitment of a completely private kind.[138] The Swedish-Norwegian Consul at New York refused to endorse the American Emigrant Company as John Williams had requested and instead sent warnings home about its activities, noting that amendments were being considered to the original act which would make it possible to arrest immigrants who did not fulfill their contracts.[139] Partly as a result of these warnings, the King issued a proclamation in April 1865, which was posted in Stockholm and the provinces from which emigration was taking place, cautioning "those who may be enticed to emigrate not to thoughtlessly abandon their fatherland." The proclamation was directed specifically against the agent of the American Emigrant Company in Gothenberg.[140]

In spite of the warnings of the government and the newspapers, the American Emigrant Company appears to have succeeded in bringing out a large number of Scandinavians under its care. Few, if any, however, came on contracts to work. Many came to purchase land and others turned to the American Emigrant Company after their arrival in America for aid in finding jobs.[141]

The Company was aided by an early endorsement from Swedish religious leaders in Chicago and their influential newspaper, *Hemlandet*.[142] P. L. Hawkinson, the Swedish Consul in Chicago, a man deeply involved in immigrant traffic, headed the Company's office in that city.[143] Before the end of its first year of recruitment in Scandinavia, stories began to get back to Sweden of emigrants, sent out by Nelson in Gothenberg under vague promises of work, who were disappointed with the jobs they obtained.[144] The previously friendly *Hemlandet* warned intending emigrants that they should not depend upon the American Emigrant Company to find them suitable jobs.[145]

Within a year the Company began to change its recruitment policy in Scandinavia. During 1866 when it extended its agencies in Sweden and Norway, the expansion was into rural areas with the appointment of agents in Jönköping, Skåne, and northern Sweden.[146] This step was an admission of their failure in industrial areas. From this time on the Company's activities became more and more concerned with selling steamship tickets, handling baggage, exchanging money, and selling Iowa land.

Although in February 1866 the Company offered to find jobs for Swedish immigrants in the southern part of the United States, and Nelson's large brochure published in Gothenberg in March encouraged ironworkers and miners to emigrate, no free passages were offered.[147] The Company's increasing advertisements in rural areas made no mention at all of assisting immigrants to find jobs. The United States Consul in Jönköping, who served as agent of the Company, insisted that the firm did not even encourage emigration. It was established, he claimed, to provide protection for those who were financially able to undertake the journey themselves.[148] It was not to the Company's advantage, he explained later, to have its agents in American cities burdened with pauperous emigrants who had used up their money on the trip and arrived helpless.[149]

Thus after 1866 the American Emigrant Company competed with steamship companies on their own ground. It had no special advantages or free passages to offer. Advertising itself as the "oldest and best established company" in the business, it reminded readers of its connections with the government through the Act to Encourage Immigration. It did not remind them of the purpose of that Act.[150]

While its failure to gain wide support from either American employers or European skilled workers might have crushed a less optimistic and promotion-minded spirit than John Williams, the American Emigrant Company chose to put the blame on the legal weakness of the contract itself. Before the Civil War ended, the Company's directors had concluded that the agency could be made to work if the employer's legal redress when contractees left before their contracts expired were tightened.

They argued that a lien upon land acquired by the immigrant was not sufficient guarantee against contract-breaking since industrial immigrants were more likely to leave for higher wages, or the same wages without deductions for transportation, than they were to take up a homestead. The president of the Company, John Hooker, claimed that if sufficient protection against contract-breaking were provided by Congress, the American Emigrant Company could import twenty thousand skilled workers a year. In a letter to Senator Sherman, he outlined the Company's proposals. The absconding worker should be required by law to forfeit double the amount remaining unpaid of the money advanced by his employer, and the employer should have the right to follow the deserting workmen to his new job in order to impound his wages. The new employer should be given the option of deciding whether to retain or dismiss the workman: if he decided to keep him the new employer must assume the importing employer's unpaid bill of advances, "taking it afterwards out of the wages of the workman." The Company further requested that contracts with minors or married women be held valid in law and that contracts made in New York City for work inland be brought under the terms of the Act to Encourage Immigration.[151]

Unable to secure these amendments in Congress, H. C. K. Welch, one of the directors of the American Emigrant Company, introduced a bill which contained the desired provisions in the Connecticut legislature in May, 1865.[152] In the Connecticut legislature the American Emigrant Company's bill had smooth sailing. Within two weeks of introduction it had been passed. The Connecticut Act to Encourage the Importation of Laborers contained all the securities demanded by the American Emigrant Company. Employers not residing in Connecticut could enforce their contracts in the Connecticut courts.[153]

This sweeping legislation was not enough. In 1866 John Williams again asked for a federal amendment to make possible the impounding of wages.[154] The federal Commissioner of Immigration, E. Peshine Smith, following the lead of the American Emigrant Company, recommended to the House Committee on Immigration an amendment which incorporated the provisions of the Connecticut law. He assured Congressmen that although there might be some apprehension that the Connecticut law was passed "in the interest of individuals or companies making advances to immigrants," these companies were serving an important public interest and therefore deserved consideration from the legislators.[155]

These efforts were of no avail. No bill was even introduced into Congress. Immigration had begun to climb again after 1863; but neither the American Emigrant Company nor its friends in the Bureau of Immigration had been able to establish the agency as an important distributor of the skilled workers who were landing daily at New York City. When business slackened in 1867 Congressmen saw even less need to take any action with respect to immigration. In 1868 they repealed the Act to Encourage Immigration.

After the repeal of this Act the government continued, through its consuls, to promote the emigration of skilled workers, whenever and wherever diplomatic considerations allowed. Consuls in

Great Britain, Ireland, the North German Confederation, Austria, Sweden, and Norway were instructed in 1868 to induce "persons of capital, industry, or skill" to emigrate to America if they could obtain permission for such activities from local authorities.[156] United States consular officials abroad served as emigration agents, distributing literature and maps.[157]

Most of the promotion work reverted to interested parties, primarily railroad and steamship agents, who suffered none of the compunctions which even the ardent advocate of immigration, Commissioner Smith, had felt as a governmental official. As one spokesman of the steamship companies expressed it, there was no need for the federal government to send special agents abroad to encourage emigration since consuls, railway and steamship agents could furnish "any information" that was required by prospective immigrants.[158] Indeed, as things were, the information supplied by consuls was not much more disinterested than that of railway and steamship companies.

The transportation interests objected even more strongly to any suggestions that the federal government's efforts to assist in the distribution and protection of immigrations be continued. Some organizations still hoped that the federal government could foster a rational distribution of immigrant labor. In 1870 the Citizens Association of New York petitioned Congress for the creation of an International Association for the Promotion and Protection of Immigration. They envisaged a federal agency which would not only protect emigrants from fraud after their arrival in America, but also aid in "transferring the surplus labor that now burdens our cities to sections of the country where labor is in demand."[159] A Convention called by governors of twenty-two western states in 1870 did not go so far as to suggest a federal labor distributing agency since representatives of steamship lines and railways were among those invited; but it did propose a federal agency to protect immigrants from deception.[160]

The recommendations of the governors' convention were received coldly by Boards of Trade and Chambers of Commerce. Pronouncing its opinion that federal protection and control of immigration was neither necessary nor desirable, the Boston Board of Trade urged western governors who wanted to "promote the well-being of the immigrant" to "use their influence to turn the tide of population by the European steam lines running to Boston, and over the railways, connecting this port with the interior . . ." In the interests of expanding her own trade, Boston was ready to admit that abuses at Castle Garden were excessive.[161] The New York Commissioners of Emigration and the New York Chamber of Commerce similarly objected to federal intervention. "Everything is done for the protection of the person and property of the emigrant" once he entered the port of New York, they maintained, in striking contrast to Boston's view of their work.[162]

Transportation interests and public apathy carried the day for laissez-faire in immigration matters. American industry had neither patronized the labor agency nor coöperated with government immigration commissioners. Having failed abysmally to attract either American manufacturers or European skilled labor, in spite of its near-government-sponsored status, the skilled labor agency was no longer in a position to raise any objections to the withdrawal of the federal government from the field of immigration promotion.

Chapter 2

PATTERNS OF PRIVATE RECRUITMENT,
1860–1885

From the flurry of newspaper reports and government proclamations abroad, one might be tempted to conclude that, for the brief period from 1864 to 1866, the skilled labor recruitment agencies were the only channels by which American industry imported skill. This, however, was not the case. Many manufacturers by-passed such agencies completely when they sought to fill wartime labor needs. Their recruitment policies bore strong continuity with prewar methods, and were to continue, along much the same lines, even after the Foran Act of 1885 had prohibited the importation of contract labor.

As the new accelerated phase of American industrial development proceeded, many spokesmen of American industry, in the iron and textile industries in particular, maintained that skilled workmen from European industry were still needed in America. At meetings of manufacturers' associations and in trade journals these spokesmen stressed that expert workmen from Europe had contributed to America's rapid industrial advance; that profit was still to be gained from a "more abundant supply of skilled hands accustomed to the more laborious and less remunerative systems of Europe"; and that even "Yankee ingenuity, in the invention of labor-saving machinery" did not abolish the usefulness of "painstaking, patient, manual skills."[1]

These exhortations on the values of European skills did not produce concerted action on the part of manufacturers to acquire them. Employers of labor remained, on the whole, content to take what they got in the normal course of immigration. They made no efforts to get government assistance, to revive the skilled labor agency or the contract system, or, in fact, to take joint action among themselves in the interests of stimulating the emigration of skilled workers from Europe. When occasion arose, familiar methods could be employed by each individual firm to satisfy its needs.

Protectionist arguments probably tended to lull manufacturers into a sense of security about their future supply of skilled labor. Tariffs were described as a guarantee that skilled workmen, attracted by the higher wages which protectionists attributed to those duties, would continue to pour into America. That arch tariff-lobbyist, John L. Hayes, Secretary of the National Association of Wool Manufacturers, struck the keynote:

Let us keep up the walls about our continent, so that there may be a sure refuge for the industries, or in other words, the capital and skill and labor which we will attract from Europe. . . . If we want the fabrics of Europe, let us not import them; but bring, by the attractions of our protective system, her capital and establishments, her skill and her workmen to our own land.[2]

Speakers at the banquets and meetings of the Association echoed the point of view of the Secretary.[3] The same argument was used by James Swank, the president of the Iron and Steel Association.[4]

These arguments were undoubtedly influential. The optimistic economics of Henry Carey promised that labor supply and capital would follow adequate protective tariffs. If the government would not invest in the passages of skilled workers, neither would manufacturers as long as there were tariffs. All one need do was wait for European workers to read the message of high wages in tables prepared by Edward Young for the Bureau of Statistics of the Treasury Department. Official editions were available in English, French, German, and Swedish, which consuls, steamship companies, and railroad and land companies could be depended upon to circulate in Europe.[5]

One of the lessons of the American Emigrant Company experiment was that American manufacturers did not want to invest large sums of money in obtaining skilled workers. They were willing to take their chances of filling their requirements from a high immigrant stream. Confident that, when necessary, they could get European workers for particular tasks, and to oversee learners, they looked askance on trade-union apprenticeship schemes or any labor system which necessitated a long-term investment in skill.[6]

The general atmosphere after the war appears to have been one of confidence that the revived flow of immigration would fill most of industry's needs for skill. Nevertheless, recruitment abroad continued on a small scale and sporadically. The evidence lies primarily in company letter books and labor journals. More individual cases of recruitment of contract labor abroad may be turned up in time, as more company files are examined by scholars. Enough is already known to give a reasonably clear picture of the purposes and method of this recruitment in the textile, mining, iron, and steel industries.

The cotton manufacturers of New England who had been so conspicuous in the committees of the Boston Foreign Emigrant Society and whose agents had swarmed over the Lancashire cotton towns during the "famine," still complained of an insufficiency of workers after the war.[7] The difficulty was not one of getting hands, but of getting hands with the necessary skill. Edward Atkinson was probably not alone in his opinion that the lowest-paid operatives often made the most expensive rather than the cheapest cloth.[8] Even though mills were not up to full production in 1870 there was a general scarcity of good weavers.[9] Skilled female workers were particularly hard to find.[10] American manufacturers felt keenly that they were constantly having to deal with raw recruits, while in England manufacturers could draw upon a supply of operatives who had engaged in cotton manufacturing for a lifetime.[11] In some cases mechanical improvements were not adopted because of the absence of skilled labor to operate them. The chief objection to the roller card in 1867 was that a high degree of skill was required for its proper management, demanding a class of labor not readily available.[12]

Discussing the shortage of skilled labor, cotton manufacturers blamed each other for failing to train "green hands." Many employers apparently preferred to send out their overseers to persuade skilled workmen to leave other jobs by offering them special inducements.[13] George Ward and William P. Haines submitted a manufacturers' code to the Cotton Association in 1869 under the terms of which employers were to agree not to entice help from each other and to train a certain number of workmen; but no action was taken.[14]

At the same time that New England cotton manufacturers were complaining of their need for weavers, another depression in the Lancashire industry gave them an opportunity to procure workers which some firms, at least, hastened to turn to advantage. After a series of strikes had broken out in the spring of 1869 in Blackburn, Preston, and other towns over wage cuts, United States Consul Dudley in Liverpool wrote in terms reminiscent of the "cotton famine" of the early sixties. "If means could be found to provide passages, I am convinced that almost if not quite one-half of the operatives in the manufacturing districts of this country would emigrate to the States . . ."[15]

Emigration societies, organized by the cotton spinners and weavers, sprang up all over north and west Lancashire.[16] Although their funds were limited, these societies managed to send some of their members to the United States and Canada.[17] Despite the warnings of British manufacturers that there was already a shortage of labor in the cotton textile industry and the opinion of the London labor newspaper, the *Beehive,* that sending operatives to a rival industry in America would not increase the "wages fund," the operatives persisted in their course. Because of their limited means, the emigration societies welcomed the assistance of American agents in finding jobs for emigrating members. If the agents were able to forward passage money, they were all the more welcome.

Since government immigration figures by occupation were far from reliable, it is impossible to say how many Lancashire operatives came to America at this time.[18] It was reported that "a large number of the most experienced operatives" had their passages paid to Lowell and that several agents of American manufacturers were at work in Lancashire inducing textile workers to emigrate.[19]

The agents employed at this time by American cotton manufacturers appear to have been, for the most part, residents of Britain who were connected with the New England mills as regular agents and who often recruited workers for more than one firm.[20] Another device used at this time, and in fact for the rest of the century, was that of obtaining skilled workers through British firms.[21] Cotton-spinning machinery establishments in England which sold machines to the United States helped American manufacturers recruit labor by collecting registers of persons wishing to emigrate which were made available to American concerns buying their machines.[22] A Congressional Committee in 1888 discovered similar arrangements in the woolen industry. One F. H. Johnson, who was collecting workers for at least two woolen concerns in the United States, had been hired for that purpose by a firm of brokers in Liverpool who supplied wool to the American mills, but preferred not to have it known in Britain that they were sending woolsorters, clothfinishers, and experienced dyers out of the country.[23] Manufacturers expected more satisfactory results from confiding the business of selecting skilled help to such men, who were known to them and whose knowledge of the industry assisted them in making careful selections, than they obtained from the inexpert agents of the American Emigrant Company.

Two cases of recruitment in Scotland through such agents illustrate the methods and difficulties encountered in filling "orders for labor" with any degree of precision even under these conditions. One of these cases, that of the Amoskeag Mills in Manchester, New Hampshire, has been described by David Creamer. This firm had taken advantage of the American Emigrant Company's proffered services, but found the workers sent not so skilled as they had been led to expect. When Amoskeag again decided to import workers from Britain in 1868, this time in order to begin the manufacture of fancy gingham, about ninety women were procured as weavers by George Thomson, a resident of Great Britain, who had a wide acquaintance among New England textile factory managers.[24] The other case was that of the importation of about sixty-five weavers by the Pepperell Manufacturing Company for their plant in Biddeford, Maine, in 1881. The Boston agent of the Company obtained these weavers with the help of Dr. James Houston of Glasgow, who was at the same time signing up workmen for the York Mills at Saco, Maine.[25] The aim of these importations was not to begin a new process as at Amoskeag, but rather, as the historian of the Pepperell firm has observed: that "the expense of obtaining them might be balanced by the pattern of conscientiousness and thrift which they set for the more easygoing French."[26]

In both of these instances the companies asked that any help sent to them should be, first of all, skilled, and secondly, sober, respectable, and of good moral character. Since this recruitment in Scotland was not carried out through trade-unions as it was in England, operatives who desired to be sent to America had to provide themselves with credentials attesting their ability as weavers and their good moral character. These documents had to be obtained from a local clergyman and from a former employer. Where there was doubt about the intending emigrant the agent required security from a relative, that is, a guarantee that passage money would be repaid.[27] "As we want only first class help," wrote George Dexter, treasurer for the Pepperell mills, "I must depend on you to make sure that the girls are as they should be and failing to find such I trust that you will not ship any." Although the Company generally advanced passage loans for the girls, steerage class, Dexter was willing to provide intermediate passages if they could thus get a better "class of girls."[28]

The usual procedure was for the Company to deposit passage money with an established steamship line.[29] The operatives signed contracts in which they agreed to repay the money advanced. Most of the contracts were for a year, but the Pepperell Company insisted only that they cover a long enough period to obtain repayment for the advances. Dexter calculated that women who came by steerage should be able to repay their debts in two months.[30]

The agents received a commission on each operative sent out. James Houston received $195 for procuring 65 weavers; this was two dollars less each than the American Emigrant Company had charged for cotton operatives.[31] The evidence available indicates that George Thomson collected a fee from the operatives for "the expenses of engaging," in addition to the commission he received from Amoskeag.[32]

Little trouble was experienced by Thomson in the late sixties in finding sufficient help in Glasgow to fill the orders from Amoskeag, although he complained of the "unpleasantness connected with making these engagements, and the necessary inquiries regarding them."[33] When he had completed the selection of 40 women required in 1870, he noted that he still had a list of 112 applicants "many of whom seem very likely women." The "unpleasantness" seems to have arisen from the fact that manufacturers did not coöperate readily in giving references. As one applicant put it, "Our master is not very willing to part with his weavers for he has lost a great many emigrating to America."[34] Applications were so numerous, in spite of the opposition of manufacturers, that Thomson sent to Amoskeag several weavers who were able to pay their own passages, giving them letters of recommendation but no promises of jobs.[35]

The Pepperell Company had less success in getting a full complement of skilled weavers for their plant in Maine. Pleased with the first shipment of nineteen girls, Dexter began to think of a "large-scale" importation. Before they had arrived, he ordered twenty more girls and twenty men for wide looms.[36] However, the second set of girls turned out to be unskilled and had to be instructed, while the men for the wide looms left for other mills soon after their arrival.

It soon became apparent that a large number of skilled female weavers could not be obtained in Glasgow. Glasgow was reported to be "exhausted" of potential emigrants late in 1881.[37] That it was lack of supply rather than demand which cut off the importations is indicated by Dexter's eager inquiry early in 1882: "I saw some time since that one of your mills was burned. Were there many good girls thrown out of employment & what became of them?"[38] Early in 1882 Dexter had agents scouting for skilled help in Ireland and ordered one hundred workers to be sent during March.[39]

Textile companies were sometimes willing to make loans for transporting the families of immigrant workers if this would keep their skilled workmen with them. Once a workman proved himself to be satisfactory, he might get a loan from his employer to bring out his wife and children.[40] In 1881 the Pepperell Company hoped to get additional skilled help by sending for the husbands of women who had proved satisfactory.

Specific problems of skilled labor supply were less frequently discussed in the meetings of the National Association of Wool Manufacturers, which represented the portion of the industry primarily concerned with tariff legislation,[41] than they were among the cotton manufacturers. From the evidence available it seems reasonably clear that the wool manufacturers were also less ambitious than the cotton men in making the necessary temporary outlay to import skill. One commentator stated that Europe's ascendancy in wool manufacture was based on her command of certain varieties of wool without which Americans could not make the best face goods. With the proper raw material he thought that all the difficulties of manufacture could be overcome by importing German workmen.[42]

The Slater Woollen Mills in Webster had, in fact, already succeeded in obtaining German workmen, and this company was held

up as an example to the trade of the ease with which this factor of
skill could be met. When the Slater mills needed finishers in 1865,
an agent in New York was requested to notify them of the approach of ships from Antwerp, Bremen, or other German ports.
The arrival of a telegram saying that a ship had been sighted off
Sandy Hook sent the manager of the finishing department off to
New York where, by special permission of the Commissioners of
Immigration, he was admitted to Castle Garden. By interviewing
German workmen as they landed, he succeeded in procuring the
necessary help.[43] The mills also found themselves in need of a
dyer. After borrowing a man from a Connecticut mill for half of
each week, Slater's finally obtained an experienced dyer from
England through a wool brokerage firm in Liverpool.[44]

Slater's was also trying to procure fine drawers at this time.
New York agents of the firm advertised in German and English
newspapers and visited tailors in New York in search of men with
skill. Finally a German immigrant was obtained in New York
City and forwarded to the mills. Other fine drawers were procured
through relatives of the dyer, James Berry, who had been brought
out from England.[45] The order was placed with the same firm of
wool brokers in Liverpool whom the Ford Committee found
twenty years later to be supplying American woolen mills with
labor.

> You will much oblige us [the company wrote], if you will call on
> Mr. Sm.l Berry Fine drawers at Lockwood, near Huddersfield, and
> obtain his aid in this matter—Mr. B. is cousin to the Dyer whom you
> sent us. . . . He also suggests that his cousin will doubtless be able to
> obtain Fine drawers of excellent qualifications in every respect in skill,
> habits, temper, & character. . . .[46]

How many woolen concerns followed the example of the Slater
mills it is impossible to say. By the seventies the American woolen
industry had dispensed with the need for highly trained operatives
in the spinning department by introducing mules. In 1871 the
American Social Science Association's *Handbook,* which was circulated in Great Britain, promised woolen weavers that they
would be "very sure to find work" in New England, but warned
carders and spinners not to emigrate "unless they have work
secured before leaving."[47]

In some branches of the iron and steel industry there were

similar cases of the selection of highly skilled labor abroad during this period. Before the Bessemer process of making steel was introduced in America after 1865, the manufacture of steel and wrought iron was an expensive, laborious process which required highly skilled workers. While puddlers and heaters were still needed to handle molten iron, skilled labor from England, Wales, and Germany was at a premium. Although Irish workers were numerous both at the blast furnaces and in the puddling process, they were not so highly in demand. Irish workers frequently came to ironworking areas, but according to Abraham Hewitt, they were not skilled puddlers as a rule (unless they had first worked in England and learned the skill there) and had to start as puddler's helpers.[48]

Some of the demand for foreign skill in the blast furnaces and puddling and molding processes was met in the mid-sixties by the recruitment through emigrant agencies; but private recruitment by the manufacturers concerned was also a feature of the period. Few records of this search for skill have been found; yet enough evidence is available to indicate that there was some small-scale importation of key workmen on contracts.

In some cases manufacturers sent foremen or department managers who knew the exact type of skill required to England.[49] Isaac Jones, a partner of Jones, Boyd and Company, Pittsburgh, went to Sheffield himself in 1863 and picked out twenty workmen for various branches of the steel industry—melters, forgemen, tilters, and rollers.[50]

Profiting from the experience of the American Emigrant Company, Americans kept a weather eye out for trade disputes abroad which might yield skilled workers. The Iron Workers Association of Staffordshire continued throughout the sixties to turn to emigration schemes in times of trade disputes. Faced with wage reductions in 1868, the union immediately organized an emigration scheme and appealed to the United States Consul in Birmingham for assistance in carrying it out.[51] Trade journals and local newspapers objected strongly to the movement, but nevertheless reports came from the center of the Black Country that the chief desire of the ironworkers, urged on by glowing accounts and free passages, was to get to the United States.[52] While British employers warned their workmen of the high cost of living in America, reports continued to be published in Britain of higher wages at American furnaces and rolling mills. The American Social Science Association *Handbook* stated with reference to employment in rolling mills: "sober, industrious men can hardly fail of good employment, if well skilled in their work."[53]

Prussian ironworkers, noted for their high degree of skill, were also imported to new and expanding iron and steel works particularly in the Pittsburgh area. In 1867, ignoring the emigration societies, several manufacturers participated in an assessment on each furnace to raise money for importing Prussian workmen. Eight hundred recruits selected by the American Consul were distributed among several furnaces. One group of men who knew no English at all was sent to work under Andrew Kloman at Carnegie's Union Iron Mills.[54] In 1864 Prussian iron molders were brought on contracts to St. Louis, Missouri.[55]

The finished steel and hardware industries were also making great strides. Advances in machinery for grinding and cutting cutlery were being made in America during the sixties as workmen in Sheffield fought bitterly the introduction of new machinery.[56] However, skilled workmen were still wanted in America in spite of the progress in machine-production.

Sheffield, the center of the English cutlery industry, was the site of most of the recruitment for American factories. Sheffield cutlers were sought for many different branches of the iron industry because of their remarkable versatility, a product of long and careful training, which enabled them to shift from one job to another.[57] American manufacturers put this versatility to good account as is illustrated in this description by one Sheffielder of the system which operated in Connecticut cutlery factories:

The superintendent is the head "boss" over the men, lets the job, sets the price, turns off and sets on, and keeps a few hands always at liberty to go from job to job when needed; and these are called "company hands." All are Englishmen, who know where to go to any part of a knife, for the Yankees are brought up to one or two jobs and cannot shift about. Men who have jobs, matching and resining, for instances, set on and turn off their extra hands as they like, and if any of them are stuck with their work, the "company hands" are sent to help them out, and he has to pay them after the rate the company pays.[58]

During the bitter disputes of 1866 in Sheffield, rumors circulated that the demand for men in America was so great that strikers could "easily" obtain assisted passages. As was the case with the unions in the heavy iron and textile industries in England during this period, the Sheffield cutlers were not slow to organize an emigration society and to coöperate with American agents seeking workmen.[59]

When British capital was invested in American cutlery works, Sheffield manufacturers sometimes assisted the recruitment of workers. The leading Sheffield firm of Wade and Butcher appears to have helped to recruit workmen for the Pennsylvania Steel Company in Harrisburg, "the two works being connected together by mutual interest and association."[60] One group of Sheffield cutlers in Connecticut described their transfer to America thus: "A Sheffield manufacturer advertised for a lot of cutlers, forgers, and grinders, and we unfortunately were picked out and invoiced to a cutlery company in Union City."[61] Similar instances of the movement of workers along with capital to America were to be found in the heavy iron and steel industry.[62]

Other Sheffield workmen were sent to America by former immigrants who returned to England for visits which combined business and pleasure. When one of the partners of a cutlery firm in Walden, New York, returned to his native city for an extended visit in 1869, he used the occasion to pick workmen, advancing their passages, as the president of the company kept him posted by letter on the firm's needs.[63] Similarly the Wahlstanholme File Company of Buffalo sent its English superintendent to Sheffield in 1864 to procure about twenty operatives.[64] Information and contacts supplied by Sheffield workmen already in their employ were exploited in these recruitment ventures.

The facts about recruitment abroad by the mining industry are even more difficult to uncover than those in the industries discussed above. What is known indicates that contract labor was probably rarer in the mines after the Civil War than it was in the textile and metal industries. Miners from Durham, Scotland, and Wales continued to flock into American bituminous coalfields;[65] they came, as Francis Walker remarked of the Welsh, "under intelligent direction and [went] straight to the place where they were wanted."[66] This "direction" was not primarily the work of the coal operators, however.

Pressed by serious labor shortages in opening up new mines during the Civil War, a number of mine operators participated in attempts at large-scale recruitment abroad independent of agencies like the American Emigrant Company. Through the columns of the Durham *Chronicle,* the Commissioners of Immigration in West Virginia urged Durham miners to emigrate to West Virginia's coal mines.[67] Western mine operators invited the British to come to the Far West where labor was needed in the mines and well compensated.[68] Some efforts were also made on the Continent. Illinois coal operators, through their agent L. A. Bochez, obtained miners from Belgium.[69] The Coal Exchange in Philadelphia approached the American Consul in Hamburg for assistance in obtaining miners.[70]

One of the most ambitious projects was organized by a group of operators in the Lake Superior region to obtain help for the copper mines. Their aim was to get experienced copper miners from Sweden and Norway, and they were prepared to advance passage money in return for contracts.

The mining companies found the United States consuls eager to assist them. O. E. Dreutzer, the Consul at Bergen, undertook to find Norwegian copper miners in spite of newspaper charges that he was prostituting his office.[71] B. F. Tefft, the Consul at Stockholm, handed over the consulate to his son, George, in order to concentrate upon the recruitment of workers for the Maine Foreign Emigrant Association, while another son, Henry, took charge of forwarding Swedish emigrants to the Lake Superior copper mines.

Advertisements offering jobs to miners in the Lake Superior region, signed by Tefft, began to appear in Stockholm newspapers in June 1864.[72] Persons who applied to go as miners were offered $260 per year; if they fulfilled their part of the contracts and proved to be "faithful and experienced" miners they were to get an additional forty dollars at the end of the year. The mining companies agreed to lend the miner his own passage and one-third of the passage of his family to the Lake Superior region. Since the sum to be deducted for repayment was half the monthly pay and the emigrant had to sign a two-year contract, the actual wages to be received by experienced miners amounted to little more than ten dollars a month.[73]

The first shipload of emigrants for Maine and Michigan sent out by Dreutzer and the Teffts was also the last they managed. The *Ernest Merck* was ready to sail early in July 1864, with 258 emigrants on board bound for the Michigan mines and 220 for Maine. The sailing of the ship was forbidden by the Governor of Stockholm because the consignees had not presented it for inspection required under Swedish law. Investigation revealed an inadequate number of lifeboats on board; but when that matter was cleared up, the ship departed.[74] A very bad impression was left in Scandinavia by the affair, one which Dreutzer thought might injure the general cause of emigration. More than a hundred families who had come to Bergen from the interior of Norway in hope of engaging with Lake Superior mining companies, remained there until they had used up all their means, and had to be sent home at public expense. Several persons who had signed contracts with the T.toffts were refused aid when the final selections were made.[75]

 • The unpleasant publicity resulting from this incident did not terminate the recruitment of miners for Lake Superior. In the spring of 1865, C. Taftezon, a returned Norwegian emigrant, was in Norway collecting a shipment for the mines. He advertised wages for miners, engineers, and smiths at $2.50 to $3.00 a day, and for laborers at $1.75 to $2.00, while board and room would amount to only $.66 to $.75 a day. The Lake Superior region, according to Taftezon, was admirably suited to Norwegian emigrants for there they could enter their customary occupations.[76] Unlike the consuls in 1864, Taftezon operated through a firm of steamship agents, and did not offer "free" passages, although he did offer to forward a part of traveling expenses which prospective emigrants might lack.[77] In spite of newspaper opposition, Taftezon was able to collect about 150 Norwegian emigrants, exclusive of women and children.[78] One authority states that most of them came from the Kaafjord copper mines in Norway.[79]

No such clear evidence of importations on contract has been found for the period after the Civil War. There was surely a heavy emigration from the British mine fields in the late sixties and early seventies.[80] The editor of the *Workman's Advocate* of Chicago claimed that on landing in Liverpool in 1869 he had seen billboard posters advertising for miners to come to areas in which thousands were out of work.[81] Again in 1879 and 1882 labor papers charged that Pennsylvania operators were advertising for miners in England.[82] The United States Consul in Newcastle published a pamphlet in 1882 which contained advertisements for miners.[83] No such advertisements appeared in the press in Britain. If these reports were accurate, the inducements must have been distributed in the form of handbills and posters. Twenty years later in one of the most important cases instituted to try to convict coal operators of importing contract labor, the government was able to prove only that an employee of the company had visited Wales and "both orally and in writing" let miners know the wants of his company.[84] All of this adds up to a certain amount of solicitation for miner emigrants but does not confirm that miners were brought on contracts.

Another method of recruitment employed by the coal operators, and, indeed, by many industrialists, was the emigrant letter. If feasible, this method had the inestimable advantage of costing the employer nothing at all.

At the moment [wrote William Wilson, an English miner in Pittston, in 1864], there are outside hands wanted at this place where I am, and at several places adjoining. But miners will not work on the outside. Our "boss" asks me frequently if I can get him some good outside workmen, and I can assure you the work is not hard. . . .[85]

Nearly thirty years later a United States contract labor inspector pointed out that the same kind of thing was still an everyday occurrence. "Generally the method is that the foreman of a mine will say 'how do you like your job here?' 'Pretty well.' 'Have you not a brother or a cousin or some friends in your home that you would like to bring out?' 'Yes.' 'If they come here we think we can put them to work.' "[86]

Certain facts stand out about the contract labor recruitment of the last half of the nineteenth century. After the war and immediate postwar period, the temporary organization of groups of manufacturers disappeared from the scene as did the recruitment agencies. Effective recruitment thereafter was carried out only on a very small scale, probably by relatively few firms. Connections with emigrant-yielding countries through immigrant employees, capital investments or customary business transactions were exploited as the most reliable and least expensive channels by which to secure individuals with specific skills on contract. To understand why the contract labor system was not used more frequently, one must examine the experience of manufacturers with contract labor, once it had been imported.

Chapter 3

UNCERTAINTIES OF
THE CONTRACT LABOR SYSTEM

The contract labor system did not gain a firm foothold in late-nineteenth-century America in spite of her industries' demands for skilled labor and the efforts of some to revive the system. Frequent misunderstandings over the terms of contracts, the relative mobility of skilled labor, and the growing strength of the trade unions in certain crafts and their international contacts all combined to inhibit the efforts of agents of American industry to obtain satisfactory contract laborers.

The emigrant agencies had been the first to point out how difficult it was to enforce contracts. One spokesman of the American Emigrant Company regretted that "a very large proportion [of the immigrants] have failed to fulfill their contracts."[1] The Boston Foreign Emigrant Society blamed the federal commissioners of immigration for not giving sufficient aid in seeing that immigrants adhered to their agreements.[2] Both organizations maintained that contract-breaking was the major handicap to their work and deplored the "lack of faith" of immigrants in failing to carry out the terms of their contracts.

More significant was the fact that even industrialists who imported workers through their own trusted agents had reason to be disappointed with the results. In most cases neither the importing employer nor the immigrant was satisfied with the arrangements which had been made in Europe. Misled by statements on wages and cost of living, immigrants frequently accused their employers

46

of deception and held their contracts to be void on that account. Employers whose imported workers left before repaying transportation loans lost on their investment in labor. Moreover immigrants were often not so skilled as employers had expected.

Nearly every textile firm known to have recruited skilled workers on contract ran into difficulties with the immigrants after they arrived at the mills. Vera Shlakman noted that one mill in Chicopee which assisted Irish immigrants to come to work for them lost many to rival companies before transportation costs were repaid.[3] To try to extract repayment for transportation loans, the Amoskeag Mills hired a collector to follow defaulters.[4]

Lancashire immigrants brought to Webster, Massachusetts, by the Slater Mills were shocked to discover that their luggage was being held by their employers as security and that workers in nearby mills were receiving higher wages. These people sent out delegates to canvass other factories secretly in order to find better positions than they had under their contracts.[5] Many of the recruits left the Slater Mills. Those who remained appear to have succeeded in getting their passage loans reduced to nine pounds from an exorbitant twelve pounds and in obtaining a promise that their wages would be brought up to the level of the other mills.[6]

Similar difficulties arose with the second lot of immigrants sent to the Pepperell mills in the 1880's. The agent of the company in Manchester, England, promised this group of Lancashire weavers two pounds a week, a higher rate of wage than the mills were paying for weavers, and the immigrants brought with them the letters to "prove" that the company was not living up to the promises of its agent.[7] With reference to this "shipment," the Boston agent of the firm wrote back to England: "A poorer lot of men never came to any mill. Half of them have left & we are out the passage money paid them & we are well rid of them. They were not skilled help & your brother was very wrong to send them out as such."[8] When the imported men left, the Company tried to trace their whereabouts in order to get their new employers to help recover the loans.[9]

In all likelihood, manufacturers who imported contract labor to meet legitimate labor shortages or skill requirements, only to lose the importees to rivals, did not take the cases to court. No test case reached the superior courts under any of the state laws on contract enforcement during the sixties. Civil action against immigrants was probably far too costly, cumbersome, and futile a procedure to be seriously considered. The most important result of the defaulting of contract labor was to discourage manufacturers from prepaying passages. Thus the president of a cutlery firm which had experimented with contract labor wrote:

Tom wrote for one of our cutlers to some relations of his to come out here and work for us. as this man has left our employment we don't want you to find any money for anyone to come out here. but if you can find two or three cutlers good workmen and steady men. who will pay their own passages out here we can find them steady work.[10]

The experience with skilled contract laborers was no more satisfactory in a region somewhat isolated from alternative employment like the Lake Superior copper mining region. There the disappointment of Scandinavian immigrants with conditions of work was used as justification for breaking contracts in order to join Swedish and Norwegian fellow-countrymen in neighboring states. An immigrant at the Quincy mine pointed out that the land which had been advertised as an inducement was stubbly and stony; the cost of board and room was between $20 and $24 a month, while miners who were brought on contract to the mines were to receive only $260 a year, from which transportation loans had to be repaid as well. At the Ontonagon mine, where wages were higher, board cost $35 a month.[11]

Some of Taftezon's party stayed at the mines only two and a half months and then left, with only ten dollars clear, to wander for months in Wisconsin in search of work during the dull winter, depending on the charity of other immigrants.[12] As one party of Norwegians was being guided up to the mines, they met a party of Swedes coming back who warned them not to proceed farther.[13] Johann Schröder, who visited nearly two hundred Scandinavian settlements in the United States and Canada just after the Civil War, said that many immigrants, who landed at Quebec penniless, accepted contracts offered by mining companies for the sole purpose of getting farther inland.[14] Others who arrived at New York on contracts made with Tefft in Sweden did not go to the mines at all when they were told by the Swedish Consul that the agreements were worthless if they did not freely recognize them.[15] Efforts to retain workers by the organization of accident and death benefits, the building of churches, and even restricting the use of vessels on Lake Superior failed to prevent the exodus of contract laborers.[16]

The relative mobility of the skilled workers which enabled them to break unsatisfactory contracts for other jobs in the United States was also evidenced by the frequency with which they returned to the old country if disappointed with what they found. Many of those induced to try America by the recruiting agencies later returned to England. In 1864 textile workers were reported as going back to Lancashire from America;[17] British iron and coal workers left for England in the fall of 1865,[18] and again in 1866.[19] The Minutes of the Scottish Iron Moulders during 1866 and 1867 are spotted with notices of men formerly assisted to emigrate to America, who had returned and reapplied for membership in the union.[20] G. T. Clark, the resident trustee of the great Dowlais works in South Wales, stated in 1867 that it was the skilled workers who most frequently came back from America because they were able to get the means to do so.[21] In 1869 Gideon Welles reported that he was "assured by the manufacturers that at the present time especially the tendency among skilled workmen, brought from Europe in pursuance of special arrangements for the extension of special branches of industry, is rather to return to the Old World than to remain in the United States."[22]

Although immigration statistics give no basis for judgment, other contemporary comments indicate that the Europe-ward stream during the long depression of the seventies contained a high proportion of skilled workers.[23] In fact, the depression years witnessed a number of cases of recruitment of skilled workers by agents of German and British industry in America.[24] Lancashire cotton mill owners, for example, were said to have had agents in New England with orders to obtain a thousand mill hands.[25]

There are many other cases of skilled immigrants who went back to their homelands when they concluded that they had made a mistake in emigrating. Sheffielders were reported as returning home when they heard of the revival in trade there in the early seventies.[26] Others who found that they had been imported as strikebreakers left America sometimes with the aid of the trade-union involved in the strike.[27] A skilled designer of calico prints testified in 1883 that a considerable number of highly trained Englishmen in his trade went back to England permanently, although he did not know of any such cases among the ordinary mill help.[28] The wages commanded by skilled workers in America enabled them, more easily than laborers, to take advantage of low steamship passage prices. Many British building trades workers became frequent "Atlantic migrators," coming to America for the boom months each year.[29]

If American capitalists had reason to be discouraged in their attempts to secure a stable skilled labor force through contract labor because of the loss of importees either to rivals or through re-emigration, their efforts to break strikes with imported skilled labor proved, if anything, even more costly and futile. During the war and immediate postwar period, iron manufacturers and coal mine operators made use of emigrant agencies primarily for obtaining strikebreakers. In so doing they had to contend not only with the attempts of strikers to frustrate their efforts, but also with a predisposition in favor of trade-unions among many of the skilled men they attempted to introduce. The result, in skilled branches of these two industries, was the creation and nourishment of ties between British and American trade unions which further counteracted the effectiveness of policies of recruitment of contract labor among skilled European workers.

During the war, when the labor scarcity was acute and miners' wages were rising, coal miners in the Belleville Tract in Illinois succeeded in a strike in spite of the importation of strikebreakers. Many of the Belgian workmen brought in by the coal companies were sent away from the area at the expense of the Miners Association.[30]

In 1865 and 1866 when wage reductions in the coal mines of Pennsylvania, West Virginia, and Illinois were being met with strikes, British workmen were frequently brought in as strikebreakers by means of the emigrant agencies.[31] When they came from areas where unions were relatively strong the British often flatly refused to take up work. A good example is that of John James, later Secretary of the Miners National Union, who emigrated after the war, and, with other miners from the North of England and Scotland, was shipped to a West Virginia mine with transportation advanced from New York City. After learning from local miners that there was a strike, James served as spokesman for the British immigrants who refused in a body to work while a strike was in progress and denied the validity of their contracts and debts to the company on the grounds that no contracts made under "false pretenses" were binding.[32] The trade-union mindedness of British miner immigrants is apparent in many of the letters they wrote to friends and to trade-union journals in the old country.[33]

On the other hand, immigrant miners imported from South Wales where strong trade-unions had not developed up to this time sometimes behaved quite differently from John James and his companions. During 1865 many Welsh miners were said to have contributed to the successful cutting of wages.[34] One of them wrote to a friend in Wales, criticizing the latter's "misrepresentations" of the motives of the American Emigrant Company, and expressing his gratefulness to the Company for "paying" his passage:

We were all very kindly treated when we arrived in New York and all the way until we came to Thomas Town. We left Thomastown through the warnings of some Irishmen, who said there was nothing but Irish working in that place, and that they would not allow us to work there. They also threatened to throw some stones at us, and fire some pistols![35]

Because of these threats, not because of hesitancy to interfere in a trade dispute, this group of Welsh miners moved on to Pittston and Ashland.

Importation of workmen for American iron manufacturers produced a vehement reaction against the emigrant agency and led to sustained efforts to frustrate subsequent attempts to obtain skilled British strikebreakers in the iron industry. The trade unions involved in this fight against recruitment were the Iron Molders Union, founded in 1859 by William Sylvis, the leading personality in the labor movement of the sixties; the Sons of Vulcan, organized among puddlers and boilers of the Pittsburgh area in 1858; and later, the Amalgamated Association of Iron and Steel Workers, formed in 1876, in which the skilled puddlers of the Sons of Vulcan formed the backbone. Having gained in strength during the Civil War, the Iron Molders Union and the Sons of Vulcan made the first experiment in a national labor federation in America when, in 1866, under Sylvis' leadership, they took the initiative in forming the National Labor Union.

An incident occurred in St. Louis early in 1864 which placed the Iron Molders in opposition to the recruitment of any labor on contract, whether the approval of government officials was affixed to the agreements or not. After a long strike in the stove and machine foundries of that city, one employer, Giles Filley, refused to settle with the union, and instead arranged through the State Board of Immigration to import twenty-five sand molders from

Berlin under one-year contracts in which the workmen obligated themselves "not to join any clubs or associations, of which in any way harm or disadvantage could arise to Mr. Filley, but to make the entrance in of such workmen or similar associations always dependent upon the permission of Mr. Filley." The contracts fixed wages at $2.00 a day while other employers in St. Louis had agreed to pay $3.00 to skilled molders.[36]

Representatives of the Iron Molders Union managed to make contact with the Prussian workers during a change of trains in Indianapolis to warn them of the situation, and then telegraphed to the local in St. Louis the exact time the men were due to arrive. Union members met the new men at the railroad station in St. Louis as did guards sent by Filley. The union representatives persuaded the Prussians to put themselves in the union's care.[37] All of these contract laborers joined the union, broke their contracts with Filley, and managed to obtain jobs elsewhere in St. Louis.[38] With its large German population, St. Louis was a poor city in which to try to use German strikebreakers!

The iron molders did not forget the Filley incident.[39] Once the American Emigrant Company's operations were fairly under way, William Sylvis laid down a steady barrage of denunciations of it in the column of *Fincher's Trades Review,* citing the Filley case as evidence that the Company's aim was to overstock the labor market and thereby reduce wages.[40] In the summer of 1865, the molders had positive proof, from their standpoint, that their charges against the American Emigrant Company were true. During a foundry strike at the Eagle Iron Works in Chicago, Scottish molders, recruited by the American Emigrant Company, were sent on prepaid passages from New York City to Chicago. Much to the alarm of the union, these men went to work.[41] What was even more disturbing was that when two strikebreakers, who were discharged by the Eagle Works, wrote to Glasgow denouncing the American Emigrant Company, the Scottish union leaders, in the midst of organizing an emigration scheme, labeled their former members' warnings untrue, accepted "explanations" offered by Peter Sinclair and the president of the Eagle Company, and advised members to take advantage of the opportunities offered by the American Emigrant Company.[42]

After this shock the International Molders Union of North America did not rest until it had arrived at a formal agreement with the British unions on the subject of emigration.

The members of the Sons of Vulcan also had to cope with imported strikebreakers during these years. When iron manufacturers of Pittsburgh and vicinity decided to reduce wages in February 1866, the puddlers and boilers in the Sons of Vulcan lodges united to resist the reductions by strikes throughout the iron mills of Pittsburgh and Allegheny county.[43] The American Emigrant Company offered to supply the manufacturers with strikebreakers. The union reported that they were "triumphantly told by our employers that 800 puddlers from England were hourly expected at New York, and were coming on here to take our places at reduced wages."[44] The employers were, however, unable to carry out the threat. When one company actually did receive nineteen boilers through the American Emigrant Company, the union was able to persuade them not to fulfill their contracts.[45]

Furthermore, the Sons of Vulcan saw to it that the affair got publicity among British ironworkers. At the request of the union the imported strikebreakers sent letters to their friends and relatives explaining that they had been "sadly deceived" and "gulled" into coming to America, since they had been sent to Pittsburgh to break a strike.[46] Patrick Graham was commissioned by the union to write an "Address to the Iron Workers of Great Britain" to counteract the effect that the circulation of the American Emigrant Company's *Reporter* was having upon Welsh ironworkers in particular. Graham maintained that neither puddlers nor boilers nor hammermen nor rollers were needed in America and pointed out some of the inaccuracies in prices listed in the *American Reporter*.[47]

The strike ended in March 1866, a victory for the union as the reduction was not effected.[48] But the dispute was not really settled. In December of the same year, the manufacturers again tried to enforce a wage reduction, and its announcement gave birth to a strike which lasted until May 1867.[49] Having failed to break the 1866 strike with British workmen, the employers now turned to the continent in hope of getting effective strikebreakers. Two hundred Belgian ironworkers were brought in;[50] and it was in order to break this strike that the manufacturers of the area pooled resources to import eight hundred puddlers and boilers from Prussia.[51]

Again the experiment did not work. After a few weeks, the union reported, the employers "were fully convinced . . . that the importation business would not work" and opened negotiations with the Sons of Vulcan.[52] The Belgian workers turned out to be incompetent, inefficient, and slow because of their unfamiliarity with American methods and standards.[53] As for the Prussian puddlers, the only record we have is that of Sylvis, and he stated that many did not go to work, but were reduced to utmost poverty because of the strike, some of them receiving private charity and others forced to go to the poorhouse.[54]

By the end of the period of the skilled labor agencies, the American unions in the iron industry were highly incensed about the importation of contract labor.

Ever since the completion of the Atlantic telegraph [observed the editor of the *Workingman's Advocate*], it has been the threat of unprincipled employers, in every state where an unpleasantness has occurred, to threaten the importation of foreign workmen, and in many instances they have been enabled to put their threats into execution. . . .[55]

Before the emigrant agencies had really begun their work, Sylvis summarized the policy toward immigrant molders thus:

These men should not be spurned and treated as enemies, because they are only the dupes of wiley agents. We should rather seek to show them that they have been imposed upon; and it is our duty to aid them in retrieving what has wrongfully been taken from them. Bring them to our standards, . . . and by their co-operation, we will diligently work for their as well as our good.[56]

Compare this statement with the words of Patrick Graham after the puddlers strike of 1866:

Heretofore when men came from England and presented a card of your English union, we gave them the hand of fellowship and used them as brothers. Hereafter this will be reversed, as men who will allow themselves to be used as tools to injure us need to expect no other treatment at our hands than that of enemies.[57]

The iron molders took the lead among American trade-unions in seeking ways and means of weaning British unionists away from the blandishments of recruiting agents and finding a modus vivendi with the British unions by which emigration within the craft could be regulated according to genuine employment opportunities in the United States. While he was at the head of the union, William Sylvis made several attempts to open negotiations with the English and Scottish Friendly Societies for an agreement to regulate the emigration of iron molders. His efforts met with no success. From the English Society he received "polite replies," while the Scottish Society did not even acknowledge his letters.[58] Sylvis' letters represented a low water mark in diplomacy. No wonder the English Secretary found them "insulting" when Sylvis denounced their emigration scheme as "a direct and outrageous FRAUD."[59]

Softer words enabled Sylvis' successor, William Saffin, to secure the desired agreement a few years later. Saffin's suggestions were substantially the same as those put forward by Sylvis: that the *Monthly Journal* of the American union be used in Britain as a guide to the state of trade and that a system be worked out whereby emigrant molders arriving with clear British cards should be received by the American union, aided in obtaining jobs, and advised on money, customs, and cost of living.[60]

By August 1871, the American union was able to announce that a "friendly business correspondence" with the English Society had been begun.[61] The following year, the Secretary of the Scottish Society took the initiative in suggesting to Saffin that the American union supply the societies with monthly reports on the state of trade in various districts in America. Again planning an emigration scheme, the union executive did not want to repeat its experience of the sixties when assisted emigrants returned home disappointed after spending only a few months or years abroad.[62]

On the basis of this correspondence the American union reached an agreement with the English union in October 1872, and with the Scottish Society, in February 1873.[63] The Americans had to compromise on two issues. An amendment to their request that British molders undertake not to sign any contracts to work in America was adopted by which the British agreed not to sign contracts to work in places where workmen were on strike or in dispute with their employers. The Americans were also unable to obtain assurance that a Friendly Society member not turning in his card to the American union be dealt with as an excluded member if he returned to Britain. The rest of the American propositions were adopted. The Iron Molders Union agreed to designate one member in each seaport city to give advice and information to immigrating members of the British societies. Monthly correspondence was to be maintained and a summary published in the British trade journal. Any Friendly Society member could become a member of the United States Union without paying an initiation fee, once he had found a job.[64]

Two years later, when both British and American molders began arriving on British shores as the depression deepened, the British societies took steps to protect themselves as well.[65] In 1875 the English voted to deduct a pound from the initiation fee charged Americans who came to England with clear cards. The Americans were required, however, to work three months in England, paying contributions, before they were eligible for membership since they did not have the "versatile skill" of English founders.[66] Correspondence was continued between the British and American unions, and in 1880 the American union reviewed the agreements of 1872 and 1874, commenting that they were still in operation.[67] Under these arrangements the iron molders appear not to have been troubled again with strikebreaking by skilled immigrants from Britain.

Although they were the first, the iron molders were not the only American craftsmen to have formal agreements with British unions. As might be expected, the two British societies which established branches in the United States during the sixties, the Amalgamated Society of Engineers and the Amalgamated Association of Carpenters, remained in close touch with employment conditions in America.[68] In 1871 the Engineers ruled that no member could receive an emigration benefit to go to a place where more than $7\frac{1}{2}$ per cent of the members of the society were unemployed.[69] Other American unions, including the brickmakers and plasterers of New York and the Window Glass Workers of America, also took steps to control the inward movement of members of their crafts.[70] By the end of the century E. Dana Durand was able to state to the United States Industrial Commission that "in occupations controlled by strong labor organizations, there is entire reciprocity between American and European unions."[71]

Agreements of this kind were not characteristic of the basic industries with which this study is concerned. Trade unions in the heavy iron and steel industry, the mines, and textiles did, however, establish certain connections with European trade unions. Tenuous and informal though these relations were, they did undoubtedly have some influence upon the distribution of skilled union members by providing them with information about American conditions.

The Sons of Vulcan had joined the iron molders in attacking

the work of the emigrant agencies in the late sixties. Copies of their journal, *Fincher's Trades Review,* with its condemnations of the American Emigrant Company, were sent regularly to the Merthyr *Telegraph,* the London *Miners Advocate,* the *Beehive,* and other British labor journals.[72] When the American Emigrant Company extended its agencies to Ohio, the Cleveland branch of the Sons of Vulcan appointed a protection committee to warn British workmen against the Company and to urge them to emigrate only on the assurance of a job from a friend in America, not on the promises of emigrant agents.[73] In 1870 there was some talk on both sides of the Atlantic of uniting the Iron Workers Association of Great Britain with the Sons of Vulcan.[74]

Although nothing of this nature was accomplished, the contacts established by the Sons of Vulcan during this period were to prove useful to the Amalgamated Association of Iron and Steel Workers when, with the revival of trade in the late seventies, iron manufacturers again threatened to import ironworkers from Great Britain. In 1879 American agents were reported as seeking "puddlers, rollers, roughers and furnacemen" in the Cleveland iron area of northeastern England, going "so far as to pay the passages of a few men in order to delude others to follow." Unable to find jobs in the Pittsburgh region, a number of men induced to come out by these agents turned to the American union for aid. Letters from these unemployed men and discouraging reports forwarded to the Secretary of the Amalgamated Association of Iron and Steel Workers of Great Britain "had the desired effect," according to William Martin, Secretary of the American union, for he received no further applications for assistance from recent British immigrants.[75]

During strikes of the early eighties the Amalgamated Association was able to frustrate efforts of the manufacturers to import British workers. A good example was the Cincinnati strike of 1881. As soon as the union heard that manufacturers of the region were planning to bring men out from Britain a cablegram was sent:

> We desire to inform you that the iron workers of Cincinnati, Covington, Newport, Aurora, Terre Haute and Portsmouth have been for the past sixteen weeks and still continue, on strike . . . we believe [the employers at these works] have now sent agents to Great Britain to try and induce men to leave that country for the purpose of taking the situations of the men on strike here. We have reasons for believing that Leeds will be the first place visited by the agents from this country,

and to prevent men being deluded under false pretenses we send this information for circulation, and request all British workmen not to be induced by the plausible tales of the employers' agents to come to this country and aid in our defeat.[76]

In response, the General Secretary of the British Association wrote:

I enclose a copy of circular letter, 2,000 of which will be distributed amongst the principal workmen in various districts of England, Scotland and Wales, on 26th and 27th. I will also go up to Leeds on 27th, and see some of the leaders and do all in my power to counteract the attempts of unprincipled agents who desire to induce workmen to cross the Atlantic for the purpose of blacklegging. . . . The letter will also appear in "Journal," issued and circulated on October 1st. . . .[77]

Again prompt coöperation and assistance from the British union prevented strikebreaking with British ironworkers.

Similar cables cut off any possibility of obtaining British strikebreakers during a boilermakers' strike in New York City in 1882, a strike at the Pacific Iron Nail Company in San Francisco in 1883,[78] and a nailers' strike in Oakland, California, and the east in 1884.[79] During the New York City dispute the president of the American union, James Curran, remarked that the cablegram to the British boilermakers "amounted to an order" that no boilermaker be allowed to come to America.[80] The Amalgamated Association of Iron and Steel Workers was confident that foreign skilled workers could not be imported as strikebreakers "for the English workmen are as well organized as we are, and the importation of Germans is almost an impossibility, for the German method of work is altogether different from the American mode of producing."[81]

Informal connections between American miners' unions and British unions during the seventies and eighties were particularly strong. Scores of American miners' leaders were men who had been introduced to trade-unionism in Britain.[82] One striking bit of evidence of the influence of such immigrants in miners' organizations in the United States was the fact that the constitution adopted by the short-lived Miners National Association in 1873 was patterned on the British organization of the same name.[83]

The initiative in turning these personal links to account in aiding the rational distribution of emigrant miners from Britain was taken by the British miner leaders themselves. The most outstanding work was that of Alexander MacDonald, the vigorous president of the Miners National Association, after he stopped listening to the overtures of American mine agents. Three times, in 1867, 1869, and 1876, MacDonald visited the United States, stopping at scores of mines, so that he was in a position to advise men where to go in America and what kind of mining they could expect to find.[84] After each trip, he submitted reports to conferences of British miners and spoke at local meetings, recommending the western part of the United States—Kansas in 1870, and Nevada and California in 1877—and urging intending emigrants to put themselves in touch with local trade-unions in America.[85] In addition to his journeys to America, MacDonald received frequent letters from acquaintances there and claimed to take thirty American newspapers each week.[86] Through the columns of the Glasgow *Sentinel,* he kept Scottish miners informed of conditions in the various coalfields of the United States and gave them notice of strike districts.[87]

MacDonald was not the only leader among British miners to take part in encouraging and advising emigrants. In 1876 and 1877 the Durham miners' agents served as an emigration committee until charges from local lodges that they were deriving profit from the undertaking put an end to it.[88] The General Secretary of the Durham miners, William Crawford, and also the head of the Northumberland miners, Thomas Burt, both visited the United States in the interests of advising emigrants.[89]

Because of unemployment and strikes, thousands of miners left the Durham area between 1879 and 1881. One writer estimated that three thousand departed in 1881 alone.[90] Crawford cautioned the men who were leaving: "What I want to do is to warn you against speculating rascals, who have inveigled some men away to where they are not wanted, and work not plentiful. Trust no adventurers."[91] These skilled miners did not go out to become wage cutters abroad. In fact, in this very group were men who became leaders in the Knights of Labor and later in the United Mine Workers.[92]

In the textile industry, unions were weak or nonexistent, except among the Lancashire mule spinners clustered in Fall River and New Bedford. Although the cotton spinners were not able to influence the flow of skilled emigrants from Britain to the same extent as miners and ironworkers, they did what they could to prevent strikebreaking by their own people. One mill operative, testifying before a Senate committee in 1883, said that he had written hundreds of letters to secretaries of operative associations in England warning men not to come to Fall River, but the unions generally answered that textile workers insisted upon coming to see for themselves.[93] Another defense adopted by the mule spinners in Fall River, Newburyport, and Lowell, when they could afford it, was to assist strikers to return to England.[94]

The work of the American and British trade unions in providing prospective emigrants with information and assistance was undoubtedly an important factor in making many skilled British workmen relatively impervious to exaggerated statements of recruiting agents as well as to offers of "free passages." It must not be inferred from this account that the skilled British workers were the only potential emigrants who were reached by warnings from America about agents of American industry. While the British were preponderant among the skilled foreign born in the mines, iron and steel works and textile factories, German industrial workers—blacksmiths, butchers, shoemakers, carpenters, and tailors— were found in trade-union lodges in America in the seventies.[95] While there were isolated cases of German trade-unions in the United States notifying their countrymen of unfavorable conditions in America, the inferior state of organization of trade-unions in Germany in the sixties and seventies, as compared with British, prevented the establishment of close communication.[96]

In addition to the warnings, advice, and information which issued forth from local workmen and trade-union lodges, as well as national craft unions in America, to defeat attempts at the recruitment of skilled contract labor, some efforts were made by the first national federation of unions, the National Labor Union, to deal with the problem of immigrant distribution on a broader front. William Sylvis, the "leading light" of the National Labor Union, was not satisfied with attempts to regulate immigration within the foundry industry alone. The tasks they set themselves were too big for this top-heavy organization which Professor Ware characterized as an "organization of leaders without unions."[97] Nevertheless, their projects have a good bit of intrinsic interest. While their ideas were too grandiose for their weak organization, they came closer to the heart of the problem than did the Knights of Labor, fifteen years later, when it fought for an anti-contract labor law.

After its first meeting, held in Baltimore in 1866, a committee from the National Labor Union called upon President Johnson and, among other items, stated their position on the relationship between tariffs and immigration, an argument which was later to be exploited by the Federation of Organized Trades and Labor Unions. In an argument to which Johnson did not deign to refer in his response, the delegates requested that labor be given some protection against "foreign pauper labor" commensurate with manufacturers' protection from the importation of foreign goods.[98]

The following year Sylvis began to take cognizance of "the great reform movement abroad," the International Workingman's Association, for the same reason that British trade unionists had been active in founding it at the time of the American Civil War: British trade unionists had also been confronted with foreign strikebreakers.[99] Influenced by Sylvis' hopes that some system of warning Europeans of trade disputes in America might be worked out, the N. L. U. convention of 1867 elected a delegate to go to Europe with "power to enter into such arrangements by treaty or otherwise, as he may deem best for the prevention of special importations to impoverish the Workingmen of America and Europe."[100]

Although this plan collapsed at the time, two years later Andrew C. Cameron, editor of the Chicago *Workingman's Advocate,* one of the many free-lance reformers who attended the congresses of the N. L. U., did attend the I. W. A. meeting at Basle, Switzerland. Cameron asked the I. W. A. to coöperate in setting up an emigration bureau, and although the Convention adopted the idea, the actual organizational work was tossed back directly at Cameron and the N. L. U. by the decision that definite organization of a bureau was to be postponed until Cameron furnished information on hours, wages, the demand for labor, and access to the land in different sections of America.[101] Such a task was far beyond the resources of the N. L. U., for it had only slender contact with local trades unions throughout the United States from whom it could get information on the state of trade from the workingman's standpoint.

In 1870 the National Labor Union tried to implement the program drawn up in Basle. A committee of five was appointed to act as the International Bureau of Labor and Emigration. The duties assigned to the bureau are a clue in themselves to the lack of local organization within the National Labor Union which blocked any real action:

> That the duties of this Bureau shall be generally to enter into correspondence with Trades, Labor and Emigrant Associations in Europe; obtain and forward information as to the condition of trade and labor, rates of wages, strikes and other such intelligence as may be valuable in the work of ameliorating the condition of labor here and in the Old World; to publish the same as may be desirable, and otherwise aid the one high purpose of all who work for our reform—that of complete unity and enfranchisement of labor everywhere.[102]

Backed by high-sounding phrases and little or no organization, the emigration bureau had no chance of influencing significantly the distribution of labor.

The fact remains that although the N. L. U. was unable to organize the distribution of immigrant labor in the United States to suit the trade-unionists, neither were the emigrant agencies able to control the recruitment of skilled immigrant labor to satisfy employers. Given the fluid job conditions of America and the channels of information open to the skilled European workers, the difficulties of the contract labor system clearly discouraged its large-scale use. Indeed, as time went on, employers doubted that they wanted to have to deal with British workers.

The opinion expressed in the columns of the New York *Herald Tribune* that English workmen "must change their habits if they are to make good in the United States. No longer can they give the worst work for the highest wages" found seconders among industrialists.[103] The attitude of Captain William R. Jones who became superintendent of Carnegie's Edgar Thompson Steelworks at Braddock, Pennsylvania, was significant. Outlining the labor policy to be carried out in the new works, he wrote:

> We must be careful of what class of men we collect. We must steer clear of the West where men are accustomed to infernal high wages. We must steer clear as far as we can of Englishmen who are great sticklers for high wages, small production and strikes. My experience has shown that Germans and Irish, Swedes and what I denominate "Buckwheats"—young American country boys, judiciously mixed, make the most effective and tractable force you can find. Scotsmen do very well, are honest and faithful. Welsh can be used in limited num-

bers. But mark me, Englishmen have been the worst class of men I have had anything to do with; and this is the opinion of Mr. Holley, George and John Fritz. . . .[104]

Such complaints against English workmen were frequently voiced in the textile industry. The greater number of strikes in Fall River was attributed to the English element in that city.[105] All the leaders of the Fall River strike of 1879 had come to Fall River since 1871, wrote the *Tribune,* from those two centers of trade-unionism and communism, Blackburn and Preston.[106] The English workmen were considered to be the most skillful operatives in the textile mills, but conditions in their native country were said to render them "peculiarly difficult to deal with" from the manufacturers' point of view. "Many of these men," wrote Carroll Wright, "came hither from Preston and Blackburn districts of England, bringing their inherited distrust of the employer, and accompanied by their old leaders who were not long in establishing here the customs and regulations of their craft."[107] An English observer in 1879 found this same attitude toward English workmen prevalent among Fall River employers. The Englishman was considered skillful and capable of turning out a large amount of work, but his "discontent" made him less satisfactory in the long run than the more "reliable and persevering" natives of other countries.[108]

To the American employer, the scarcity of skilled labor, his unwillingness to train it, the difficulties of recruiting it abroad, and the unsatisfactory result in trade-unions when he did, combined to recommend a policy of increased mechanization to free him from the demands of the skilled European workman.

PART II

FROM EUROPEAN FARMS TO AMERICAN INDUSTRY

Chapter 4

AGENCIES IN EUROPE FOR RECRUITING
UNSKILLED INDUSTRIAL LABOR

A great majority of the European immigrants during the nine-teenth century were not skilled and experienced industrial work-ers but people from European farms and villages whose skills and knowledge were agricultural. These former agriculturists became the "hewers of wood and drawers of water" for the developing American industrial giant. Their hands built the canals and rail-roads, performed "outside" labor at the mines, and handled fac-tory work which required little or no training.

The source of these agricultural migrants to American indus-try shifted several times during the century. This moving frontier of mass emigration—from Ireland and the Rhine provinces in mid-century, to the Scandinavian countries and northern and eastern Germany in the sixties, and the beginnings of the exodus from Italy and the Austro-Hungarian Empire in the eighties—is familiar. Several writers have demonstrated the remarkable way in which this vast emigration from European agriculture followed the trends of the American business cycle particularly after 1860 or 1870. Good business years in the United States were bumper years for immigration.[1]

This correlation between American business conditions and immigration in the last third of the nineteenth century might sug-gest, on the face of it, that American industry recruited common labor in Europe during boom years. Even if the powerful changes taking place in European agriculture be recognized (as in some

67

areas increased population pressed upon peasant freeholds and in others the breakup of feudalist relationships gave way to capitalist farming with hired labor), the ebb and flow of migration lends itself readily to a theory of recruitment by industry. In the movement of the early eighties to induce Congress to prohibit the importation of contract labor the charge was made and apparently widely believed that industrial capitalists were importing large numbers of Hungarian and Italian peasants.

This charge is not substantiated by either an investigation of the contemporary records in European countries or a careful analysis of the evidence submitted to Congressmen. To be sure, recruitment agencies were at work in the countryside in areas where agricultural circumstances produced the urge to move; but they were neither financed by nor directly connected with American industry, and contract labor played little if any part in their activities.

The most important groups at work in Europe after the Civil War were agents from western and southern state governments which continued to support the search for new blood to develop their industry and agriculture after the federal government withdrew from the field; railroad land companies eager to settle prospective customers and land purchasers along the line of their roads; steamship companies determined to carry full cargoes of immigrants on each trip to America; and independent commission agents who helped them to fill those ships. The "America letter" was probably equal in importance to all the formal agencies in impressing upon the European the opportunities which awaited him in America. Its influence became significant, however, only after the flow from a particular village or region had begun.

Scholars have paid far more attention to the activities of the railroads and states than they have to the steamship companies and other emigrant agencies. Yet it was in connection with the sale of steamship tickets that a new type of labor agency developed after the Civil War. These new agencies undertook both the recruitment in Europe and the distribution in America of immigrant labor for American industry. Widely different from the American Emigrant Company, these labor agencies dealt in unskilled labor and did not sign immigrants on contracts for American employers.

The circumstances which gave rise to these labor bureaus arose primarily in Europe. The agricultural laborer, the cotter, and the small tenant farmer responded eagerly to glowing descriptions of life in America which were laid before him. His chief difficulty was to get, somehow, the money necessary to transport himself, and perhaps his family, to America, once he had given up hope for the future at home and settled in his mind that he must seek his fortune elsewhere. If, by selling his plot of land or his household goods, he could manage his passage money, the assurance of a job soon after his arrival could be the deciding factor. Clearly those agents interested primarily in selling him his ticket had much to gain from being able to offer him a job on his arrival.

Out of these conditions came a system of distribution of unskilled labor to American industry far more efficient than anything which had operated before the Civil War. In the early railroad building era of the forties and fifties there was little systematic organization of the supplying of immigrant labor to industry. Irish and German agriculturists landing in America were left almost entirely to their own devices in finding work. Employers of labor, too, were for the most part dependent upon their own recruitment activities to collect workmen.

None of the important immigrant-receiving ports, New York, Boston, or New Orleans, offered public assistance to immigrants in locating jobs or to employers seeking help. Throughout the nineteenth century, in fact, almost the only disinterested work in rationalizing the immigrant labor market was done by voluntary national societies, founded by former immigrants themselves; but these efforts, hampered by inadequate funds and the stigma of charity, were not really significant. An Irish Emigrant Assistance Society, founded in New York City in 1825, tried to direct new arrivals into canal building.[2] Its successor, the Irish Emigrant Society, launched in 1841, organized a labor bureau which directed about 2,500 immigrants to jobs in 1842 and 1843.[3] In 1847 this Society and the German Emigrant Society, both woefully short of funds, urged the state of New York to take over the work of protecting and advising immigrants. When the state did step in the following year, these organizations discontinued their work among the newly arrived, since both their presidents sat as ex officio members on the Board of the State Emigration Commission. From the proceeds of the head tax levied in the 1847 Act, New York did make efforts to protect immigrants from fraud; but it had only a perfunctory labor bureau before 1867. Massachusetts never established a labor bureau for immigrants at Boston even though an investigation of the late fifties revealed a substantial surplus from the head tax paid by immigrants beyond the expenses of caring for those immigrants who later became public charges.[4]

Private labor agencies, dealing in large numbers of unskilled immigrants for canal and railroad work, do not appear to have been firmly established as middlemen as they were to be later in the century. Both New York and Boston had "intelligence offices" during the fifties which fleeced job-seeking immigrants of all they could.[5] There is nothing to suggest, however, that these offices supplied large numbers of workmen for construction projects. The few New York labor bureaus handling German and Irish immigrant labor which advertised in the newspapers stressed jobs for servants, laundresses, and clerks and probably served no more than a limited local market.[6] Immigrant labor was to be found in New York and Boston but construction bosses, or their agents, had to collect it themselves.

While New England and other eastern railroads and canals had a convenient source of labor, the contractors on projects distant from both large cities and a settled rural population faced rather serious problems in acquiring and keeping an adequate force. There is little evidence of their resorting to direct recruitment in Europe. As the mid-nineteenth-century German and Irish emigration climbed to the hundreds of thousands, port cities became convenient pools from which to obtain immigrant labor for construction works undertaken during the fifties.

Getting the men from these cities to isolated construction projects, and keeping them there, housed in rude temporary shacks, separated from their families, and facing disease, floods, and severe cold, were not easy tasks. During the construction of the St. Mary's Falls Ship Canal begun in 1854 far from any local sources of labor, labor shortages constantly delayed the work.[7] The canal company had to employ its own agents to collect workmen, chiefly in New York City. The Michigan Central Railroad agreed to transport construction workers for the canal from Buffalo to Detroit at a dollar a passage to be paid in the first instance by the Canal Company which presumably reimbursed itself later from the immigrants' wages. Many of the men thus forwarded, having been recently subjected to the ravages of the immigrant sailing vessel, were "sick, tired, lean, lank, slim, light built fellows"; some were "not well enough to hardly sit up, certainly not well enough to stand or walk."[8] Confronted with this situation one of the contractors suggested employing an agent who "is acquainted with laboring men to select them and not paying any base for those of inferior stature. . . ."[9]

The Illinois Central Railroad, which started construction in Illinois in 1852, also had to depend chiefly on its own agents to get workers from port cities. To secure men, the Illinois Central authorized its agents to advance to immigrants the $4.50 or $4.75 necessary for transportation from New York to Chicago as a loan to be repaid from wages.[10]

In 1852, Roswell B. Mason, the engineer in charge of construction for the Central, appointed H. Phelps as agent in New York to collect and forward immigrants. The first group of six hundred whom Phelps forwarded arrived in Chicago completely destitute. The Company had made no preparations to handle their distribution out from Chicago. About a hundred were sent to the works at La Salle; but the others remained in Chicago because Mason Brayman, the solicitor to the railroad, who was in charge in Mason's absence, lacked authority to send them to the various construction sites. The delay brought the mayor of Chicago on the scene insisting that the company get the immigrants to work so that they would not have to be supported by the city.[11]

By 1853 the system of recruiting and forwarding men was working somewhat more efficiently. At first, attempts were made to get enough men in Chicago and St. Louis by providing teams to bring them to the work and paying their expenses; but since no men were to be found in either city, further arrangements had to be made with the New York agent.[12] The contractor on the twelfth division promised to pay Phelps a dollar for each man shipped who worked at least a month. In order to avoid the bottleneck in Chicago which had occurred the previous year, Phelps made agreements with various railroad companies to send men from New York to Kankakee, Illinois, by way of the Great Lakes. Even under this system, however, men bound for the twelfth division were set down one hundred miles from the actual construction site.[13]

The Illinois Central also dispatched an agent to New Orleans in 1853 to tap the spring flow of German immigrants. Having made arrangements for cheap rail fares,[14] this agent arrived in Jonesboro on March 10th with five hundred men and promised to supply five hundred a week for the six-week period of heavy immigration. By April 3rd he had sent twelve hundred men to the southern division "which about kept the force good."[15]

As immigration through New Orleans diminished with the approach of summer, the possible shortage of men led the Company's engineer to try to procure labor in New York from other sources than its labor agent there.[16] In April Mason "arranged with one concern in New York to send 1,500 Germans and with an Irish Emigrant Society to send a large number."[17] In July Mason recommended hiring still another New York agent to forward two thousand men.[18]

The difficulties which these contractors of the fifties met in trying to keep an adequate labor force on the job, in the face of a constant turnover and makeshift arrangements for getting labor in the ports, make the laying of 21,000 miles of road during the decade a most remarkable achievement. Although in emergency men could be obtained through Irish and German emigrant aid societies, it was clear that the specialized private labor agency could fulfill several useful functions for western railroad builders. It might take over the troublesome functions of selecting men of sufficient physical strength, of seeing that enough were supplied, and of conducting them from the ports to construction sites. Moreover, the development of labor agencies might shift the site of railroad labor pools from New York to Chicago. As the system developed, the labor agent was also frequently to undertake to feed and house his men on the job; such a man, when he operated among Italian immigrants, was often called a "padrone." This arrangement was probably unusual in the fifties: the Illinois Central, in fact, fired one of its foremen who appeared with his own crew and was suspected of being "in collusion with the men."[19]

Although more than 150,000 miles of railroad track were laid between the end of the Civil War and the panic of 1893, their builders probably had less difficulty than those of the earlier generation in meeting labor force requirements. As recruitment agencies in Europe, whether interested primarily in a large turnover of immigrant passages or the luring of great numbers of people to particular areas, discovered that what the poorer agricultural emigrant longed for most of all was the assurance of a job on arrival in America, they found it to their advantage to establish some liaison with American industry in the interests of prying the potential emigrant loose. Industrialists and railroad builders had little need to participate in the traffic themselves. Even the work that railroad agents had had to do in the fifties was now done for them, at a price, of course.

The pressure upon recruitment agencies operating in Europe to give assurances about jobs is clearly demonstrated in the activities of both state immigration bureaus and railroad land companies. These organizations also learned that the contract labor system was unsuitable for bringing unskilled agricultural immigrants to America.

Several southern states which established immigration bureaus, or licensed private immigration agencies, aimed at recruiting industrial labor as well as plantation labor and servants, and, toward that end, legalized contract labor.[20] Their failure to attract the immigrant is well known; and offering assisted passages to unskilled workers did their cause no good.

The German Consul in Galveston warned prospective emigrants against the Texas scheme through an official letter to the state governments in the North German Confederation.[21] *Hemlandet,* perhaps the most influential of Swedish-American newspapers, ridiculed rumors of assisted passages.

How could any sensible man believe that any company here in America would pay the travel expenses for emigrants from Sweden on terms that the emigrants should work off the advance? There isn't the slightest guarantee that the emigrant will fulfill the agreement on arrival.[22]

The contract labor system was completely unsuitable for the importation of unskilled plantation and railroad labor. The Missouri Board of Immigration, which had planned in 1864 to assist the importation of contract labor with high hopes of success, concluded by 1870 that "Man is not a merchandise that can be imported. All attempts to do this have proved failures . . . forced importation . . . will prove as unprofitable as it is unwise."[23]

The western states—Iowa, Colorado, Missouri, Wisconsin, Minnesota, and Michigan—which supported state immigration agencies abroad after the war had already discovered the futility of promoting contract labor in large-scale recruitment. In most cases they did, however, emphasize opportunities for work immediately on arrival in America in their publicity abroad.

When the Wisconsin State Immigration Commission, for example, decided to send agents to Europe in 1871, they stressed that one of Wisconsin's chief selling points was constant employment for laborers at high wages, recognizing that "this is a very important item to the immigrant without means . . ."[24] Wisconsin closed its European agency during the depression of the seventies but renewed its activities as prosperity returned. Again opportunities for work in the lumber industry were featured in their pamphlets.[25] In 1881, K. K. Kennan, who had originally been sent to Europe by the Wisconsin Central Railroad to sell land, was appointed agent of the State Commission. Setting up headquarters in Basle, Switzerland, Kennan advertised in Germany, Bavaria, and Sweden, offering "just as cordial and ready assistance to the mechanic bound for Milwaukee as to the farmer who proposes to buy lands . . ."[26] He claimed that many Bavarians were induced to come to Wisconsin by assurances of work in the lumber camps of the northern counties.[27]

Other states which aimed primarily at recruiting farmers advertised jobs and wages in railroads and other private industrial undertakings within their states. Michigan mine owners exported state pamphlets describing the inducements of Michigan copper mines,[28] and Minnesota's commissioner advertised abundant employment for mechanics of all kinds.[29] Since the difficulties with unskilled contract labor had been discovered in 1864 by Maine enthusiasts, the colony of "New Sweden" planned and started in 1870, instead of promoting contracts simply advertised "work opportunities" on railroads, in lumber camps, and in trades.[30] The need of the prospective emigrant for a job was probably fully as important as requests by employers for workers in encouraging state agents to advertise industrial jobs.

Similar considerations colored the statements of railroad land companies with agents in Europe. In the midst of the Civil War labor shortage the land commissioner of the Hannibal and St. Joseph Railroad publicized in his letters to agents in Ireland the road's need for "common laborers." "Our Rail Road want a great many," he wrote. "So do the other Roads & they have to pay the highest wages to them—So you see here is full & complete remedy to the 'famine for employment' in Ireland, which you speak of . . ."[31] In Wales, where coal miners formed a large body of potential emigrants, the agents of the Company were instructed to stress that "New Cambria, Mo. is in a Coal Region & Coal Miners are naturally attracted to it."[32]

As railroad building boomed in the northern interior states,

Illinois, Wisconsin, Minnesota, Iowa, Missouri, Ohio, Kansas, and Nebraska, during the late sixties and seventies,[33] many agents for the land companies of railroads constructing new lines landed in Europe. In spite of the fact that their job was to attract land purchasers, these agents took advantage of the fact that construction was in progress to give settlers general assurances of employment.

The Central Pacific of California offered to "employ all the labor that may be offered" on construction at thirty dollars a month plus board.[34] Agents sent abroad by the Northern Pacific in 1870 offered "abundant employment" for a year or two on the road.[35] One of their pamphlets stated more cautiously that although the Northern Pacific did not guarantee employment to anyone, in a new and rapidly growing country like central and western Minnesota, "willing hands do not wait long for employment."[36] Hans Mattson, representing the Lake Superior and St. Paul Railroad, maintained that, for the poor who had "nothing but their good will and bodies" to depend upon, there was an unusually large amount of opportunity for work at $2.50 to $3.00 a day in the neighborhood of the railroad's lands, particularly at lumber camps and sawmills.[37] One advertisement of the Lake Superior and Mississippi Railroad Land Company, which appeared in nearly every issue of *Skandinavisk Post* between 1870 and 1873, offered steady work for two thousand on railroad construction.[38]

Pamphlets issued for American readers during these years by land agencies of roads which did not have construction projects in hand held out no inducements to laborers, clearly stipulating that they wanted men with capital.[39] Agents in the European field perhaps yielded more readily to the temptation to mention job opportunities and high wages. The policy of the Burlington Railroad during the sixties was to sell land, not recruit labor; yet Henry Wilson, its agent in Liverpool, had to emphasize this policy constantly in letters to sub-agents in terms such as these: "You make the same error as do most agents, by not striking for *men with money*. We do not want men who have barely the means to emigrate, but farmers, their sons, etc., and people who have capital."[40] In spite of warnings from George Harris, the Road's land commissioner, that he had no knowledge of the labor needs of corporations and no time to find out,[41] the Burlington subagents continued to promise job opportunities, claiming that wages in Nebraska were "higher than in any other state."[42] On seeing such an advertisement from one of his agents Wilson wrote: "from your advt such people as navvy's labourers, colliers, etc., are calculated to make a rush for the new country whereas we do not actually want to send them."[43]

When the new construction boom began in 1879, representatives of American railways were again to be found stimulating the emigration of the humbler agricultural peoples of Europe. The *Railroad Gazette* watched indices of immigrant arrivals from 1879 to 1882, noting that unless the rate of immigration continued high, contemplated construction would be handicapped.[44] The editor commented with satisfaction that large numbers were arriving from Ireland, the Scandinavian countries, and Italy who would be likely to seek employment in railroad construction.[45] By 1883 the boom was over, the rate of building retarded, and the *Gazette* was happy to see that fewer immigrants were landing.[46]

The construction frontier had shifted westward by the time of the boom of the early eighties, the heaviest building taking place in the tier of states west of the Mississippi and in the Rocky Mountain states.[47] One of the roads under construction in the Dakotas, a region which added 724 miles of track in 1880 alone,[48] encouraged farm laborers to come as well as "the industrious classes of Europe, who make a scant living on rented farms."[49] In 1881 the Denver and Rio Grande Railroad was building 400 miles of road in Colorado and contemplated another 800 miles to extend the line to Mexico. Faced with this enormous program, the road took extraordinary measures, quite apart from land-selling activities, to obtain workers. Advertisements appeared in Great Britain to the effect that 10,000 workers were needed at $1.25 to $1.75 a day plus board.[50] The line was reported as treating with several Italian labor agents and sending a man abroad to try to get French workers. In all their extraordinary measures to get workers, the construction agents made it clear that the road was unwilling to pay the transportation costs of immigrants because they were not sure they could keep them in service once they arrived in Colorado.[51]

Both state bureaus and railroad land departments concentrated their activities in northern Europe—in Great Britain, Switzerland, the Scandinavian countries, and the German states. In the case of the Burlington this reflected George Harris' view: "I have so poor an opinion of the French and Italian immigrants for agriculturalists that I shall not issue any circulars in their language."[52]

Steamship companies, on the other hand, did not discriminate between areas of recruitment for they were primarily interested in filling the ships and it did not matter whether potential agriculturists or railroad laborers were in the cargo. Their agents followed the push of emigration throughout Europe, as active in Sweden and Norway in the early seventies as they were in Italy and Hungary in the eighties and nineties. In fact, as one follows this moving frontier of recruitment the traditional classification of "new" and "old" immigration which has guided so much of American thinking on the subject of immigration in the past is an obstacle rather than a guide to uncovering the facts.

The assumption that the immigrants of the eighties and nineties from southern and eastern Europe were "imported" in any unique way which differed markedly from the steerage immigrant traffic of the sixties cannot be substantiated. If there was a watershed in recruitment, after which more people came in response to job advertisements from America, the victory of the steamship on the Atlantic by the mid-sixties marks the beginning of the "new era" rather than the start of southern and eastern European emigration to the United States two decades later.[53] The steamship companies honeycombed potential emigration areas with agencies, sub-agencies, and individual agents, thrusting down recruitment roots more firmly and widely than either state governments or railroad land companies.

The real transcendance of the steamship over the sailing vessel for transatlantic emigrant shipping coincided with the beginnings of an important emigrant traffic from Scandinavia.[54] Sweden and Norway thus provide a good model of the "new type" of recruitment. Unfortunately a definitive study of steamship activities will probably only be possible when and if the records of the older companies are made available to scholars. Something can be learned about the appeals they made and their methods of operation among the poorer classes of agricultural migrants, many of whom were ultimately distributed as unskilled workers to American industry, from newspaper advertisements, records of government investigations, and discussions in the emigrant press.

Before 1864, steamship companies did not advertise in the rural press of Sweden. They depended largely upon emigrant companies and private individuals to bring them business. But by 1867, their advertisements began to appear regularly and in large quantities in Swedish and Norwegian newspapers. By 1870, six different lines were competing for the Scandinavian traffic, offering to carry emigrants either through Hull and Liverpool or via Hamburg, Bremen, or Copenhagen.[55] The competition did not express itself in rivalry over which line provided the most comfortable crossing. An investigator for the British Board of Trade of the handling of Scandinavians remarked as late as 1882 that "although the accommodation offered for the money is not of the sort that would satisfy an ordinary English mechanic I am satisfied . . . that it is equal to if not ahead of the wants and experience of these emigrants. . . ."[56] A very important aspect of the competition was, however, the offer of steamship agents to help emigrants to find jobs upon their arrival in New York or Chicago.

Late in 1869, Captain H. A. Burger was appointed general agent for the Anchor Line in Sweden and Norway.[57] Burger was an experienced operator in the emigrant business, having worked for the American Emigrant Company and founded a prominent emigrant newspaper, *Amerika*. At the time of his new appointment he was serving as agent for several railroads as well as a shady sort of emigrant agency, the Swedish Commercial Company.[58] Partly at Burger's suggestion, the Anchor Line set up labor bureaus in Chicago in 1869 and in New York in 1870 in order to attract people who needed assurance of work before they would buy steamship tickets to America. Burger's sub-agents in Sweden advertised in the rural press that passengers could get suitable work "with respectable entrepreneurs" at the going wages in different states at the Anchor Line's labor bureaus.[59] After the depression of the seventies, the new agents of the Anchor Line in Norway, Henderson Brothers, again found it useful to advertise "good work at high daily wages is procured" for all its passengers.[60]

Other steamship companies followed the Anchor Line's lead. Cunard advertised its labor bureau in 1870, and by 1871 had procured the services of a returned Swedish emigrant who offered to find "favorable jobs for men and women" in Boston through the supposedly philanthropic American Industrial Aid Society.[61] An interpreter was to go with Inman Line passengers on the voyage. They would be met in New York by a Captain Anderson who would give them advice on work and arrange for their safe conduct to Chicago with another interpreter who would help them obtain jobs there.[62] The Allan Line and the Montreal Steamship Companies also advertised labor bureaus in the early seventies, while in the eighties two more lines, the State Line and the Dominion Line, claimed to have arrangements for finding jobs for emigrants in America.[63]

Usually the advertisements of these labor bureaus were vague and gave no evidence that they were operating "to orders" from American employers. Only rarely did industrialists in need of labor make use of the steamship company offices in Sweden to obtain a load of workers. John Newberry, who in 1872 was seeking 400 workers for the Lake Superior region, established headquarters in the Allan Line offices in Gothenberg.[64] In 1881 the Dominion Line offered to take emigrants to work on "a new railroad line" in Canada,[65] while the Inman Line was also asking for railroad labor.[66] These tempting offers were sometimes spurious. On 6 April 1881, a shipload of 235 men, many of whom had borrowed money from friends and relatives to answer an Inman Line agent's advertisement that he had been requested to furnish 400 Swedish miners for a Pennsylvania mining company at $1.75 a day for miners and $1.25 for other workers,[67] embarked with their families, only to find when they arrived that the mining company denied it had asked Inman agents to get workers for it.[68]

Besides the actual steamship company offices a number of emigrant agencies which, like the American Emigrant Company after it had given up trying to get American employers to invest in passages, were interested primarily in steamship ticket commissions, exchanging of money, and the sale of land, began offering industrial jobs to immigrants.

One of these, the American Emigrant Aid and Homestead Company, found, much to its regret, that advancing passage money on the strength of emigrants' future jobs was risky. Although this firm wanted chiefly to sell certain lands in Pennsylvania and the south, it advertised through its agents in Sweden and Norway that it was prepared to find jobs for needy emigrants.[69] "Our corporation," ran one of its brochures, "is in communication with many large factories, railroad construction companies, etc., and can usually find employment for those who seek it. . . ."[70]

Such advertising attracted emigrants, but not people able to buy land. Of the passengers sent by their agents to the *Ottawa*, the first ship chartered by this company, only 40 were able to pay their fares. Having collected only 22, instead of an expected 300 self-paying passengers at Gothenberg, the Company took on, at Christiania, some 230 emigrants, chiefly laborers and handicraftsmen, as a speculation. The Company hoped to reimburse itself later from their wages.[71]

Finding jobs for these emigrants, to pay for the speculation in fares, was difficult. Many of the *Ottawa's* passengers registered complaints with their Consul in New York.[72] Others refused jobs with plantation owners. About 250 finally went to Missouri to work off their passages on contracts with the Southern Pacific Railroad. While the American Emigrant Aid and Homestead Company received $5000 from the railroad for getting it laborers, the railroad was not likely to enter into such an arrangement again. Soon after the immigrants arrived they went on strike, charging both the railroad and the recruiting company with bad faith.[73] The directors described the venture as a "wretched failure, and a dead loss of some forty thousand dollars."[74]

One of the most widely publicized of these emigrant agencies was the Scandinavian Emigrant Agency, founded in 1868, which appointed Frans Peterson general agent for Sweden in November 1869. Peterson soon became deeply involved in labor recruitment.[75] He offered to procure jobs for laborers with farmers and contractors, with tradesmen, factory owners, and innkeepers, through a Chicago branch which was headed by A. E. Johnson, a man of very doubtful reputation, and Peter Peterson.[76] Claiming to have entered into agreements with businessmen in several states, Peterson was ready to "guarantee" work right after their arrival to all who applied, whatever time of year they came.[77]

Of particular interest is the fact that Peterson offered free board and room in Chicago for all who came out with him, as well as promising that he could "advance transportation costs" to the southern states where workers were needed.[78] He encouraged one of the licensed boardinghouse keepers in New York City, a Dane, to offer work for large numbers of railroad and canal laborers in New York and surrounding states,[79] promising "free" passage to the working place from New York City.[80] These inducements were strikingly similar to those made by Italian "bankers"; and the system of distribution, to be discussed in the next chapter, was also much the same.

Peterson's promises of work, like those of the steamship company labor bureaus, were usually vague and general. The fact that occasionally more specific jobs were advertised only serves to highlight the probability that the "agreements" he claimed to have with American employers were not of a very binding kind. In the spring of 1872 a Swedish-American work foreman on the New Jersey and Midland Railroad arrived in Sweden to collect 600 railroad workers through Peterson's office.[81] During 1870, 500 workers were ordered for both the Lake Superior and Mississippi River Railroad and the Southern Minnesota, and 1,000 more for the McGregor and Missouri Railroad through the Scandinavian Emigrant Agency's offices in Sweden.[82] After the Chicago fire, one Chicago labor bureau offered to get jobs at $5.00 a day for laborers who came with letters of recommendation from Peterson.[83] Again completely spurious offers were interspersed with others which may have had some basis.[84]

Other such companies plowed the Scandinavian emigration field. Count Edward Taube for the Great European and American Land Company claimed to have entered into association "with several honorable persons in the large cities of America to obtain information on the demand for work . . ."[85] until his sales of spurious land certificates for the Company's Wisconsin land forced the Company itself to print warnings in the European press and led its president, Caleb Cushing, to resign after trying to redeem some of Taube's pledges.[86] Another company, the Scandinavian Head Office, had arrangements to board its immigrants with a Chicago Swede until it found them work.[87]

Steamship companies and closely allied recruitment agencies also operated in Great Britain during the seventies and eighties. A. A. Wise, Cunard's agent in London, published a newspaper called *Free West,* comparable to *Amerika* or *Amerika-Bladet* in Sweden, which advised emigrants on employment, or, in other words, held out the same vague offers of work to potential passengers on their lines. In *Free West* and in labor journals, Wise and the Allan Line's London agent advertised the American Emigrant Agency which offered to issue, free of charge, letters of "Endorsement and Recommendation to the largest Employers of Labour of all kinds—such as Machine Shops, Railroad Companies, Builders, Farmers, Printers, Lithographers, Factories, and All the Various Branches of Labour, insuring employment on arrival" to all who brought them "Certificates of Character."[88] Rail fare advances from ports to the interior were offered, and intending emigrants were invited to advertise at low rates in *Free West* to contact employers willing to advance ocean fares as well.[89] Other examples could be given.[90] In an investigation made in 1891 for the United States Commissioners of Immigration, Joseph Powderly found that steamship company and emigration agency officers in London were still advising applicants on work in America, though not "guaranteeing" situations.[91]

Reports of former emigrants returning to Germany to recruit labor and of labor exchanges in America were also to be found in German emigrant journals in the late sixties.[92] However, the German government strictly enforced regulations against labor agents after representatives of American manufacturers were thrown out of Germany in 1870.[93] In spite of these restrictions there is some evidence of recruitment of miners and iron workers in the coal and iron district of the Rhineland and Westphalia, Galicia, and Silesia, carried on apparently by former emigrants.[94] One agent of the North German Lloyd Steamship Company told a reporter from John Swinton's newspaper in 1884 that their manager received many applications for German men and women in small gangs of one or two hundred who were wanted for cotton mills, iron mines, and factories, but that this company, which did the largest transatlantic passenger business, was too busy to deal with such orders.[95]

This kind of recruitment for industry which went on in Britain, Scandinavia, and Germany involved little expense by industry itself; and yet these activities were intensified at exactly those times when American industry needed more workers. Railroad land companies and state governments invested in expensive foreign agencies only during prosperous times, and steamship companies had more ships going west with space for immigrants in good years. The discussions of immigration which preceded the Foran Act to prohibit the importation of contract labor in 1885 were based on the assumption that radically different forms of recruitment of agricultural workers were being used in Italy and Hungary, that mine operators and railroad companies were actually engaged in importing unskilled workers on contracts. The evidence offered in these discussions suggests, on the contrary, that what was really happening was that steamship companies, emigrant agencies, and independent commission men were merely expanding their base of operations into new areas, using much the same inducements and methods which had been developed in northern Europe.

For one thing, the term "contract labor" was used very loosely in the discussions of the eighties. One witness before a House Committee said that Slavonians were "contract laborers" in that "importers" had made a special contract with a steamship company at a low rate for their delivery in America.[96] There was no suggestion in his evidence that contracts had been drawn up between industrialists and immigrants such as one found in skilled labor recruitment. The Pennsylvania Secretary of Internal Affairs maintained that the "great part" of Italians arriving were under contract. As he described it, "A railroad contractor tells a man going abroad the amount of men he wants and in a specified time they arrive."[97] Such agents might well have been Italian bankers or operators of labor agencies, and the arrival of the immigrants did not prove that they came on contracts. Consul Starkloff in Bremen "suspected" that Polish, Bohemian, and Hungarian miners were being engaged on contract by Pennsylvania mining companies. His evidence was that the emigrants came in groups, spoke to no one, and followed their "leader" blindly.[98] Such a scene in a European railway station gave no proof as to whether the men were being brought on contracts or merely the kind of promises which Frans Peterson gave to intending Swedish emigrants.

Although one Hungarian interviewed by the New York *Sun* maintained that "nearly all" the Hungarians came to America on contracts, the Pennsylvania Secretary of Internal Affairs thought they came voluntarily.[99] Old inhabitants of the Connellsville coke region remembered that in 1882 some companies had agents in Europe soliciting the emigration of Slovaks, Poles, and Bohemians, but they could only guess that "some may have been imported as contract laborers."[100]

There is nothing definite in these reminiscences and statements to suggest that coal operators and railroad contractors were actually forwarding passage money and signing contracts with peasants of Hungary, Italy, and Poland. It seems far more likely that industry was depending upon steamship companies and private labor agents to collect workers for them in Italy and Hungary as they had in the Scandinavian countries.

Steamship companies and their agents were certainly actively engaged in trying to fill ships by recruitment in rural areas of Italy, Hungary, and Poland. The New York Emigration Commissioners spoke of the steamship company agents "sweeping into their vessels all they can induce to emigrate," with the result that many came who had passage money and no more.[101] As was the case in their activities in the Scandinavian countries, the agents of steamship companies were interested in selling tickets for fees; and, if statements about jobs and wages in America helped toward that end, they were made. Circulars thrown into their huts and villages by steamship company agents told Italian peasants that they could make from $2.50 to $3.50 a day in the Pennsylvania coal regions.[102] Some steamship companies were said to have as many as two thousand agents in Europe in every district on the continent. These sub-agents got commissions of between fifty cents and two dollars on every emigrant passenger obtained.[103]

Some people thought that steamship company agents made a practice of advancing "free" tickets on contracts. P. J. McGuire, General Secretary of the Brotherhood of Carpenters and Joiners, said in testimony before a congressional committee: "[The Hungarians] come under contract—to fulfill contracts. They receive a certain compensation, and a percentage goes to the parties who make the contracts, generally transportation companies combined . . ."[104] The implication is that transportation companies made work contracts; there is no other evidence in congressional committee reports except this vague statement. The Pennsylvania Secretary of Internal Affairs did not think that steamship companies "made a business of importing labor on contract."[105] Certainly the financial dispositions for such a venture would have been vast and risky. One type of arrangement which might have been confused with labor contracts was the fairly common practice by which a ticket agent advanced a loan for the ticket money at exorbitant interest taking a mortgage on whatever property, a small farm, a house, or a vineyard, the prospective emigrant had.[106]

Next in order of respectability to steamship companies among recruiters of labor in southern Europe were the Italian "banks" which were in many ways comparable to firms like the Swedish Commercial Company, the Scandinavian Head Office, and the Scandinavian Emigrant Agency. Such firms were interested in handling currency for immigrants; often they ran boardinghouses for recent arrivals; and many were prepared to supply immigrant labor to contractors who requested it. The owner of Banca Italiano told a reporter who posed as an iron manufacturer that he had imported 14,000 Italians over a period of twenty years. When necessary he advanced about $34 for traveling expenses. This is where the "contract system" entered. The immigrant was to repay the loan at 6 per cent interest.[107] Joseph Powderly reported as late as 1892 that he was told in Naples that Italian bankers and hotel keepers were inducing emigration to the United States through their agents there, although no direct evidence of contracts was to be found.[108] A representative of one agency told editor John Swinton that it had given up making contracts in Europe because they were unenforceable in court. Contracts were signed in New York City instead for a period of six months.[109] They preferred immigrants who paid their own fares.[110]

A labor "syndicate" in Denver had agents in Italy "enthusing the poor workingmen with a desire to come to this country," in order to hire them out to railroads and public works projects in Colorado. The immigrant had to pay his own passage. To secure the job he had to deposit a fee of three, five, or ten dollars, and contract to pay his importer 20 per cent of his wages for three years.[111] The system was extortionate, but not very different from some modern private labor bureaus as to the principles on which fees were to be paid: a fee and a percentage of the wage for a stipulated period of time.[112]

These bankers and labor agents were probably comparable to other intelligence and labor bureaus in every way except that some of them risked advancing passage money from Europe. In this way the unscrupulous operator often gained a whip-hand over the immigrant so long as the latter believed the contract which he made for repayment enforceable. The immigrant was in virtual subjection to these men who were in some cases only a "shade better than padroni."[113] This type of banker boarded the immigrant until he was placed in a job, charged food and lodging up to his debt, and tried to get the immigrant work with a railroad or public works contractor or coal-mine operator to enable him to repay the advances. Several immigrants brought out on such terms appeared before the Ford Committee in 1888. Immigrants committed themselves to pay forty, fifty, sixty-five, or seventy dollars in return for passage advances which probably amounted to about twenty-one dollars.[114] Many had pledged property as security.

The real padroni class can be divided into two groups. One type of padroni imported children, dwarfs, and cripples to exploit them as bootblacks, street musicians, ragpickers, and street acrobats.[115] The other class which served American industry was, like the banker, an importer of labor, but the contracts he made bound the immigrant to him in a personal relationship more akin to servitude. The differences between the padrone and the unscrupulous type of intelligence bureau agent were that the padrone hired the immigrant at a fixed rate and stood to profit from whatever wage he could get for him above that rate; and that the padrone kept his men with him, accompanied them to the job, and handled all the relations between them and contractors. The padrone was their employer.[116] In the summer of 1888 the Italian Vice-Consul in New York stated that there were no longer padroni in New York City.[117] At any rate, the system was already very much weakened. The labor bureau was not so shortlived.

In addition to these institutions which helped recruit labor for American industry, the emigrant letter must be mentioned as another typical and cheap method by which industry obtained immigrant labor. This method was certainly used to some extent for getting unskilled workers as well as skilled men. Railroad companies encouraged employees to send for their families. T. V. Powderly maintained that superintendents "bribed" Hungarian, Greek, Italian, and Slavonian workers to write to their acquaintances to induce them to emigrate.[118] Swedish and Norwegian workers in the Wisconsin lumber industry also wrote letters home stipulating their wages and working conditions.[119] At the end of the century the United States Industrial Commission concluded that American letters were

the principal means by which, at the present time, employers desiring to import laborers secure their immigration. They simply speak to their friends, advising them of the opportunities for employment, and the latter attend to the correspondence . . . necessary to bring the foreigners to these shores.[120]

The actual recruitment in Europe of unskilled immigrant labor for American industry was not undertaken by industry itself, but by a variety of other institutions which, in the interests of encouraging a poor man to emigrate, offered to find him a job in the United States. If the agriculturist had sold all he owned to pay his passage and was without contacts in America he was almost certain to have to turn to one of the private labor agencies when he landed. While American industry was clearly not involved in importing unskilled contract labor, some immigrants did arrive on contracts with ticket agents and bankers under which they agreed to repay loans for passage from their first wage packets. Such arrangements were probably a feature of the early days of emigration from any country and were designed to stimulate the general flow of immigration. Thus the American Emigrant Aid and Homestead Company made a speculation in fares in Sweden during the sixties as did some Italian bankers in the eighties. The evidence suggests that agencies or agents making such loans soon ceased the practice on finding the risks greater than the profits.

Chapter 5

THE DISTRIBUTION OF
UNSKILLED IMMIGRANTS TO INDUSTRY

As he comes down the gangplank, staggering under the weight of baggage that would break the back of a mule, wrote the editor of the Philadelphia *Times,* the average European immigrant knows nothing about American institutions. He dumps his trap on the wharf, sits down to eat his bread and cheese, and then moves on. In twelve hours he has disappeared. "It has puzzled many people to discover how he becomes welded with the population, how he finds employment and what he does when unable to get it."[1]

The pioneer emigrants from any particular village, region, or country in Europe had neither personal, nor often institutional, ties in the United States. To them organizations engaged in distributing immigrant labor to industry were important and often necessary. Once the people of a European village had established links with America through former emigrants they had less need for institutional assistance in finding jobs. Emigration was planned in private letters, and arrangements for finding employment were made through friends and relatives in the United States. This type of individual planning determined the distribution of thousands of late-comers from an area even though many migrants were thus led into towns and cities where their townspeople were more plentiful than were jobs.

This chapter is concerned with the institutions which distributed unskilled industrial labor to jobs during the last part of the nineteenth century. Whether he came from Scandinavia or eastern

Germany in the sixties or Italy in the eighties, the facilities offered by both public and private labor agencies were of great importance to the "new" immigrant. The chapter is divided into two sections. Chicago as a distributing center is discussed first as affording a clear picture of the problems Scandinavian emigrants faced in finding work in America after they had fled from famine in the late sixties. More particularly it is the sequel to the story of recruitment in Scandinavia outlined in the previous chapter. The rest of the chapter is devoted to a description of the more varied institutions of New York City as they appeared to the Italian or Hungarian immigrant of the eighties.

The Swedish agricultural laborer or "torpare" often arrived in America with little money remaining after he had paid his travel expenses.[2] Scandinavian consular officials estimated that the average amount carried by emigrants in 1869 was $54.[3] According to one observer, many brought about $100 thinking that would last three months while they looked for work, but found it was gone in half the time and they still did not have jobs.[4] Cases of destitute Swedes and Norwegians in the late sixties were by no means infrequent. Swedish-Norwegian consuls in Baltimore, New York City, Washington, Cincinnati, and Chicago wrote of the increasing number of recent emigrants who came to them, without jobs, without knowledge of the language, requesting some kind of aid. Some, it was said, had had no food for three or four days and were sleeping in Battery Park with no means of getting out of New York City.[5]

Chicago became the chief distributing point for Swedish and Norwegian immigrants. Many came directly to that city via Quebec and Montreal. In 1869, 24,260 Swedes and 15,172 Norwegians arrived in Chicago. According to the Scandinavian Consul, most of them, having brought their tickets through to that city, were quite penniless when they arrived and unable to proceed farther inland.[6] At the Chicago railroad stations, and frequently on the trains a few miles outside the city, immigrant runners, scrambling to divide the spoils, swarmed down upon the newly arrived, offering to take them to their "patrons," which were usually labor agencies or "intelligence offices."[7] This fast-growing metropolis gave no public assistance to newcomers, and the runners were not even licensed as they were in New York City.[8]

Characteristically, the first efforts to assist immigrants were made by Scandinavians already settled in the city. In the face of the indifference of the public at large, both the greatest assistance and also the greatest frauds were rendered newcomers by their fellow-countrymen.

A Scandinavian emigrant "Hjelp-Förening" was organized in 1865, supported by voluntary gifts from Lutheran church people in Chicago.[9] This society was able to handle only a small number of immigrants and was obliged to use the freight depot of the Northwestern Railroad as a free lodging place for them.[10] In 1868, the anticlerical party, Svea, whose newspaper, *Svenska-Amerikanaren,* rivaled the Lutheran church's *Hemlandet,* founded another benevolent society for immigrants.[11] Both organizations built immigrant homes on Illinois Street in 1870, apparently competing with each other in conspicuous benevolence.[12]

Neither of these homes continued for long as a philanthropic organization. The agent of the Lutheran home, Frederick Nelson, had previously worked for the American Emigrant Company. Its treasurer, F. S. Winslow, head of the Skandinavisk Bank och Wechsel, became agent for the Montreal Steamship Company in 1867. The house built by the church party was sold later in the year, by auction, to one of the many labor bureaus operating in the city, Henry Hjorth and Company, which retained the old name, Scandinavian Emigrant Benevolent Society.[13] The Svea house was also managed by men who were in some way interested in the immigration business.[14] Its facilities were in any case woefully inadequate; during the last half of 1870, it handled only 534 Swedish and Norwegian immigrants.[15] By 1871 it, too, had fallen into the hands of "runners," who sold it late in the year.[16]

The situation became so bad in Chicago that the Wisconsin Commissioner of Immigration advocated abolishing their Chicago office on the grounds that "it is impossible to get any co-operation from either the city or police authorities and emigrants there are at the mercy of runners and boarding house keepers."[17]

The combination of banker, boardinghouse keeper, and labor agent, which Americans have associated with the southern European immigration, partly because the first government investigations were not made until the 1900 decade, was to be found in Chicago both before and after the great fire. No fewer than eleven labor agencies dealing in Scandinavian labor advertised in the newspapers during this period, most of them concentrated on

North Clark Street and East Kinzie Street, which might almost be called the Mulberry and Greenwich streets of Chicago.[18] Among them was the Scandinavian Emigrant Agency which handled Guion Line passengers, and after 1871, Cunard Line passengers as well, who were sent by Frans Peterson in Gothenberg.[19]

These labor bureaus dealt primarily in railroad labor. Whereas in the fifties, the Illinois Central had had to send its agent to New York City to find immigrant labor, the flood of Scandinavian immigrants into Chicago after the war transformed Chicago into the center of railway employment in the country.[20] Although some roads continued to hire their own agents to obtain labor for them in Chicago, others gave contracts to one or more labor agencies to keep them supplied. The agencies usually charged employers a dollar for each worker furnished.[21] The contractors or subcontractors frequently agreed to lend money for transportation, all or part of the way from Chicago to the job, the advance to be repaid from the immigrant workman's wages.[22] Occasionally the employers offered to refund the workman's travel money if the latter remained on the job for a minimum of three or four months.[23] Sometimes the labor bureau itself advanced travel money if the work were not so far out of Chicago as to make collection difficult.[24] Roads which had lines running out of Chicago were able to transport their workmen free, and others were frequently able to get a reduction in rates.[25]

From October to March the Chicago labor bureaus advertised southern railroad jobs almost exclusively. In spring when construction picked up again in the north, contractors from Illinois, Wisconsin, Indiana, Michigan, Minnesota, Iowa, and Kansas submitted their orders to the Chicago agencies. Both construction and repair work provided jobs for newly arrived Swedish and Norwegian immigrants.

The labor bureau advertised the number of workers for which they had orders in the Scandinavian papers in Chicago. When the job was a good distance from Chicago, the name of the railroad being built or repaired was given, but even that information would not guide the immigrant to the location of construction without applying at the labor bureau. Frequently the advertisements were as vague as these: 500 railroad and canal works needed for Iowa, Illinois, Michigan, and Minnesota;[26] 300 railroad workers needed for Illinois, Iowa, Michigan, and Wisconsin;[27] 1,000 railroad workers needed for Tennessee;[28] 2,000 railroad workers needed for Kansas.[29] To get specific information the worker had to turn to a labor bureau.

Once he did turn to such an agency for assistance, he was required to make a deposit of one or two dollars for advice as to where a job could be found. The usual charge was a dollar for information on a job less than a hundred miles from Chicago and two dollars for anything more than a hundred miles away.[30] If the immigrant was unable to pay the fee, he was obliged to deposit his luggage as security. If he was prepared to pay his own way to the construction site, the bureau sold him a railroad ticket at a commission.[31] When large groups, of fifty men or more, were dispatched from the agencies, the bureau usually sent along an interpreter.[32] Such interpreters were often loosely called padroni when they appeared with Italian or Greek railroad laborers in a later period. It was more common for the subcontractor himself or one of his agents to conduct workers to the job.[33]

No public investigations of the work of labor bureaus in Chicago enable us to estimate the proportion of railroad labor distributed through them. When railroad construction again increased after the depression of the seventies, there were only four or five permanent railroad labor agencies in the city, along with numerous seasonal ones, fewer than during the period when the first large numbers of Scandinavian immigrants, fleeing from harvest failures, flocked into the city. By the eighties the agencies dealing exclusively in Swedish and Norwegian labor had disappeared.[34] The system of distribution underwent little change although the composition of the labor force did change. Fairchild reported that in 1908 he found fifty Greek workers ballasting track along the new Burlington and Missouri Railroad out of Lincoln, Nebraska; they had been hired by the road's passenger agent through a Greek labor agency in Chicago.[35]

Neither the railroads nor immigrant workers were satisfied with the system. Contractors complained particularly of the tendency of workers to leave without notice before a job was finished; for that reason contractors paid a bonus, in the form of transportation money, to those who stayed. Workers were accused of using railroad transportation facilities with no intention of working on the road at all. Harvest season lured them from construction sites to the land where wages were twice as high. During the summer of 1880 contractors were said to have written and wired constantly to the agencies in Chicago to fill the places of deserters. These uncertainties led one road to order fifteen hundred men when forty or fifty would have sufficed.[36]

Immigrants who turned to the labor agencies in order to get employment also ran risks. The familiar story of immigrant runners who had preyed upon the helpless German and Irish immigrants in the late forties was again repeated. In the absence of any public intervention such as was obtained in New York in 1847, the Scandinavian immigrant population itself had to deal with the problem as best it could. The church people connected with *Hemlandet* and editors of secular newspapers like *Justitia* and *Nya Welden* united in 1871 in an effort to expose the iniquities of the Scandinavian Emigrant Agency and the Swedish Commercial Company. These companies were denounced for directing Swedish immigrants to the south where they found no work or work at extremely low wages. The officers of the Scandinavian Emigrant Agency, as well as the head of its labor bureau, were shown to be men with shady pasts, who left town, two of them with money collected from immigrants to bring over relatives, as soon as the exposé began. It was also made clear that the company had never been incorporated although it had claimed to be.[37]

Even when immigrants were directed to bona fide jobs, they sometimes encountered difficulties. Frequently contractors skipped off with considerable wages outstanding to laborers who were paid by the month.[38] A Swedish representative introduced a bill into the Illinois House in 1871 "to protect laborers upon Rail Roads," which proposed to give workers six months' lien for wages on any company which hired irresponsible subcontractors.[39] By 1881 Illinois, Minnesota, Iowa, and Wisconsin had such laws.[40] Workers also complained of having to spend most of their savings traveling from job to job because each was short-lived.[41]

Immigrants who obtained jobs through the Chicago labor agencies usually had to make their own arrangements with employers about pay and board, sometimes at a lower rate of wages than that which had been advertised.[42] Even the advertised wage rates suggest that the western roads were not paying above the New York scale in the early seventies, so readily were labor agencies able to supply men. Railroad wages in the south and middle west were advertised at $1.75 or $2.00 a day without board between 1868 and 1871. The rate of board varied with the wage paid. At $1.75 a day, board and room were generally $4.00 a week, while in Kansas in 1870 wages were $2.25 a day and board and room, $5.00 a week.[43] If the contractor lodged and boarded the workers, wages were a dollar a day in most sites obtaining workers out of Chicago;[44] nevertheless railroad jobs were advertised in Tennessee in 1869 at $16 a month plus board.[45] Average wages for unskilled labor were listed in the New York labor exchanges in 1869 and 1870 at from $1.75 to $2.00 a day, a rate certainly not lower than was being paid in the middle west.[46]

The Chicago labor agencies also handled orders from the mining and lumbering industries. Occasionally coal-mine operators advertised directly in Chicago for miners, "experienced or inexperienced," as did railroad contractors.[47] The labor agencies were also useful, however. "Through the labor agencies of Chicago," wrote the agents of the Lake Superior mines in 1880, "we have been able to supply ourselves with all the common labor we required, and at the present time are out of all danger of labor troubles for this year at least . . ."[48]

Although immigrants who found their first jobs through Chicago labor bureaus were often imposed upon, as they were wherever runners' activities were not regulated by law, the city was probably a better starting point for eventual settlement on the land than were the eastern port cities. Railroad work and lumbering were sometimes the steppingstones to landownership for Scandinavian agricultural immigrants who came during the post-Civil War boom, as they were for Polish immigrants to Portage Lake, Wisconsin, during the same period.[49]

Far more important than Chicago as an immigrant receiving and distributing center was, of course, the port of New York which gained and held a strong lead over all other United States ports in this respect after the Civil War. While in Chicago, the private labor bureau was the only institution engaged in supplying immigrants to industry, in New York the picture was more varied. At least three types of organizations assisted immigrants in finding jobs in the eastern metropolis: the public labor bureau at Castle Garden, benevolent or philanthropic societies, and the private labor bureaus.

After hearing the report of a legislative committee which uncovered a shocking picture of frauds and impositions upon immigrants, among them the iniquities of the "intelligence offices," the

New York legislature had in 1847 provided for a head tax which was to be used in part to finance the inspection and protection of newcomers.[50] From the outset, the two oldest mass immigration nationalities gained a favored position in that city, with the heads of the German and Irish Emigrant Societies sitting as ex officio state commissioners. Since the agents of these societies were officially recognized by the state, they were in an admirable position to advise and assist their countrymen who landed in that city during the great emigration of 1848 to 1854.

At first the state commission did not undertake to carry on the work which the Irish Emigrant Society had begun in a modest way during the forties of assisting immigrants to find jobs. Not until the fifties was a labor bureau started at Castle Garden. This early bureau was far from satisfactory. Its records were described as "confused and fragmentary," and it made no effort to provide immigrants with work outside the vicinity of New York City.[51]

The Castle Garden Labor Bureau was reorganized and put upon a more satisfactory footing in 1867 when a one-story building, eighty by fifty-two feet, was erected as its headquarters, adjoining the old Revolutionary fort which served as the immigrant receiving depot. The new building was planned as a place where immigrants could meet prospective employers. There they could record in a register their names, nationalities, and occupational skills. Employers, or their agents, were invited to come direct to the labor exchange. After providing suitable references, they could register their labor needs, and clerks would assist in bringing employers and immigrants together. The bureau also forwarded immigrants to "approved" employers on receipt of transportation advances from them.[52] Special agents were assigned to Buffalo, Albany, and Rochester to help place immigrant workmen.[53] Employers of New York and New Jersey received by far the greatest numbers of immigrant workmen from the Castle Garden exchange, with Connecticut and Pennsylvania running third and fourth.[54]

Although the clerks at the labor bureau did not interfere in negotiations between immigrant and employer as to terms of wages and permitted contracts under which immigrants had rail fare to repay from wages, the immigrant who obtained a job at this bureau had some protection. The state required that all contracts made at the Bureau be registered with it;[55] and its officers undertook to investigate and reclaim wages for workers from employers who did not pay according to the terms of the registered contracts.[56]

The Castle Garden Labor Bureau failed to become a central clearing house for immigrant labor. According to a report of the state Commissioners of Emigration in 1875, countless employers, even in New York State itself, did not even know of the bureau's existence.[57] Few requests from employers for skilled workers reached the rotunda at Castle Garden. During the good times of 1868 to 1873 about five-sixths of the jobs provided through the bureau were labor or servant positions. With the advent of depression, the proportion of skilled positions declined further to about one in ten of the total workers placed.[58] Between 1875 and mid-1879 the commissioners commented in every report upon their inability to place skilled workers. Not until 1880 did requests for miners, furnace hands, skilled ironworkers, weavers, and molders exceed the supply of appropriate immigrants who applied at the bureau.[59]

It was German and Irish agricultural immigrants who were assisted in finding jobs by the Castle Garden bureau; in fact, the bureau served these two established immigrant nationalities almost exclusively.[60] From the founding of the new bureau right through the eighties only German and Irish clerks were to be found at the rotunda at the labor exchange.[61] The close connections of the emigrant societies of these two groups with the state organization was reflected in the fact that during the depression, when the state legislature stopped appropriating enough money to pay the salaries of labor bureau officials, the German and Irish emigrant societies took over and maintained the labor bureau.[62] It is little wonder that the Irish clerk, William Connelly, told a reporter in 1885 that few Italians even applied there for jobs.[63]

British, Irish, and German immigrants appear to have been better informed about, as well as better served by, the Castle Garden labor exchange. As early as 1852 Vere Foster wrote in the *Irish Farmers Gazette* that the commissioners of immigration at New York would "most probably" be able to "put all laboring men in the way of getting situations, chiefly on railways and on canals."[64] Literature available to intending emigrants in Britain and Ireland frequently discussed the work of the Castle Garden labor bureau.[65] Similarly German emigrant papers commented on the reorganization of the bureau in 1867,[66] and emigrant guides recommended its facilities.[67] The chief Irish clerk at the bureau in 1885 wrote regularly to London newspapers and to members of Parliament about the state of the labor market in New York City. "Those who come here," he intimated, "are pretty well posted and know just what to expect."[68]

The first references to the work of the Castle Garden labor exchange did not appear in Scandinavian newspapers and consular reports until 1870.[69] The previous year a Swedish family, with no member able to speak English, had been found ill and in great distress in Jersey City. After this event the *Skandinavisk Post* of New York began to urge the formation of an immigrant aid society to be represented, like the German and Irish societies, on the state board of immigration, and also suggested the hiring of an intelligent Scandinavian official to be stationed within the Garden to assist and advise immigrants.[70] Having explored the possibilities of acting upon these suggestions, the Scandinavian Consul in New York reported to his government the following year that such an agent would not be permitted to operate within Castle Garden; nor did he see any hope that a Scandinavian agent could have success in finding jobs for immigrants since his resources and information would be relatively limited if he had to work outside the state organization.[71]

German and Irish immigrants were also favored during these years by extensive private philanthropic organizations, established by earlier immigrants, which were prepared to give assistance to the needy. Both groups had sound savings banks to handle remittances to Europe. The Deutsche Gesellschaft, which had an office in lower Broadway, not far from Castle Garden, had facilities for receiving German immigrants, housing them, and helping them to find jobs in most important cities including Chicago, St. Louis, Baltimore, and New Orleans.[72] The St. Louis branch, working in close coöperation with the Missouri State Commissioners of Immigration, placed German immigrants in jobs, sometimes advanced their rail fares from New York City, and spent a good deal of money advertising to warn immigrants to stear clear of intelligence offices.[73]

Closely associated with the New York Deutsche Gesellschaft was the German Mission at Castle Garden, managed during the sixties and seventies by Rev. Robert Neumann, pastor of a Lutheran church in Brooklyn, who contributed articles to *Der An-*

siedler im Westen, a German emigrant newspaper published in Berlin. In 1873 a German immigrant house was established opposite the entrance to Castle Garden by the Lutherans.[74] Pastor Neumann worked among German immigrants who arrived penniless or had spent their last savings. During the bad winter of 1868, three thousand German immigrants were fed at the mission.[75] Writing in *Der Ansiedler im Westen,* Neumann described some of the cases in which the mission had aided immigrants. It is probably significant that most of them concerned immigrants from eastern Germany who found themselves destitute in New York City. Lutheran immigrants from Pomerania, Saxony, Brandenburg, and East Prussia who sought help in finding jobs were "new immigrants" during the sixties in that they came from areas which had not yet built up ties of kinship and acquaintance in the United States. In this sense, they were comparable to many of the Scandinavian immigrants of this period. Often these people had already spent their small savings trying to procure jobs through private intelligence bureaus before they appeared at the mission.[76]

These benevolent societies had a decided handicap as distributors of labor in that their existence and resources depended more on what immigration had been than upon what it was or would be. Both national and religious characteristics of established immigrant groups influenced their outlook. Irish aid in the nineteenth century was almost entirely Catholic. While the German Society of New York operating through the New York commissioners was a secular organization, the other early German benevolent societies were Protestant, and primarily Lutheran, until the St. Raphael Society's branch in New York City began to gain some support in the eighties.[77] Efforts to aid Scandinavian immigrants in New York City failed miserably during these important years. A Catholic Society to help Italian immigrants was not started in New York until 1891, and a secular organization, the Society for Italian Immigrants, in 1901.[78] Only the Hebrew Emigrant Society had some organization during the eighties when it was most needed. When the Hebrew Society gave up its labor bureau in 1903, after twenty-seven years of operation, its board noted other weaknesses of the philanthropic labor bureau. Many immigrants avoided calling where charity was involved; and employers, if willing to take its applicants, expected to get labor below the going rates.[79]

In addition to these ethnic organizations, a few other institutions existed in New York City to assist the unemployed to find work. Although they served immigrants, they were not exclusively immigrant-distributing agencies. The Commissioners of Charities and Correction organized a labor bureau in 1868 with the view to carrying off the unemployed to the interior of the country. In order to protect the worker, employers were required to supply references and security of fifty dollars; on this basis the Commissioners would supervise the drawing up of "binding contracts" as to wages and the repayment of transportation loans.[80] The state subsidized this labor bureau to the extent of ten thousand dollars a year. During the first few months of its operation, in the summer of 1869, about five thousand workers found jobs through its offices.[81] Plans to set up depots in the Middle West and to obtain public aid from interior cities were never realized, however, and its work remained local in scope. The Y. M. C. A., which also found jobs for about two hundred persons a month during good times, had the reputation among trade-unionists for furnishing strikebreakers and cheap labor.[82]

The third type of institution in New York City engaged in placing immigrants in industry, the private labor bureau, flourished during the early eighties. In fact, during this decade its function came to be a matter of interest to the public at large, not merely to immigrant groups concerned with the problems of the newly arrived. In the minds of many people the labor agency came to be associated with the introduction of Italian and Hungarian labor to railroad work, city construction projects, the mines, and the steel industry because in this decade bureaus handling these nationalities first appeared. At this time the term "contract labor" also began to be used with reference to the private labor bureau. In the following two chapters an attempt will be made to explain why these private labor bureaus suddenly appeared in an invidious role which aroused widespread criticism. For the moment, the discussion is limited to the question of whether or not the labor agencies which dealt in Hungarian and Italian immigrant labor were different in principle from either those described earlier in connection with the Scandinavian immigrants in Chicago or their predecessors in New York City itself among other immigrant nationalities.

The private labor bureau catering to immigrants was certainly not new to New York City. A German "Arbeits-Nachweisungs Bureau" was advertised in 1853.[83] During the Civil War and postwar period, at least two or three agencies supplying German labor to railroad companies operated in Greenwich Street opposite the exit from Castle Garden, a street which two decades later became a synonym for "cheap labor."[84] Several labor bureaus handled Swedish and Norwegian immigrants during the early seventies.[85] Often for a fee of five or ten dollars the inquiring immigrant was merely told, "You go to such and such a place and you will find railroad work."[86] Swindles like the case of Totten and Company which collected five dollars from each of a hundred and fifty workers on the promise that they would have free trips to jobs at New Orleans at $3.75 a day, and abruptly closed the office and disappeared, were not uncommon.[87]

By the eighties, private labor bureaus, often operating boardinghouses and banks as well, were to be found all along Greenwich and Mulberry streets near the place where immigrants left the Castle Garden depot. Some agencies had licenses to send their runners into the depot to solicit clients; others placed their representatives outside the gates through which all immigrants had to pass. Many of these boardinghouses were in basements; beds were lined along the walls, one above the other, as in the steerage of a ship.[88] Some agencies lodged fifty or more immigrants in these close basement rooms, and kept other houses uptown for the overflow.

John Swinton's reporter found ten agencies within two blocks on Greenwich Street in February 1885.[89] During the Ford Committee hearings three years later, the head of the Italian Bureau listed eighteen Italian bosses in New York City who were supplying labor.[90] Herman J. Schulteis, once a special commissioner of immigration, estimated in 1899 that there were eighty Italian banks in New York City most of which operated labor bureaus.[91] In 1906, two years after New York City began to require the licensing of labor bureaus, sixty-one agencies reported to the Commissioner of Licenses.[92] On the eve of the First World War it was estimated that there were eight hundred odd private labor bureaus in New York City alone, fifty-eight of them handling unskilled industrial labor as distinct from domestic servants.[93]

Labor agencies sent out circulars to employers of unskilled labor, offering to furnish large quantities of immigrant workers and stressing that they could be supplied "at a moment's notice."[94] One agent boasted that he could collect twenty thousand workers and mentioned a contract which he had for the summer of 1885 to supply one concern with five thousand.[95] Eleven thousand were reported as sent to the New York and West Shore Railroad in 1883.[96] Another Greenwich Street office sent three thousand in one lot to Pennsylvania via the Baltimore and Ohio Railroad.[97] The only official figures available on the numbers of workers placed by private labor bureaus appeared twenty years later, after state licensing was begun in New York. Between June 1904 and June 1906 it was estimated that 40,737 immigrants obtained jobs through licensed labor bureaus. Over half of the immigrants thus placed were sent to railroad construction (55 per cent) and 8½ per cent to coal mining.[98]

Although Italians, as a "new" immigrant strain, were prominent among the workers placed by labor bureaus during the eighties, Italian labor was far from being the only nationality furnished at this time. One contractor on Greenwich Street, who claimed that he could furnish three hundred men on a moment's notice, handled Swedish, German, and Hungarian labor.[99] Achilles J. Oshei, a Buffalo labor agent who got his men through a bureau in New York City, supplied Swedish, Polish, and German as well as Italian workmen.[100] Many bureaus had a space in their order blanks which allowed employers to stipulate the "nationality preferred."[101]

The mode of operation of the labor agencies of the eighties does not seem to have differed significantly from earlier private labor bureaus in Chicago. A dollar was the usual price charged the employer for each man sent to him.[102] If the immigrant were unable to pay the cost of transportation to the job, the employer frequently lent him the money through the labor bureau.[103] Sometimes the labor agency itself advanced railway fare, particularly when it sent someone with the immigrants as an interpreter.[104] The immigrant was also charged a deposit of one or two dollars; if unable to pay he left his baggage as security or agreed to repay the fee from his wages. When the agency sold railroad tickets to its clients, commissions of two or three dollars were added.[105]

Some of the New York labor exchanges were reported to be supplying labor at very low wages, far below going scales. The New York City Italian Labor Bureau advertised workmen at fifty or sixty cents or a dollar a day.[106] Swinton said that Poles, Hungarians, and Italians were working in the Pennsylvania coal mines for eighty cents to a dollar a day while the regular rates were $1.50 to $1.75.[107] These low wages were usually reported in cases in which the immigrant had transportation loans to repay.[108] The wages at which railroad laborers obtained jobs through the bureaus were more frequently $1.25, $1.35, or $1.50 a day.[109] But there were cases of Italian and Hungarians being sent out, both to railroads and mines, at a dollar a day. One contractor lamented that others were underselling him with railroad labor at a dollar a day.[110]

Many instances could be cited of Swedish, Norwegian, and German immigrants in an earlier generation, who, like the Irish before them, took jobs below the going wage in the face of their temporary helplessness on arrival in America.[111] In 1865 the American Emigrant Company had complained to the Commissioners of Immigration against other emigrant agencies which were supplying workers for southern plantations below what it considered to be the "going rates."[112] Furthermore, it did not take immigrants of any nationality long to discover what the going rates were, and to demand them. One unemployed Italian workman after another, whom the Ford Committee members tried to lure into admitting that he would work at sixty cents a day, replied that he preferred to return to Italy, since he had come over expecting to make $1.25 or $1.50 a day.[113]

When labor bureaus had orders for large numbers of men they sent an interpreter with the immigrants as did the Chicago exchanges. This is the point at which a relationship which was often loosely called a padrone system entered. The padrone, it will be recalled, had long-term contracts with his men himself, often on the security of ocean transportation advances; workers who went with an interpreter to a railroad contractor or mine, if they had a contract at all, usually had one with the contractor for advancing the rail fare from New York City to the site of work. Under the real padrone system the padrone collected wages from the employer and dispersed a small, contracted portion to his men. This system was really practicable only in cities, and that is why the padrone was found, for a while, in sewer building and street railway projects. The coal-mine operator or railroad contractor appears to have paid his men directly, albeit infrequently. A great deal of confusion surrounds the term "padrone," and I am adopting what I consider to be a useful and consistent definition. A differentiation between the padrone as here defined and the "boss" interpreter seems a useful one.[114]

The interpreter, or "boss," who accompanied men to the work, stayed with them if he was able to obtain from the contractor or foreman the privilege of provisioning or housing the men.[115] Upon arriving at the construction site, the boss bought a hundred dollars' worth of lumber and put up a shanty. For a bed in such a squalid overcrowded shanty a man paid from seventy-five cents to a dollar a month. In some cases the boss rented shanties which the contractor had already built, or commandeered old boxcars.[116] All supplies were furnished to the men by the boss who either boarded them or ran a store. Groceries and clothing went at so high a price in his store that the boss often did not bother his men with a commission for finding them the job if he had commissary privileges.[117]

This system of "bossage" had decided advantages for the railroad contractor, solving many of the problems which had been encountered by the Illinois Central in the fifties. So lucrative was the commissary privilege that bosses often demanded no hiring fee from employers in such cases, particularly when they secured an agreement that the contractor was to dun the men's wages and pay the boss directly the amount owed him for provisions. The labor agencies which sent out bosses offered the employer a number of useful services: collecting men, conducting them to the job, lodging and feeding them on the way, sometimes making transportation advances, interpreting on the job, and taking care of "discipline." State free employment bureaus, on limited budgets, later found themselves unable to compete with the private agency because of the variety of services offered by the latter.[118] A research committee in New York City in 1909 which investigated the possibilities of establishing a model labor bureau, free of the abuses of the commercial agencies, concluded that, in order to capture any of the business of distributing railroad labor, it would be necessary to imitate the methods of the boss.[119]

Whatever the advantages to employers of the system of private labor agencies, to the immigrant they were but a necessary evil. Italian and Hungarian immigrants who turned to New York labor bureaus encountered the same difficulties of vague offers of work in areas already overcrowded that were met by Swedish workers who paid their fees to Chicago labor bureaus. Even when an interpreter was sent with the men to distant jobs, work sometimes was not available when they arrived. This was the case with a contingent of three thousand laborers who had been accompanied by bosses to the site of construction on the Canadian Pacific Railway on the north shore of Lake Superior in December 1883. When they arrived, it was late in the season and work had been partially disbanded. The agents from the labor bureaus merely left the men destitute with no means to get back to New York City.[120]

Irregularity of employment, particularly on construction work, often kept immigrants under the virtual rule of a labor agency or a boss. Winter was always a time when railroad construction virtually ceased. When men were released, the problem of getting back to New York City, or another urban center, was acute.[121] Sometimes the workmen accompanied the boss back to the city during the winter where either he or the banker allowed them to mortgage future earnings in return for lodging during the winter.[122] Many had to seek their own way back to the city, however; and winter was often a time of hardship at Five Points. An investigation made in 1884 of idleness in New York City revealed that about five thousand Italians in the Sixth Ward were men who came to the city when railroad construction or other work outside the city stopped for the winter.[123]

If they complained of their treatment on the job, sometimes the boss incited his men to riot against the contractor who employed them. Such incidents also terminated the job. In any case the boss stood to gain in the way of commissions from changes of job.[124] A survey of Italians in Chicago in 1896 showed that of persons who said they worked for a "padrone" the average time on the last job was eleven weeks and four days.[125]

Although the immigrant often suffered, the private labor agencies of New York, Chicago, and other cities afforded a necessary link between him and prospective employers. The system of private labor exchanges took root and flourished not only because immigrants demanded some kind of job assurance before crossing the Atlantic, but also because it enabled railroad contractors and mine operators to get supplies of unskilled immigrant labor adequate to their needs without direct recruitment in Europe. Even had employers been willing to invest in contract labor in Europe, they had no need to incur such expenses or to run the obvious risks of importing on contracts. T. V. Powderly and H. J. Schulteis discovered this, when as government investigators, after the contract labor laws were passed, they tried to find evidence of contract labor recruitment in Italy. Posing as employers looking for contract laborers, they found a sub-agent of the Anchor Line in Italy quite willing to furnish them with workers but "astonished" that they "had taken the trouble to come to Italy for that purpose when it could have been done just as well by the agents in Mulberry Street, New York." [126]

It seems clear that the system of private labor agencies developed in response to the economic requirements of agricultural emigrants and American employers and was a feature of the adjustment of the agricultural worker and American industry to each other. American investigators and reformers who sought to link the labor agency with the submissive qualities of particular nationalities were not getting to the heart of the matter. It is also clear that contract labor was not an essential element in this system of distribution. When immigrant workmen did sign labor contracts, they were usually drawn up in American cities rather than in Europe.

Chapter 6

REACTIONS IN THE MINES
AND ON THE RAILROADS

The labor exchanges of Greenwich and Mulberry streets in New York City, as well as similar companies in other large cities, provided American industries with convenient pools of unskilled immigrant labor which could be readily tapped without the inconvenience, risk, and expense of importing contract labor. The private labor agencies became specialists in selecting and supplying to order the labor requirements of employers who could use workers only recently separated from agriculture.[1] Since the agencies were run for profit, they had little or no interest in such problems as the adjustment of the immigrant to American industry. Their profits were made from fees charged the immigrant for finding him a job and the employer for supplying him with workmen. Considerations like the state of the labor market in an industry and area to which immigrants were being forwarded did not concern them.

The years following the great depression of the seventies witnessed the rise of a national labor movement which embraced unskilled and semiskilled workers as well as craftsmen. As the Knights of Labor grew, one of its important political aims came to be the restriction of contract labor. Yet, it seems clear that industry was not importing laborers from Europe on contracts to any significant degree. The struggles of the Knights against the combination of widespread employer determination to resist trade unionism as such and the constant supply of immigrant labor furnished by the labor agencies form an important part of the psychological preparation of union leaders for legislation which purported to restrict immigration.

The decline of the Knights of Labor has been explained in terms of the ineptness of its leaders, its ill-defined aims, and the hysteria produced by the Haymarket Affair.[2] The constant undermining of Knights' locals through strikebreaking with immigrant labor furnished by the labor exchanges has probably not been sufficiently recognized as an important factor in the defeat of the "one big union" which for a short time seemed likely to organize the bulk of the American labor force.

An increased flow of immigrants from urban labor exchanges into both anthracite and bituminous mines followed the first successful attempts at union organization in those industries. The way in which immigrant labor was introduced into the mines, via the labor exchanges, could not have been better calculated to estrange the "old" and the "new" miners and to feed prejudices.

It is well known that until the 1870's the immigrant strains in the American mining industry were largely Irish, Welsh, English, and Scottish. According to the Census of 1870 there were 22,822 Irish, 28,877 English and Welsh, and 5,515 Scottish miners in the United States as against 58,388 American-born miners.[3] In Pennsylvania and Ohio the British made up more than a third of the total labor force, while farther west, in Illinois, they comprised about 45 per cent of mine labor in 1870. The channels by which the English, Welsh, and Scottish miners, as well as many Irish who had worked for a spell in Northumberland or Glamorgan, were able to distribute themselves to mine fields where their labor was needed, without turning to private labor exchanges, have already been described.[4] Although these British miners came to the United States in large numbers during the booms of the late sixties and early eighties, they had an important failing according to American entrepreneurs: the British tended to gravitate to trade-unions where they existed and to be active in organizing them where they did not.

Welsh and Irish immigrants and their children formed the backbone of the labor force in the anthracite mines.[5] In 1870, of nearly a hundred thousand foreign-born miners in the five anthracite counties in northeastern Pennsylvania, 44,122 were Irish and 30,785 were Welsh; English and German miners made up another

18,410.[6] Men from the northern coal beds in England were said to shun the anthracite region because of the dangers of mining there and their lack of experience of mining anthracite.[7] The Welsh formed the aristocracy of the workmen in the anthracite mines while less experienced Irish miners or German immigrants, who had mined in the old country with less progressive methods than those employed by the Welsh, could be used in the thick veins.[8]

After the Civil War period of prosperity for the mining industry, the Workingmen's Benevolent Association was organized in the anthracite region, largely by men who had previous experience in British trade-unions and who introduced the benefit features of the National Miners Association of Britain. The union won quick gains. A strike in 1868 resulted in a 10 per cent wage increase, and by the close of the year the union had organized 85 per cent of the miners of the area. Keen rivalry among the operators in the three main beds—the Northern or Wyoming field, the Lehigh field, and the Schuylkill or Southern field—assisted the union in its meteoric rise.[9] These gains were short-lived, however. In 1870, after the union had succeeded in pushing wages to a higher point than they had ever been, the sliding scale, adopted in 1869, was turned back upon it to reduce wages by 30 per cent.[10]

At the peak of the Workingman's Benevolent Association's power, the directors of both the Lehigh Coal Company and the Philadelphia and Reading Railroad, two of the largest operators in the area, expressed the fear that Civil War profits had resulted in the construction of collieries beyond the consumption capacity of the postwar market.[11] The diagnosis of this chronic disease of excessive capacity led to centralization of ownership of the mines in the hands of the railroads carrying the coal in an effort to regulate production and fix transportation rates. The destruction of the W. B. A. became, however, a major aim of the combination. "Notwithstanding the prospect of a serious loss from a long suspension," wrote the president of the Lehigh Coal Company, "it was thought better to suspend operations for the year, if necessary, than to fasten a policy upon the company which would subject its property to the demands of others and result in the employment of its whole capital solely for the benefit of hostile organizations. . . ."[12] The views of President Gowen of the Philadelphia and Reading on trade-unions are too well known to require repetition.

A major weapon in this fight against the union was the build up of labor surpluses. There were two reasons for labor surplus inherent in the move toward combination. For one thing, demand for coal was strong only in certain months, and, since storing coal was considered wasteful, the miners were idle in the dull months. Secondly, the system adopted by the carrying companies of determining the annual tonnage which each was to market, according to the capacity of the mines in their territory, increased the tendency to overexpansion. The larger the potential output of the mines it served, the greater the market reserved for the individual carrier.[13]

The operators also actively fostered the building up of excess labor near the mines. During the early seventies the railroads brought into the region Irish laborers, inexperienced as miners, from the labor exchanges of New York and Philadelphia.[14] When agents of the companies had obtained a consignment of workers, a passenger car was attached to a coal train to carry the immigrants to the anthracite regions. There they were assigned to company houses for which they paid four dollars a month. Little more than wooden shanties, these houses were often barren of furniture when the immigrants arrived. As long as the new arrivals were fellow countrymen, the miners often helped newcomers to get stoves and furniture from abandoned houses.[15]

When the long depression began, the railroads were ready to move against the union. In 1874 thousands were out of work in the Wyoming and Lackawanna valleys.[16] The union was completely smashed during a strike involving forty thousand miners in the Schuylkill, Wyoming, and Lehigh regions, which lasted from December 1874 to June 1875. The railroads would listen to no offers of compromise.[17] The collapse of the union cleared the way for the reign of terror of the Molly Maguires.[18] When the Mollies, too, had been broken through the determined efforts of Gowen and Pinkerton detectives, wages reached their lowest point since 1864. How could unionism survive when, as one Englishman remarked, "There are two or three to do the work of one. . . ."[19]

As trade unionism revived in the northern and southern beds of the anthracite region in 1884, reports again appeared that employers were collecting immigrants from the city labor exchanges. This time the immigrants were Italians, Hungarians, and Poles.[20] In 1887 a strike against wage reductions was defeated by the mine owners, freeing them from unions for another twelve years.[21] The presence of surplus labor in the area again contributed to the employer victory in the strike and the destruction of unions. At the time of the strike there were five thousand Polish, Hungarian, and Italian immigrants in the Lehigh District and twice as many in the Wyoming area.[22]

Trade-union organization presented more serious initial problems in the bituminous mines which were spread out over a number of states including parts of Pennsylvania, Ohio, Indiana, Illinois, West Virginia, and Maryland. British miners also constituted an important part of the labor force in the bituminous mines, with respect to both numbers and skill. Possibly not unrelated to the persistent urging by British miner leaders that emigrants seek the west was the fact that the British-born made up a larger proportion of the workers west of Pennsylvania. The Census of 1880 stated that of the 5,575 miners in Ohio, 5,047 were English or Welsh by birth.[23]

After the close of the Civil War, trade unions disappeared from the bituminous mine fields when the short-lived American Miners Association was blotted out of existence. Not until 1872 was the Miners and Laborers Benevolent Protective Association organized in the western fields of Illinois, Missouri, and Indiana. The following year this organization united with miners in Ohio, Pennsylvania, and West Virginia to form the Miners National Association under the presidency of John Siney.[24] In spite of the depression, membership rose to 21,177 in 1874, and at the end of 1875 the union claimed over thirty-five thousand members.[25] Between 1866 and 1872 when the bituminous miners had no national organization, I have found record of only one case of strikebreaking with immigrant labor.[26] From 1872 until the end of 1875 when the Miners National Association began to disintegrate, there were no less than fourteen strikes in Ohio, Pennsylvania, and Indiana into which immigrants were brought as strikebreakers.

Swedish, German, and Italian immigrants were imported into the bituminous fields as strikebreakers during these years. Swedish miners were brought to a strike in the Blossburg district, Pennsylvania in 1873; to a strike near Harmony, Clay County, Indiana, in June 1875; to the Mahoning Valley in 1873; and to both the Shenango and Mahoning valleys in Pennsylvania in 1875.[27] German strikebreakers entered Clearfield County, Pennsylvania, in May 1875; the strike at Harmony; and also one at the Castle Shannon mines in Pennsylvania.[28] Operators in the Mahoning Valley and in Clearfield and Westmoreland counties shipped in Italians to help break strikes during these years.[29] The nationality of the strikebreaker mattered little. The only requirement was that he be sufficiently inexperienced in industry or sufficiently destitute to be willing to serve as a strikebreaker. Negroes were also used in the mines during this period.[30] Even an occasional British miner appeared in the role of a "blackleg." A Scottish and an English miner who had served as strikebreakers in Harmony were warned by the union that if they intended to return to England, the *National Labor Tribune* circulated there as well.[31]

New men obtained for the mines from labor exchanges in New York, Philadelphia, and Cleveland were generally brought in under heavy guard. Swedish immigrants shipped into the Blossburg district in 1873 were taken by the operators to large barracks built to house them and "surrounded by special constables sworn in by the coal companies . . ."[32] It was reported that Italians came into western Pennsylvania from New York City in 1874 "armed as a regiment of soldiers."[33] Italians were shipped into Clearfield County in 1875 in boxcars, "like cattle," and conducted to the mines under police protection.[34] Other immigrants brought into Westmoreland County were armed with breech-loading rifles.[35]

These precautions were taken, not so much to protect strikebreakers from injury by strikers, but rather to seal them off from hearing the strikers' explanation of the situation. The first step that the unions took, when strikebreakers arrived, was to try to persuade them to leave the area or join the strike. Members of the Miners and Laborers Benefit Association lined the highway outside the barracks where Swedish strikebreakers were housed during the Blossburg strike. In spite of the efforts of the managers to prevent the union members from speaking to the strikebreakers, when one Swedish union member finally managed to get in among the new men, he succeeded in persuading them to join the strikers.[36] In this instance the strike succeeded. In other cases, in which operators were able to isolate strikebreakers from union members, the strikers were moved to take more direct action against strikebreakers, and violence sometimes resulted. Prevented from explaining the situation to new men, miners at Goss Run in 1875 armed themselves with clubs, forced their way into the mines, and marched the strikebreakers thirty miles away from the area.[37]

The final deathblows were dealt the Miners National Association during the summer of 1875. The arbitration award handed down in 1875 under the leadership of Mark Hanna, the largest operator in the Tuscarawas Valley, crumbled when one mining company offered to pay its men higher rates.[38] After this, according to Perlman, the miners exhibited an "uncontrollable passion" to "strike against every reduction in wages."[39] During the summer of 1875, strikes took place both in Clearfield County and in Westmoreland County, Pennsylvania. Although not all these strikes were authorized by the Miners National Association, the union leaders did what they could to help the beleaguered strikers, as agents of the mining companies recruited both Negro and immigrant strikebreakers in Cleveland for the Ohio strikes, and in New York and Philadelphia for those in Pennsylvania.[40] In the famous strike in Clearfield County, Pennsylvania, where John Siney and Xingo Parks were arrested on charges of conspiracy and incitement to riot, their crime had been to address meetings of the miners advising them as to how best to prevent the imported men from taking over the mines.[41] In the Shenango Valley that summer operators were reported to be paying unskilled immigrant miners five to thirty-five cents a ton more than the strikers asked, proof to the union men that the fight was directed primarily against the union.[42]

With the return of prosperity in 1879 and 1880, Knights of Labor locals began to appear in the bituminous mines of Pennsylvania and Ohio. Again the importation of immigrant strikebreakers became a feature of nearly every important strike, official or unofficial, by members of the Knights of Labor. Experience in these uneven struggles finally brought the miner leaders to Washington petitioning for an anti-contract labor law.

One strike can serve as an example of the problems faced by the Knights. On 14 March 1882, about three thousand miners in the Cumberland region in western Maryland walked out in response to a notice of wage reductions and the institution of a twelve-hour day issued by the presidents of twelve companies in the area.[43] By the end of May, eight thousand were on strike, virtually all the miners in the area.[44]

The coal companies clearly viewed their duty to be the destruction of the Knights of Labor in the locality. They refused all offers to negotiate the dispute, declaring "that the laws and regulations governing . . . employees in and about the mines at the present are unjust and embarrassing to the companies and really advantageous to no one."[45] In a letter addressed for the attention of Archbishop

Gibbons in Baltimore, the president of the Consolidated Coal Company asked for the recall of a local priest who was suspected of sympathizing with the strikers, a priest who two years earlier had counseled Catholics not to join the Knights of Labor.[46] The plea was based on the following argument:

This is not a question that interests *us only*—it is one of vital importance to society. The organization [Knights of Labor] by which our property has almost been ruined, and against which we are now contending, is one that if permitted to continue to grow in numbers and power as it has in the past three years, may be expected before many years to enact in this country scenes not less terrible than those committed by the Commune in Paris.[47]

After two months, when the strikers had not yielded, the mining companies began to put up buildings to house a thousand imported laborers. The mine operators announced that special police would be brought into the area and that one of the three houses being built was for lodging police. Captain Benjamin Hancock, ex-Confederate officer, who had helped quell the railroad strike of 1877, was to have on hand two hundred men, in blue uniforms with brass buttons and black slouch hats, armed with revolvers, to guard the immigrants. Fences were built around the barracks and around the mouths of the pits at Eckhart so that miners could not approach the new men.[48] Carpenters constructing the barracks were accompanied by special officers to their work near the mines each morning.[49] "It is evident," remarked a New York *World* reporter, surveying the preparations, "the companies will succeed in their efforts to crush the Knights of Labor in this region."[50]

On May 31st the first group of immigrants arrived with Captain Hancock. Fifty coal company policemen sent to meet the train in Cumberland quickly surrounded the cars to prevent any of the Knights of Labor officers from speaking to the new men. In addition to Hungarians, thirty-one Poles and sixty Germans were among the importees. Only twenty-five were reported as having any mining experience, and these few were to be depended upon to begin mining operations, each instructing two "greenhands" in the rudiments of mining. Within a few days mining operations had been started; striking miners were served with notices of eviction from the company houses in which they lived; and during June and July a second and third group of immigrants were brought to the area.[51] Coal officials told the press they would take no notice of a proposal from the Executive Board of the Knights of Labor to negotiate a settlement of the dispute.[52]

Careful precautions continued to be taken by the operators to keep the immigrants isolated. The local priest wrote to Archbishop Gibbons, "The camp which in every respect looks like a military camp contains about fifty different nationalities even some Russians."[53] The immigrants were not allowed to leave the barracks to attend religious services; the president of Consolidated was prepared to pay the expenses of a German Redemptionist brother to conduct mass inside the barracks not only on Sunday, but during the week as well, because the local priest was not acceptable to the company.[54]

Several observers feared that there would be bloodshed before the summer was out. With reference to evictions, the local priest thought, "This thing has very much embittered them and if it comes to the enforcing of the law I am afraid that there will be bloodshed and burning of property."[55] Myles McPadden, the Knights of Labor organizer arrested the same summer in Clearfield County, Pennsylvania, noted after a visit to the region that as the Central Company prepared to bring in foreign labor the revolver of every one of their guards could be seen.[56] The kind of incident which might at any time break into a riot was described by the priest:

When the new men arrived yesterday there was great danger of a riot. One worker said to Mayer: I see you are bringing your cattle into pen and cursed Mayer's answer in most horrible way. Mayer then laid his hand on his revolver, Crowly challenging him to fire. They tell me Crowly does not belong to the K. of L. they considered him too bad to belong to any society. But he is a desperado, a sort of Jesse James and there is every danger that he will break the peace. . . .[57]

In spite of these dangers, little violence occurred.[58] The miners did, however, take what steps they could to counter importations. Regardless of the precautions taken by the companies, the Knights succeeded in reaching strikebreakers from time to time. On June 12th, handbills printed in German asking the men to quit work and join the strikers "were mysteriously distributed within the police line."[59] The newspapers attributed the departure of a few of the immigrants to the "mysterious influence" of the Knights of Labor.[60]

Evictions and new importations continued through the summer.[61] By the end of August, the old miners began trying to get their jobs back on the operators' terms.[62] The operators victimized and black-listed 234 of the old miners after the seven months' strike had been broken.[63]

Similar stories could be recounted elsewhere during the three years preceding the passage of the anti-contract labor law. During the same summer that the Cumberland miners were out, the miners in nearby Clearfield County, Pennsylvania, struck for a wage increase to bring their wages up to the Cumberland level after three requests for some form of "arbitration or conciliation" had been ignored by the operators.[64] Agents of some of the coal companies went to New York City for strikebreakers.[65] According to a Pennsylvania state official, the strike failed because of defections in the miners' ranks and importations from abroad.[66]

A strike in the railroad mines of Pittsburgh against a wage reduction in 1882 was defeated after operators had sent to West Virginia for Negroes and to Castle Garden for immigrant strikebreakers.[67] During the six months' strike, begun in June 1884, of about three thousand miners in the Hocking Valley of Ohio, also against wage reductions, the expenses of strikebreaking and the salaries of agents to collect men at labor exchanges were paid by the recently formed syndicate of coal operators.[68] One labor agent was promised five thousand dollars, in addition to the fee of two dollars per head he received for furnishing strikebreakers, if he succeeded in breaking the strike.[69] John McBride, president of the Ohio union, reported in the middle of August that fourteen hundred immigrants, accompanied by armed Pinkertons, had been imported into the valley up to that time, including Negroes, Swedes, Italians, Poles, and Hungarians, collected at New York, Chicago, and Buffalo labor bureaus.[70] This strike too was lost, the union broken, as frightened miners returned to work on "yellow dog" contracts.[71]

In all these strikes, operators took whatever immigrant labor they could obtain from the labor exchanges. The editor of the *Engineering and Mining Journal* commented that "Castle Garden, with its hosts of immigrants, appears to be solving the labor question. . . ."[72] Although Hungarian and Italian immigrants were conspicuous among the strikebreakers of the eighties, many other nationalities were used. A union man in Tioga County, Pennsylvania, for example, complained in 1880 that the Operators have and are Still Discharging some of our Brothers at three of the four coal works of this County. at Antrim. Morris run and fallbrook for no other thing but to try and breek up our holey Order as tha are Employing others in thare places. mostley Sweds as tha Say it is not men with brains but Muccell tha want. . . .[73]

An appeal from District Assembly Number 9 of Pittsburgh, during the strike in 1882, admirably summarizes the problems facing miner unions. The appeal condemned:

The enticing of penniless and unapprised emigrants, speaking uncommon languages and just landed at Castle Garden, to the mines to undermine our wages and social welfare, and to take the place of our workmen.

The quartering and restraining of these emigrants in huts and shanties far within their property line for the sole purpose of preventing them and the old miners from holding joint meetings, where all the facts, reasons and objects of this resistance could be fully stated and fairly discussed. . . .

An attack upon our Order in District No. 9, should be the concern of the order everywhere. We were rapidly increasing in strength and members, and the object of this capitalistic assault is to check our growth, undermine our strength and destroy District No. 9; and if the operators succeed in breaking up our Assemblies and our District with cheap emigrant labor, it will encourage and lead them to use the same tactic to defeat and destroy other Districts of the Order. . . .[74]

While the use of immigrants to destroy unions was labor's primary concern, miners made other complaints against the immigrants of the eighties. Miners claimed that the presence of inexperienced workmen in the mines endangered lives. Many accidents occurred because immigrant laborers did not support loose coals properly, did not handle their safety lamps correctly, or were unable to read the danger notices written in English. Nineteen Hungarians were killed in one disaster near Connellsville, Pennsylvania, because they did not understand a danger signal.[75]

Miners also maintained that the presence of immigrants made it more difficult to enforce the Pennsylvania checkweighman's law. Often infringements occurred before immigrants learned of its provisions.[76] At the Castle Shannon mines, German immigrants who did know that the weights were given short on the scales in use, were afraid to put on a checkweighman.[77] When union men in the coke region tried to organize Hungarians to enforce these state laws, the companies discharged and black-listed the men who thus interfered with immigrant workmen.[78]

From these grievances unionists broadened their charges against the new immigrants, the Hungarians, the Italians, and the Poles, when they came to Washington to testify for an anti-contract labor law. The harrowing descriptions of crowded living conditions, poor diet, and willingness to work at low wages that the Knights submitted[79] do not differ markedly from those we have of other European agriculturists thrust unawares into the unwelcoming environment of American industry during their first years in America—the Irish in Boston or New York in the fifties, or Germans in Detroit in the eighties, for example.[80]

Protests came to be more and more directed against the Hungarian immigrants in particular. In 1882 a number of coke drawers struck against the employment of sixteen Hungarians in the Connellsville region. A hundred and fifty Irish and English miners employed by H. C. Frick and Company's coke works struck in June 1884, because seven Hungarians were introduced.[81] In the summer of 1884 feeling ran high in the anthracite regions against Hungarian workers who were thought to be "contract laborers." Meetings were called to denounce railroad and mine corporations for importing Hungarians, and societies were formed to drive out foreigners. In the Kingston area, miners stoned the houses of Hungarian workmen.[82]

How the frustrations of the miners came to be directed against contract labor, when it actually figured so insignificantly in their problems, is explained in a later chapter. It is pertinent to recall, however, in connection with the conflicts of the 1880's, that after the United Mine Workers was formed in 1890 most of its members were recent southern and eastern European immigrants. John R. Commons observed in 1907:

In the anthracite coal field I saw a dozen Slovaks just arrived from Hungary, but persuaded by their unionized precursors not to take the places of strikers. In New York a shipload of Italians in time of strike has been taken directly into the union. Such a sight would have been unlikely a dozen years ago.[83]

Conditions in railroad construction and maintenance differed considerably from those in the mines with respect to the recruitment of immigrant labor. Railroad building had always been an unskilled occupation and consequently an important introduction to America for Europe's agricultural emigrants. The Irish, who constituted the bulk of the unskilled workers in mining during the sixties and seventies, also provided the plurality of railroad workers. Nearly thirty-eight thousand "railway employees other than clerks" in 1870 were Irish born, more than a third of the total number employed.[84] "New" immigrant groups were joining them, however, so that by 1890, 21,051 Scandinavians and 10,280 Italians, along with 18,613 German immigrants were employed as "steam railway employees not otherwise specified," while the Irish had declined numerically to 33,086.[85]

While mine operators might make a sudden demand on the labor exchanges for large numbers of immigrant workmen during a strike, railroad construction, by its very nature, came to depend on the bureaus for ordinary labor needs.[86] When lines or extensions were being constructed, large groups of workers had to be found, often for relatively isolated places. The work was seasonal and temporary in any one location; and this characteristic had two important effects relevant to the introduction of immigrant labor.

First of all, the temporary nature of the work in railroad and city street railway construction encouraged the continued dependence of immigrant workmen on the interpreter boss. Furthermore, trade-unionism did not develop readily under these conditions. Thus the importation of immigrant labor to break strikes was rare on the railroads, since strikes were rare, although there were a few reports during the eighties of Italian, Swedish, and Negro workers brought in from the New York and Baltimore labor exchanges at times of wage disputes.[87] In spite of the fact that railroad and city construction conditions encouraged the use of labor in gangs under interpreters who might keep workmen in debt for a time in a relationship akin to peonage, and possibly definable as contract labor, the pressure for anti-contract labor laws did not come from the unorganized railroad construction workers.

Not all railroad labor jobs were temporary and seasonal. Work on maintenance of way or freighthandling provided more permanent employment. If trade-unions or strikes developed in these branches, workers were faced with the same employer techniques as were the miners. The strike of freighthandlers in New York City in 1882 is interesting and significant not only as an example of successful union smashing with immigrant labor, but also as an indication of the tendency of many recent immigrant groups to go over to the strikers when they heard their viewpoint.

The freighthandlers' strike was not a Knights of Labor affair. The railroad companies involved—the New York Central, the Pennsylvania, the Lake Erie and Western, and the Lehigh Valley —maintained that the workers merely left the piers in mid-June 1882, without making any formal demands. They soon announced their demand for wage increases from seventeen to twenty cents an hour which the railroads determined to resist.[88] Only after the strike began was it "rumored" that Knights of Labor organizers were working among the freighthandlers. The Freighthandlers Union itself was an *ad hoc* organization which was formed after the strike was at least a week old.[89] By that time three thousand workers were out.[90]

Since the strike involved piers in New York and Jersey City, immigrant labor sources were close at hand. Hundreds of Italians were brought from Castle Garden and from Five Points to the piers. On 23 June, 150 Italians were carried by tug from Castle Garden to the New York, Lake Erie and Western piers, and returned in the same way at the end of the day to sleep within its walls.[91] Polish, German, Hungarian, and Greek immigrants were added at other piers.[92] Each night the Pennsylvania Railroad officials took in charge the hundred Italians and Russian Jews they had collected, to prevent the strikers from approaching them.[93] Young men from the Hebrew Emigrant Aid Society, who served as interpreters, accompanied Jewish immigrants back to Castle Garden where they lodged.[94] After strikers tried to talk to some of the Italians brought to the Erie pier in Jersey City, railroad officials stationed 125 police to protect the strikebreakers from interference and had the New Jersey militia alerted.

When the strike was two weeks old, even though some of the strikers were beginning to suffer want, their outlook was quite good. Freight was bottled up in spite of the efforts of the railroads to get strikebreakers to do the work. The railroad officials maintained that the immigrants were making out very well, but shippers and tally clerks who had to deal with them, through interpreters, reported that it would take a long time to bring them up to the proficiency of the old hands.

Moreover, the union had some success in winning over the strikebreakers. When rumors reached Castle Garden of the strike, not a little persuasion was needed to get immigrants to go to the piers. By mid-July the strikers managed to persuade the Commissioners of Emigration to refuse to allow the railroads to continue to send hands drafted at Castle Garden back there at night.

The strikers also enlisted the aid of countrymen of immigrants serving as strikebreakers. They met secretly with German singing societies and labor unions to devise means of preventing German strikebreaking. On 27 July it was announced that some German strikebreakers had joined the Union. At mass meetings at Five Points Jeremiah Murphy, the president of the new union, as well as several Italian speakers, urged Italian immigrants not to fight their fellow workingmen. Strikers were up early in the morning in front of east side tenements where Italians lived, begging them not to work. P. J. Maguire of the Carpenters was active in inducing Italian and Russian Jewish immigrants to join the strike.[95] Strikers sent back to their old countries the names of men serving as scabs.

These efforts were not without some success. On 3 July, 150 of the Russian immigrants in Jersey City employed by the Erie railroad left in a body as soon as the situation was explained to them. On 13 July, three hundred Russian Jews who had been working joined the Freighthandlers Union, and the following day five hundred Jews marched from the battery to the union headquarters in the Bowery. Some Italian strikebreakers had been taken into the Union by 10 July. With their help, two hundred Italians engaged at Five Points on 12 July by agents of the Erie were persuaded to turn back. Two hundred and fifty Italians left the New York Central Yard on the 15th, and this same day a number of Italians on the Long Island Railroad freight dock also joined the Union. Italian and Jewish branches were formed, the union taking on the well-nigh impossible task of feeding and caring for Italian strikers at Five Points and in Mulberry Street. Although the strikers relied chiefly upon persuasion to get strikebreakers off the piers, in a few cases "scabs" were beaten up as they went to and from work.[96]

The railroads continued to draw upon Castle Garden and the labor exchanges and gradually were able to build up sufficient labor force to handle the freight. One foreman said that he weeded out the shipment of strikebreakers each morning, sending away the unfit. The strike began to crack the week of 7 August, and the railroads ultimately won a complete victory. Many of the strikers were not rehired. The vice-president of the local union in Jersey

City summed up the situation toward the end of the strike when he said: "It's that . . . Castle Garden that's killing us."[97]

During these critical years for the organization of unskilled workers in America, the new immigrants who often found themselves being used as strikebreakers soon discovered the meaning of industrial strife. "When first brought here," reported the New York Bureau of Labor Statistics in 1885 about immigrants, they "are willing to work for very low wages, but after a few years' residence they become sufficiently Americanized to strike."[98] The new immigrants gave much evidence of such Americanization during the eighties. "The Hungarians, against whose importation into the region there was something of a stir a short time ago," reported the Philadelphia *Times,* referring to the coke area at Mahonoy City, "went out on strike" in May 1882.[99] There were many cases of unofficial strikes among Italian, Swedish, and Hungarian workmen on the railroads.[100] When one group of Italian laborers had their wages reduced by ten cents, they were said to have cut an inch off their shovels, to shovel less dirt at the lower pay.[101] There were even instances of strikes among Italian laborers in city road building and street cleaning gangs where padroni were supposed to keep them in near-slavery.[102] But, it seemed, there were always fresh shipments of immigrants to replace strikers. In June 1882, a large body of Italians and Negroes on the Jersey Shore and Pine Creek Railroad struck, asking for $1.50 a day. The same evening a fresh installment of two hundred Swedes and Hungarians arrived to take their places.[103]

Behind all these instances of strikebreaking in the mines and among permanent railroad workers were the labor exchanges. Their organization enabled employers to get strikebreakers in a hurry when strikes broke out, and thus placed a powerful weapon in the hands of industrialists determined to resist collective bargaining and destroy unionism. Two factors worked against employers, but they were not strong enough to give the victory to unions of unskilled workers. In the first place, even in jobs usually classified as unskilled, experienced workers could produce more than recent immigrants; secondly, immigrant strikebreakers had to be kept isolated if they were not to be prevailed upon to give up work and join strikers. To defeat unions employers would and did make do with incompetent help for the duration of the emergency and invest in special buildings, guards, and policemen, and premium labor agency fees to keep strikebreakers isolated.

Contract labor was not at the root of the trouble as it concerned miners and railroad workers. Nevertheless, disappointed strikers could easily be persuaded that strikebreakers were contract laborers if under that assumption they were promised some relief from strikebreaking.

Chapter 7

MACHINERY AND IMMIGRATION

"They do far more with machinery in all kinds of trades than you do," wrote one immigrant from Sheffield to the old country. "Men never learn to do a knife through, as they do in Sheffield. The knives go through thirty or forty hands. . . . If a Yankee can resin a knife they call him a cutler; and by doing one thing all the time they become very expert and they make some very good knives. . . . such patterns as is done easiest by machinery."[1] Already in the late sixties, immigrant craftsmen found that while they might be used as foremen, supervisors, or "company hands," "there is not much need for the better-class workman,"[2] and "in a short time the services of Englishmen will no longer be required."[3]

Swedish and Norwegian immigrants were writing home in the same vein, seeking to counteract the prevalent notion that craftsmen or "hantwerkare" would benefit by emigrating to America. Only those skilled workers whose craft could not be replaced by machinery, chiefly building trades operatives, would benefit by the change. Even shoemakers, tailors, dyers, and tanners would find work in America completely unlike what they knew.[4] Many an Italian and German craftsman who arrived in America was equally unable to get work to which he was accustomed.[5]

Throughout the nineteenth century the introduction of machinery and the division of labor in industry were relentlessly outdating traditional pre-industrial revolution crafts as well as skills essential in the early phases of the industrial revolution. The progress of mechanization did not, of course, suddenly obliterate the

123

need for skilled labor, nor was the movement uniform from one industry to the next. Nevertheless, the increasing ability of American industry to employ new recruits from agriculture, whether from rural areas in the United States and Canada or from Europe, did tend to enhance the usefulness of the private labor exchanges and Castle Garden.

In mining and railway construction, machinery had not yet changed methods of production. Machines for undercutting coal in the mines to replace the miner's pick, although available by 1880, were still used in producing only about 6 per cent of the nation's coal as late as 1891.[6] In the other industries with which this study is concerned, iron and steel and textiles, important technological changes had taken place by the eighties which were making possible a greater use of "greenhands."

The search for a cause and effect relationship between machinery and immigration formed an important part of the "great debate" on immigration during the 1900 decade which culminated in the forty-two-volume Dillingham Report to Congress and laid the basis of the quota system adopted after World War I. The Commission itself tended to blame immigrants from Southern and Eastern Europe for bringing about increased mechanization.[7] Like General Francis Walker thirty-five years earlier,[8] the investigators saw a moral wrong in mechanization, associating it with the breaking of trade-unions and cheapening of wages and quality of products. This view that immigrants of particular ethnic groups, because of certain inherent characteristics, were transforming American industry for the worse had an important influence on American immigration laws. Although this charge was only one of several evils which were traced to the Southern European immigrants, it was a good example of the way in which many problems of America's industrial transformation were sidestepped by blaming them upon the immigrant. One effect of this line of thought was to lead legislators to adopt a negative policy of virtual exclusion of the new immigrant rather than attempting a constructive approach to the distribution of and maintenance of standards among immigrant workers such as the I. L. O. fostered after the First World War.

Today scholars recognize that the view that unskilled labor "caused" mechanization was grossly oversimplified, and that in its racial aspects, where it held that certain nationalities debased the industrial arts, prejudice obstructed an understanding of the economic forces at work.[9] Having seen the process at work longer, we now recognize that mechanization is not always associated with unskilled labor. While many of the "revolutionary" advances in machinery which took place in the eighteenth and nineteenth centuries anachronized craft skills, much recent mechanization, particularly since the beginning of the twentieth century, has eliminated unskilled jobs. Some of the most physically exhausting, brute force work has been taken over by cranes and dredges and automatic machinery. Furthermore we know now that considerations other than the nature of the labor supply have encouraged mechanization, for example, the expandability of the market, the nature of competition, and shifts in sources of fuel. Where the nature of the labor force does enter it is not a question of assigning blame. One might just as well argue that the difficulties which American industry experienced in attempting to recruit large numbers of skilled workers in Europe stimulated efforts to circumvent the need for their skills fully as much as did the fortuitous flow of agriculturists into America from Europe.[10]

Trade unionists of the eighties did not, of course, have the advantages of perspective upon the effects of mechanization. Instead they began to interpret mechanization as a capitalist plot to replace them with cheap immigrant labor. In the midst of the bitter trade disputes of the early eighties the puddlers and mule-spinners did not foresee that they and their children might ultimately gain, in both status and standard of living, as they moved into supervisory and white-collar positions and even into independent business.[11] Although many British and American craftsmen evinced a tendency toward national prejudices before the disputes of the early eighties, the methods adopted by many employers during that decade for making transitions to new machinery undoubtedly contributed to fear and insecurity with respect to the immigrant, inflaming prejudices to the point that craft workers were prepared to believe almost anything about new immigrants, even that they were contract laborers.

Employers' constant use of immigrants in industrial warfare taught trade-unionists to fight not the machine but the immigrant in their attempts to cling to privileged positions in the labor force which time was obliterating. The mistaken tactics of the skilled workers are not difficult to understand when even a British consul in America regarded mechanization and division of labor as "a part of the policy adopted by the Capitalists, to check the scourge of the employers—the working-men's strikes";[12] when trade publications were advising manufacturers that the introduction of machinery to do away with skilled workmen was particularly desirable when strikes threatened to prevent the filling of orders,[13] and congratulated firms which abolished trade-unionism by introducing immigrants.[14] In many cases it was clearly impossible, because of the time needed to introduce new machinery, for managers and employers to break a strike of skilled workers by such techniques. Anti-immigrant hysteria often appeared even in such disputes because concerted attempts were made to break strikes with repeated threats of importations of immigrants from city labor exchanges.

The boot and shoe industry afforded a classic example of what was happening, as trade unionists saw it. Under the stimulus of the Civil War demands for large quantities of footwear, automatic machinery, including the McKay sewing machine, was introduced into shoemaking.[15] After the war, in spite of a reduced demand for shoes, a large though not effectively centralized trade-union, the Knights of St. Crispin, was organized. The aim of these Knights was not to fight the introduction of machinery, but to try to control the training of "greenhands" in order to safeguard the wages and employment of skilled boot and shoe workers.[16]

Because the new machinery robbed these craftsmen of their only real power, that of regulating the supply of skilled operatives, the Knights failed in their attempt to claim exclusive rights to operating new machinery, a policy in which the typographers and printers succeeded at a later date. Chinese workmen were imported to North Adams, Massachusetts, to prove to skilled workmen in the Knights that they were no longer needed and no longer wanted by industrialists.[17] After 1870 the Knights of St. Crispin lost their hold upon the job in a series of strikes against the introduction of "greenhands," against wage reductions, and in defense of the order.[18]

The story was not so classically simple in either iron and steel or textiles, but for craft unionists, unwilling to unite with workers on new machinery, the results were not very different.

Before the revolutionary Bessemer process for steelmaking was gradually introduced after 1865, American ironmakers had experienced a constant shortage of skilled puddlers and boilers to produce wrought iron from the pig iron which came from the blast furnace. Puddlers had been the "oldest and most self-assertive" of iron craftsmen. Strongly trade-union minded, they had comprised the bulk of the membership of the Sons of Vulcan after 1859 and 85 per cent of the original membership of the Amalgamated Association of Iron and Steel Workers which emerged in 1876. Few other jobs in iron and steelmaking were as taxing and required such experienced hands as the manipulation of molten iron in the puddling furnaces to oxidize out the carbon through contact with air, and the formation of balls of wrought iron for the rolling mills from the hot and sticky molten mass. As steelmaking in Bessemer converters and open-hearth furnaces increased during the seventies and eighties, the number of puddlers declined from 3,331 taxable members of the Sons of Vulcan in 1873 to a total of about 2,000 puddlers in the whole country in 1908.[19]

When Bessemer and open-hearth furnaces took over the production of steel ingots, the puddler and boiler were no longer needed. Partly because of the larger capacity of the new furnaces, more unskilled workers were required than in the puddling process. One writer estimated that 132 unskilled men and only 10 skilled workers were needed to operate four fifty-ton furnaces of the early open-hearth type for twenty-four hours. Before the development of mechanical charging machines and mechanical gas producers, the open-hearth furnace depended on large numbers of unskilled laborers to shove iron into the furnaces and keep the fires going. Men with physical strength rather than skill were also needed to pour the molten metal from the furnaces, and to prepare molds for casting prior to the appearance of the traveling crane and the "thimble."[20]

In the blast furnaces, too, the dramatic increases in size made during the last third of the century at first called for more strong men to keep these huge vessels fired and stocked, and to handle the work attached to casting in the pig beds. Not until the advent of automatic hoisting machinery, piggeries, and the direct conversion of pig to steel without previous casting, were some of the most dangerous and heaviest jobs attached to blast furnace operation outmoded.[21]

It would be foolish to argue that the larger blast furnaces and the new processes of steelmaking were introduced in order to do away with skilled labor, or, in fact, that they were much influenced in the early years by the nature of the labor supply. The members of the Amalgamated Association of Iron and Steel Workers were fighting a losing battle with time and technological change. With their steadfast refusal to admit common laborers into the union,[22] the union could easily be by-passed. The experiences of these workers with strikebreaking during the eighties differed from earlier days in that for the first time employers were able to call upon the urban labor exchanges, thus circumventing all the efforts of the Union to warn European skilled ironworkers against employer recruitment. The struggles of these years, as well as the Homestead strike of 1892, convinced many that the new immigrants were responsible for having "allowed machinery to enter" the industry.[23]

Eastern foundries and rolling mills had long had an advantage over Pittsburgh firms with respect to wages. There were really three scales of wages in the industry: one in the east, one in the Pittsburgh area, and another in the middle west. The farther west one went, the higher were the wages paid in the foundries, puddling furnaces, and rolling mills.[24] Some manufacturers had encouraged the Pittsburgh boilermakers to organize the eastern rolling mills during the late sixties to equalize wages, but their efforts had little effect. The wage differentials persisted.[25]

As furnaces began to be refired after the depression, western iron manufacturers again turned their attention to the problem of doing away with wage differentials.[26] From its organization in 1876 the Amalgamated Association of Iron and Steel Workers had also been interested in the problem, and at first it seemed to western manufacturers that the union might assist in leveling wages by getting eastern mills to raise wages.[27] The Association tried, at first, to get uniform wage scales within each district but had no success in enforcing its scales in the poorly organized eastern mills.[28] As for the difference between Pittsburgh wages and and those paid farther west, all that the union could do was to try to bring about uniformity in the various districts allowing western districts a 10 per cent advantage over the Pittsburgh sliding scale. The union could not help employers to bring western wages down to the Pittsburgh level. Its strikes in the west for the Pittsburgh scale plus a percentage and in Pittsburgh against reductions under the agreed sliding scale in 1880 failed; and the union did not recover from these setbacks until 1882.[29]

Western manufacturers were finally successful in getting uniform wage rates in Pittsburgh and the west by 1885 but not by coöperation with the Amalgamated Association of Iron and Steel

Estimates of Wages Paid in Foundries and Rolling Mills for
a Six-day Week in Selected Occupations, 1869–1879

Trade	Year	Mass.	N. Y.	Penn.	Ohio	Ill.
Boiler-	1869	$(13.60)	$(14.81)	$(15.00)	$(17.50)	$ . . . . .
makers	1874	(15.75)	(15.00)	(16.00)	(15.00)	(17.30)
		15.42	13.26	13.02	15.84	19.20
	1879	13.98	11.58	10.86	15.78	17.40
Iron	1869	(16.50)	(16.50)	(17.25)	(16.47)	(18.00)
molders		14.16	14.88	15.24	. . . . .	22.50
	1874	(15.00)	(15.83)	(14.00)	(13.10)	(17.34)
		13.81	14.64	13.68	16.74	18.84
	1879	12.48	13.50	12.24	13.26	14.82
Puddlers	1869	. . . . .	. . . . .	[a]20.35	. . . . .	. . . . .
	1874	(22.56)	(22.65)	(21.15)	(24.30)	(24.80)
		. . . .	. . . .	18.24	. . . .	. . . .
	1879	. . . .	. . . . .	18.24	20.46	. . . . .

Figures in parentheses are the estimates prepared by Edward Young for circulation in Europe. (*Labor in America*, pp. 25, 26–28.)

[a]Estimate of the Secretary of Internal Affairs of Pennsylvania, *Annual Report*, vol. III (1874–75), Pt. 3, p. 530.

Other figures are taken from U. S. Bureau of Labor Statistics, *History of Wages*, *Bulletin*, no. 604, pp. 246, 283, 284, 311–313.

Note that the Pennsylvania figures do not show the wage differentials clearly because they are average estimates covering the eastern part of the state as well as the Pittsburgh area.

Workers. Renewed efforts were made to recruit skilled immigrants in the iron centers of Great Britain.[30] The union was relatively successful in counteracting these recruitment activities, after the first influx of 1879, and the immigration of British puddlers and iron molders declined steadily between 1880 and 1885.[31] Nevertheless some of the British immigrants of 1879 from Sheffield and Bradford, having been reduced to near-poverty through unemployment in the iron and steel industries of those cities, took jobs in the American industry, much to the dismay of American union members.[32] The first reports of iron manufacturers seeking workers at the labor exchanges began to appear in 1881. During that year both Scandinavian and Hungarian immigrants were obtained from eastern labor exchanges as strikebreakers. Some of the Scandinavians were reported to be skilled ironworkers.[33]

Events of 1882 convinced the skilled men in the Amalgamated Association of Iron and Steel Workers that, if the union were to live, something must be done to stop the importation of foreign labor during strikes. They were not persuaded to try to organize the unskilled, but sought, rather, some other technique by which to deal with the problem. Aided by the vigorous organizing activities of the Knights of Labor, the union had made a comeback in 1882. Most of the ironworkers of the Pittsburgh area and of Ohio were gathered into the union, although the mass of workers in the steel mills remained largely unorganized.[34] The chief threat to the organization came from the manufacturers' increasing ability to use unskilled labor. In spite of the cautious leadership of John Jarrett, the Association found itself in the middle of a severe crisis in 1882.

During the early months of that year the various Carnegie works which were making Bessemer steel were, according to Professor Nevins, "already bringing in large numbers of ignorant immigrants . . . in order to keep wages low and conditions unfavorable for organization."[35] The workers handled by the labor exchanges could readily be introduced into the new processes. What is more surprising, however, is that a few strikes in mills still making puddled iron also appear to have been defeated at this time. A strike of rivet welders for a 10 per cent wage increase at Carnegie's Keystone Rolling Mills in Pittsburgh in May 1882 was met by the departure of the superintendent to get men "in the east."[36] A large strike at the Phoenixville Iron Company was defeated by the importation of immigrants from the east the same month.[37]

The operators of the newly erected steel works in Homestead, which promised to be a major rival to Carnegie's Edgar Thompson Works, were not so successful in their struggle with the Amalgamated Association early in 1882. The directors failed to prevent a strike with arguments that reduced wages were justified by improved machinery.[38] Attempts to introduce new hands to replace strikers were successfully countered by the union, not, however, without violence.[39] It was undoubtedly in part their victory at Homestead that encouraged local branches of the Amalgamated Association to hope for success in a nation-wide strike.

Against the advice of its president, the A. A. I. S. Council agreed on a strike to begin on 1 June 1882 for a general advance of 5 to 15 per cent in puddlers' wages in all mills which had refused to adopt the union's scale. The strike involved chiefly ironworks; most steel mills agreed to the union rate because they did not employ many puddlers.[40] The Carnegies and two firms connected with the Homestead works, for example, settled with the union. On 1 June, iron mills in Pittsburgh, Wheeling, Cleveland, Cincinnati, St. Louis, Springfield, and Chicago, and other places where union labor was employed, closed their doors and allowed their furnaces to get cold.[41] Nearly twenty thousand iron workers were reported on strike in Pittsburgh alone; a hundred thousand were thrown out of work by the strike, according to the *Engineering and Mining Journal.* Many men not eligible for membership in the union became involved in the fight for the puddlers' scale.[42]

Attempts were made during this strike to start work with nonunion men, many of them recent immigrants. A few firms required strikebreakers to sign "yellow dog" contracts.[43] Swedish and Norwegian immigrants were brought from eastern port cities to western mills.[44] The Cleveland Rolling Mills, having recently ceased to operate its puddling furnaces because of the completion of a new steel plant containing five open-hearth furnaces in 1878, were among the first to import labor, and were in an excellent position to succeed in the policy.[45] Strikers looked on in "sullen silence" when heavy details of police guards protected the strikebreakers as they entered the works at Newburgh, Ohio. Additions were made to the city police force while the inexperienced men were on duty at the mills. The introduction of these strikebreakers was not a peaceful process, and at first it almost seemed it would fail. By mid-July, however, the strike at the Cleveland Rolling Mills had been broken and the mills were reported as operating "just as before the strike began" with new hands.[46] The extent of the union defeat at the Cleveland Rolling Mills may be gauged from the fact that when strikers reapplied for their old jobs, individually, they lost seniority, and some who had been earning $8.00 a day returned at $1.50.[47] It was thus that Cleveland wages were brought down to the Pittsburgh level.

Techniques used in carrying out this policy were many of them quite familiar to American manufacturers. Immigrants were not told that they were to serve as strikebreakers before they arrived on the scene. Often their baggage was confiscated as security for the repayment of loans for transportation from the east. The innovation, so far as the iron industry was concerned, was the use of labor exchanges dealing in immigrant labor to obtain strikebreakers.[48]

The strike ended in September. The men gained nothing and the Amalgamated Association lost thousands of members.[49] It was this experience which impressed the leaders of the ironworkers with the dangers of unskilled immigrant labor. They admitted in Congressional hearings that union standards were injured by foreign labor only in times of strikes.[50] Only then did skilled ironworkers feel any direct competition from the immigrants brought in to man the new processes. The wages for jobs not organized by the Association were not regarded as its concern.

Changes which were to eliminate many jobs for which mill owners had formerly recruited skilled labor abroad were also taking place in the cotton and woolen industries. Cotton manufacturers had always been able to employ unskilled workers, even children, for some operations. The years following the Civil War brought significant extensions of the jobs which could be learned quickly and performed by women and children.

The adoption of ring-spinning in place of mule-spinning was an important part of this process. Mule-spinning was a highly skilled occupation, and its displacement in American mills can probably be interpreted as a search for lower labor costs in a way that the introduction of the Bessemer converter and open-hearth furnaces cannot. Although British mule-spinners had been recruited for the American industry, they could not be obtained in sufficient numbers, nor could they be induced to give up their trade-unions.[51] Women could learn to run ring-spinning machinery in a week or two, and could be paid less, while producing at least as much yarn. In 1898, mule-spinners earned twelve to fourteen dollars a week, but women operating ring spindles received on the average from six to eight dollars a week.[52]

A striking instance of the displacement of the strongly independent mule-spinnners was recounted by a British reporter who toured the American cotton industry at the turn of the century:

"The mule-spinners," said one mill superintendent to me, "are a tough crowd to deal with. A few years ago they were giving trouble at this mill, so one Saturday afternoon, after they had gone home, we started right in and smashed up a room-full of mules with sledge-hammers. When the men came back on Monday morning, they were astonished to find that there was no work for them. That room is now full of ring frames run by girls."[53]

In other branches of textile manufacture skills were also being replaced. Dyeing textile fabrics, which had earlier in the century required the importation of skilled labor from Europe, also ceased to be a highly skilled occupation chiefly because of the large amount of information which came to be furnished by producers of dye colors to those who used them.[54]

After 1894 the Nothrup automatic weft-changing loom revolutionized weaving and did away with the constant undersupply of skilled weavers which harassed textile manufacturers during the period just after the Civil War.[55] Even before the Nothrup loom was introduced, the work of individual operatives in the weaving department of American cotton textile mills had been increased by machinery improvements. Between 1850 and 1872 the number of looms tended by one operative was increased from four to eight, the machines were speeded up, and there were fewer breaks in their operation. At the same time in England few weavers operated more than four looms and each had an assistant on these.[56] Although work became harder in the weaving departments, wages declined in inverse ratio to production.[57]

To some extent, textile manufacturers continued to seek workmen through their own agents abroad and in Canada. By the late seventies, the transatlantic centers of such recruitment had shifted from the Lancashire textile towns to Scotland, Ireland, and Sweden. French Canadians were sought in preference to any European workmen. They were near at hand and had what was becoming an important qualification for work in American factories: a complete lack of knowledge of industrial methods and trade-union standards.[58] The agents of Pepperell Company, who obtained skilled Scottish girls on contracts in 1881, expressed dissatisfaction with a group of men shipped to them from the trade-union center of Manchester, England. Labor journals charged that Rhode Island manufacturers were seeking help, not in the mills, but in the poorhouses of Scotland and England in the eighties.[59] One journal reported that "many New England mills are importing Swedish help, because it is so cheap."[60] The Pepperell Company, for one, expressed its preference for Swedish workers.[61] Cotton-mill owners were also said to have agents in Hanover, Holstein, and Oldenberg, hiring workmen on "deceptive" contracts.[62]

During the eighties textile manufacturers also began importing labor through steamship company labor bureaus and the labor exchanges. In 1883 cotton manufacturers in Lowell, Lawrence, and New Bedford were said to be contracting with steamship companies to supply them with immigrant workmen.[63] New England manufacturers were making use of the Castle Garden Labor Bureau as well.[64] Immigrant labor was even brought to a few southern textile mills through the former West Virginia Commissioner of Immigration who operated a private labor bureau in New York City in the eighties. South Carolina cotton mills obtained some workers through the Castle Garden Exchange.[65]

Trade unions in the cotton industry had not gained a strength comparable to that of the puddlers and boilers in the iron industry. At the end of the seventies, however, textile mills experienced a sudden upsurge of union organization, which embraced unskilled operatives as well as skilled. The short-lived International Labor Union, formed from a brief wedding of the remnants of the old International Workingmen's Association with Ira Seward's eight-hour movement, claimed a membership of eight thousand in 1878; most of its members were to be found in the textile centers of New England, New Jersey, and New York.[66]

The failure of a number of strikes in the cotton textile industry during the late seventies and early eighties must be attributed, at least in part, to the ability of manufacturers to make use of unskilled labor obtained from labor exchanges as strikebreakers. The unskilled were rushed to the scene whenever trouble broke out.[67] The threat that they could easily be replaced by workmen who would be willing to work at lower standards was constantly held before New England textile operatives who struck for improved conditions.[68] Workers in a cotton mill in Rhode Island who threatened to strike against a 40 per cent wage reduction in 1884, for example, were warned that such a course would be "rash and foolish" because weavers could be imported from England at sixteen dollars a head.[69] Along with threats to import workers, some manufacturers made arrangements with owners of neighboring mills to blacklist strikers.[70]

Fall River was, as before the depression, the center of trade-unionism in the cotton textile industry. In 1879 the spinners of that city struck to try to regain part of the 45 per cent wage cut they had sustained during the depression.[71] French Canadians were imported to break the strike, and it was lost in spite of efforts of the strikers' committee to persuade the new operatives to leave.[72] The recruits were too poor to listen to arguments about union standards.[73] Again in the disastrous strike of 1884, when eight thousand operatives in fifty-one mills turned out to fight wage reductions, immigrants were used successfully against the strikers. Swedish and German immigrants were among those used to defeat the strike.[74]

The Harmony Mills in Cohoes, New York, had been the scene of a succession of strikes. In 1880, the International Labor Union had won a victory at these mills in a strike which obtained for all the workers, skilled and unskilled alike, a 10 per cent wage increase.[75] Efforts of the manufacturers to get enough Canadian strikebreakers failed. In April 1882, five thousand workers again left the mills. Aided by the New York and Rochester Central Trades Councils, these cotton operatives were at first in a strong position, and many of them were assisted to get jobs elsewhere.[76] As the strikers held into the summer, the managers began to make arrangements to reopen the mills by the first of September without them. Early in June eviction notices were posted at the company tenements to provide accommodation for German and Scottish immigrants.[77]

Reports reached the press that the company had made arrangements with the Inman Steamship Line to import Swedish workers. The treasurer of the company issued a statement just before the mills reopened with strikebreakers calculated to show the strikers the company's independence of them. "In relation to the Swedes," he said, "we have not yet engaged any, but we have engaged help abroad. When it arrives we will resume work."[78] The first week in August the company was ready to proceed. The works were opened; all the strikers who refused to return were evicted from the tenements; and imported workmen replaced them. Importations continued throughout the year. Three hundred Swedes were brought in in one lot. Needless to say, the strike failed.[79] Such experiences as these convinced cotton operatives that immigrants were their enemies and gained for the latter the reputation of strikebreakers.

Thus many old crafts in both textiles and the iron industry were gradually being rendered unnecessary by machines. But for the constant strikebreaking, the process might have gone on without arousing violent prejudices against new immigrant groups. Nevertheless it is probably significant that in the accounts of strikers at puddling and rolling mills, as well as cotton mills, one rarely finds instances of these skilled unionists attempting to take immigrants into the unions as was common in the mines and as figured so spectacularly in the Freighthandlers' strike of 1882.

In all four of these industries, the recruitment of immigrant labor, by the eighties, could be left to the steamship companies. The labor exchanges of the large cities provided the institutions by which undirected immigrant labor could be distributed to industry. The use of these agencies during strikes resulted in trade-union condemnation of immigrants. Such strikebreaking depended in a great measure upon the fact that immigrants were not told the kind of situation they would find and were kept isolated after their arrival. Once that isolation was broken, usually through the medium of the trade-union, the peasant immigrant often refused to allow himself to be used as a strikebreaker.[80] Many such instances have been cited in the mines, although they depended in part of course on the ability of the local union to supply financial assistance to the immigrants. In the iron and textile industries the exclusiveness of the craft unionists aggravated their problems during strikes. Even in the many cases in which immigrants did serve as strikebreakers it was not the racial character of the new immigrants as the United States Immigration Commission decided, but "the temporary result of the necessity of finding a footing in American industry," as Leiserson concluded,[81] which enabled employers and labor agencies, without any necessity of prepaid passages or "contracts," to use them to the detriment of workers already in the country.[82]

PART III

THE ANTI-CONTRACT LABOR LAWS

Chapter 8

THE WINDOW GLASS WORKERS

There can be little doubt, as will be demonstrated later, that one Assembly of the Knights of Labor, the Window Glass Workers, Local Assembly 300, was the real initiator of the measures to counteract the importation of foreign contract labor which were incorporated in the Foran Act of 1885. The peculiar problems, as well as the strength, of the window glass workers with respect to immigrant labor were important factors in determining the precise form which restrictions on immigration took in the mid-eighties.

The window glass workers had a unique position; they alone were in no conceivable way immediately threatened by the immigration of unskilled workers. The highly skilled nature of their work prevented any direct displacement of their labor and at the same time they were not in any danger of being indirectly displaced by unskilled immigrants through mechanization as were puddlers and mule-spinners.

Until the twentieth century the process of blowing glass was not different in principle from the mode of production used in ancient Egypt.[1] While some improvements in technique were made in the United States during the 1880's and 1890's, primarily in the direction of catching up with European innovations, it was not until 1903, when the Lubber cylinder window glass machine was perfected for commercial use, that the highly skilled glassmakers who had been essential to the industry were displaced by machinery.[2] Before that date innovations were made only within

139

the handicraft system of production. The window glass workers—blowers, gatherers, flatteners and cutters—were still essentially unaffected by technological revolution.

Because of the extraordinary skill required, the recruitment of European glassmakers on contract had been, and continued to be, a feature of the window glass industry. Glassmakers had been imported on prepaid passages from France, Belgium, Germany, and Great Britain since the earliest days of the industry in America.[3] Importations continued during the sixties, as the industry expanded from 89 factories in 1860 to 154 in 1870 and the value of the output of the industry from $8,512,000 in 1860 to $18,467,000 in 1870.[4] Just as other skilled workers protested against the importation of contract labor during that decade, so also the Window Glass Blowers Union of Pittsburgh registered complaints against the recruitment of European glass blowers by Pittsburgh manufacturers at the National Labor Union convention in 1867.[5]

After the depression of the seventies a strong and long-lived organization of glassworkers emerged to challenge the importation of contract labor. This organization succeeded in establishing itself quite rapidly; within two years of its formatioon in 1881 it claimed to have enrolled all the skilled window glass workers in every factory in the country.[6] Under the leadership of the Gatherers' local at Pittsburgh, which had been granted a charter by the Knights of Labor as Local Assembly 300, the blowers and gatherers were consolidated on 15 August 1879;[7] and the flatteners and cutters amalgamated with Local 300 in February 1880.[8] Uriah Stephens himself helped in organizing the workers in the Baltimore glass industry.[9] As the second men in the hierarchy of skills in the industry, receiving only three-fifths the wages of blowers, the gatherers were particularly sensitive to the advantages of industry-wide collective bargaining. They also were strongly opposed to the importation of glass blowers from Europe, since many of them were "learning to blow" and regarded the entrance of top men from abroad as retarding their own advance.[10]

The union was organized during another period of expansion in the window glass industry. This growth was directed into new areas, most of them west of the Alleghenies. After 1882, the adoption of gas instead of coal as the fuel for glass melting accentuated the reorientation of the industry into western fields. While the numbers of window glass factories in Massachusetts and New York declined, Pennsylvania, New Jersey, Ohio, Indiana, Illinois, and

Maryland acquired 162 new factories between 1870 and 1890 out of a total of 317 in the country at the latter census year. Maryland had two window glass factories in 1870, eight in 1880; Ohio had nine in 1870, twenty in 1880, and sixty-seven in 1890. The number of factories in Pennsylvania, which had led the industry, nearly doubled between 1870 and 1890, much of the expansion going to the gas fields of northwestern Pennsylvania.[11]

The location of new factories in the west during the seventies brought to the fore the question of east-west wage differentials. As in the iron industry, western wages were higher than those in the east. As the expansion into new localities was accompanied by a shortage of skilled workers which raised wages, western manufacturers sought to bring about wage equalization by importing European glassmakers.

Importations of skilled immigrant workers to the new areas began in 1879 and 1880. The aims of the glass manufacturers were similar to those of the iron employers, who were at the same time searching in the British iron centers for workers, but were also able to utilize the labor exchanges. The glassmakers, on the other hand, could not produce at all with unskilled men. Hence the window glass manufacturers brought in skilled workmen from Germany, England, and Belgium, carefully selected and signed on contracts. In other words, the recruitment of glassworkers underwent no change in the early eighties; the old methods used to obtain skilled spinners and weavers, iron molders and puddlers, before the depression of the seventies, were employed to import glassworkers at lower wages.

"Whole sets" of blowers, gatherers, cutters, and flatteners, ranging from twenty to sixty in number, were brought to Zanesville and Kent, Ohio, to Baltimore, and to other cities during 1879 and 1880. Most of the new men were from Belgium, although at least one group came from Sunderland, the center of the British glass industry.[12]

Belgian workmen who signed contracts in Antwerp to work in Kent, Ohio, pledged themselves to work at New York rates which were admittedly lower than those in force in Ohio.[13] A tenth of these wages were to be withheld regularly as a guarantee of the faithful performance of the contract. Contracts were made for a period of three years. Furthermore, the manufacturers gave no real guarantee of wages even though mention was made of the New York rate. Flatteners, for example, were to get sixty dollars a month for work actually performed, but a supplementary clause in the contract stipulated that they were to be paid only thirty dollars a month "for all work done other than flattening." The imported workmen also pledged in these contracts that the manufacturers were to "have the right to discharge any workman who shall neglect his work through drunkenness or idleness, or who shall attempt to create dissatisfaction among the workmen."[14]

The contract laborers brought to Baltimore were used to break a strike. In an attempt to isolate the foreign workmen, the manufacturers succeeded in getting a perpetual injunction from the courts restraining the American glassworkers from interfering with the strikebreakers in any way. The union maintained that manufacturers did not pay imported workmen the rate of pay mentioned in their contracts, on the grounds that the foreigners were not able to work at the speed required in American factories. In spite of the formidable weapons of the manufacturers, the union countered their moves effectively by meetings at night with the foreigners and by using union funds to assist them in breaking their contracts. Some of the Belgian workmen refused to stay at the melting pots as soon as they learned the true state of affairs. Most of them returned to Belgium, with the aid of the union treasury and the Belgian Consul.[15] In 1880 the Window Glass Workers Assembly sent a delegation to Belgium "to prevail upon blowers" not to come to America.[16]

The importations of 1879 and 1880 did not wipe out wage differentials. As the union increased its strength in 1880 and 1881, the manufacturers also combined in the American Window Glass Manufacturers Association. Early in 1882 the western branch of this organization, meeting in Pittsburgh, decided to take action to remove the disadvantage they felt even in western markets where eastern glass was underselling theirs because eastern manufacturers could get skilled labor at from 20 to 25 per cent lower rates.[17] Since 1879 when annual wage negotiations had been instituted in the glass industry, contracts for work had been made with the union in the late summer for a period of ten months. In the summer of 1882 the western manufacturers requested a delay of a month before drawing up the contracts for the next winter's work. During the extra month, they imported glass from Belgium, enough for them to lock out union members. Then they announced that the works in 59 factories in six states would reopen at a wage reduction of 30 per cent.[18]

Local 300 was just as eager as the manufacturers to equalize wages, but their plan, in which they had been encouraged by western manufacturers, was to raise eastern wages rather than lower western.[19] During the same summer of 1882, the Window Glass Workers called a strike in the east for a 10 per cent wage increase.[20] The strike in the east lasted until February 1883, and the strike in the west, which followed the announcement of reductions, continued until early in 1884.[21]

The eastern strike, called by Local 300 for wage advances and changes in working rules, extended throughout New Jersey, eastern Pennsylvania, and Baltimore.[22] Manufacturers again brought contract labor from Belgium to New Jersey and Baltimore factories in an attempt to defeat the strikers.[23] Before these new recruits left Europe, they had agreed in writing to work at wages which were below the old union scale. Blowers imported to Baltimore were to get eighty dollars a month, and this wage was to be conditional upon their making a quality of glass which was high by American standards.[24]

Local 300 succeeded in its attempt to get the wage advance when agreements were signed with eastern manufacturers during January and February 1883.[25] Employers failed to get the industry going with imported labor. In Baltimore, where employers had brought in a steady stream of immigrants to break the strike, manufacturers finally agreed to the wage advance on condition that they be allowed to keep on the imported workmen as employees.[26] Baltimore manufacturers were handicapped by the success of the union in persuading immigrants to join the union and "stand" the strike. Police refused to arrest twenty-one union members, at the manufacturers' insistence, for persuading all but three of the Belgian workmen to quit work.[27]

An exceedingly interesting and intriguing incident occurred at Malaga, New Jersey, during the strike. It illustrated not only the potential challenge of dual unionism which the Knights of Labor's aim of organizing all workers, skilled as well as unskilled, presented to the craft unions, but also the attitudes of the "aristocracy" of the American labor force towards the semiskilled and unskilled, and the fact that the real threat to the glassworkers was the importation of foreign skilled workers on contracts rather than the influx of unskilled workmen from abroad.

Before Local 300 began its nation-wide organizing campaign, there had apparently been a Knights of Labor Local, No. 872, at the window glass plant at Malaga, which had included the unskilled labor about the factory as well as the blowers and gatherers. Local 300 had skimmed off forty of the hundred odd members of Local 872, these forty joining 300, according to one embittered member of 872, "to get clear of giving sympathy or support to unskilled labor."[28]

When Local 300 called the strike, the unskilled men in 872 were thrown out of work as a consequence, but while Local 300 paid strike benefits of $6.00 to $8.00, Local 872 members who had been getting only $1.35 a day in wages as against the $4.00 to $8.00 a day made by members of Local 300, had to try to find railroad and farm work. The same informant wrote to Powderly complaining that Local 300 had started the strike, was taking care of its own members, but never asked if Local 872 needed help. "They comport themselves as though they were a different class of beings. That they were ye Lordlings of merry England and 872 are the Peasantry. . . ."[29]

It was not until foreign blowers began to arrive at Malaga that Local 300 paid any attention to the humble members of 872. Then the Preceptor of the skilled assembly came to 872 and demanded that the latter refuse to help the manufacturers get the factory going with the European workmen. Bitter and impoverished as they were, all the members of 872 except the Recording Secretary (by his own account) went to work with the "foreign scabs," though at the same time letters were dispatched to Powderly asking for advice and financial assistance if they were to come out again for Local 300. Powderly's replies appear to have added only confusion as to the Knights of Labor's official position with respect to the strike, and no money was sent. Local 300, under the circumstances, relied on attempts to persuade the foreign blowers to join the union or accept free passages home.[30]

The Window Glass Workers faced the same methods of strikebreaking in the conflict in the west. After the eastern manufacturers had settled with the union, the Window Glass Manufacturers Association at a meeting in Long Branch, New Jersey, in July 1883, agreed "That the treasurer be authorized to pay a sum not exceeding thirty dollars per man for each blower or gatherer brought over from Europe after 1 August 1883, provided the same be employed by some member of this association, and provided they are not workmen who have been in this country within the twelve months last past."[31] Accordingly skilled window glass workers were recruited in Belgium, Germany, and England.[32] Manufacturers in Pittsburgh and Ohio, and as far west as Kentucky, Illinois, and Indiana, received consignments of Belgian, British, and German glassmakers. Since none of the glass factories was large, the importations did not have to be made in great numbers to get a factory in operation.[33] The union reported that the immigrants were working at from 30 to 50 per cent less than the old scale.[34]

The Window Glass Workers were strong enough, and had sufficient resources, to fight successfully. In the autumn of 1883 every preceptory, as the local branches of the union were called, voted to hold out through the winter until the spring trade opened in February 1884.[35] A number of the master workmen of the Local went into business for themselves, some on a coöperative basis.[36] Much to the dismay and disgust of Robert Layton, the Grand Secretary of the Knights of Labor who, with Powderly, deplored strikes, Local 300 re-elected its aggressive head, James Campbell, in 1883, and through him succeeded in putting through the executive council of the Knights of Labor an assessment on the Order to assist them in what they called a lockout, but Layton termed a strike.[37] When February arrived the manufacturers were ready to compromise: a sliding scale was adopted which was considered a victory for the union. By that time most of the immigrants to western factories had joined the union.[38]

During these struggles of 1882 and 1883, through which Local 300 gained recognition as the sole bargaining agent for the entire window glass industry of the country, the persistent and resourceful leaders of the union took the first concrete steps toward getting an anti-contract labor law adopted by Congress. The seriousness of their opposition to contract labor is evidenced by a motion carried at the second national convention in 1883 that Local 300 would withhold the suffrage from candidates for official positions who would not declare themselves opposed to the importation of foreign contract labor.[39] At the same convention a motion from the Illinois delegates was adopted debarring from membership in the union a man who was hired by the Ottawa Glass Company to go to England to hire and import two sets of workmen for them.[40]

The pressure for legislation to prohibit the importation of contract labor was only one part of this union's battle for a complete monopoly of the labor supply. The window glass workers were in a unique position in industry, since glass production in both England and Belgium was highly centralized, in Belgium, in the Charlroi district, and in England, around Sunderland. The union estimated that the entire skilled glassworker population in the United States and western Europe combined was only twelve and a half thousand. Because skilled workmen were essential to the industry, recruits were bound to come from a few places in the Old World.[41]

The high degree of localization of the industry in Europe encouraged the glassworkers to attempt to extend their organizing activities. In January 1881 it was announced that an International Association of Glass Workers to be known as District Assembly No. 300 had been formed at Pittsburgh. For the moment there was no difference between Local Assembly and District Assembly 300 except in name, but the new organization had already sent organizers to France, England, and Belgium. In the spring of 1884 the president of District Assembly 300, Isaac Cline, and Andrew Burtt set out for Belgium and England in hope of forming an international federation of glassworkers which would regulate wages throughout the industry. Relations had already been established with Belgian workers by previous visits of Americans, and the Belgian union had contributed funds to aid the strike of 1882 in the United States.[42] The visit of these officers laid the basis for an international federation. Five hundred members were gained in Britain, where little unionization had previously existed among glassworkers. Plans were made to send European delegates to the first convention of the international federation to be held in Pittsburgh in 1885. A permanent organizer left for Europe from District Assembly 300 in the summer of 1884.[43]

To the first meeting of the "Universal Federation of Window Glass Workers" in Pittsburgh in July 1885 came delegates from Belgium, France, and Italy. The English did not attend because their organization was weak, and the Germans, because of anti-union laws.[44] Among the agreements reached, after Isaac Cline was elected president, was the following:

Each National branch shall have control of its members, and no member shall be allowed to go from one country to another without first having notified the National Secretary of his desire to change. In such cases the National Secretary to which such member desires to emigrate shall be apprised of the fact, and after submitting the matter to the National Council, they shall determine whether the condition of trade and labor in their country warrant such change, and their decision shall be final. No change shall be countenanced as lawful unless the consent of the resident National Council shall have been previously obtained and certified to by the National President and Secretary, and bears the seal of the National Association. Any members going from one country to another to work, shall pay into the Association of such country the full amount of the regular initiation fee, deposit his card and pay the regular monthly dues and legal levies and assessments.[45]

The Universal Federation of Window Glass Workers is an interesting case of the development of earlier craft union schemes to control the immigration of workingmen in the same craft autonomously, without the aid of the government. At the same time, it was this type of trade-union, of which the Window Glass Workers and the Amalgamated Association of Iron, Steel and Tin-plate workers are examples, made up of skilled workers who exhibited no interest in organizing the unskilled, who felt themselves to be jeopardized by contract labor, that is, the importation of skilled workmen by industry on written agreements. Even in iron and textiles, where machinery was advancing, skilled workmen in craft unions were not in direct competition with agricultural immigrants, and when they castigated the new immigrants, prejudice and scapegoating operated in those denunciations more than did direct threats to their jobs.

Chapter 9

THE FORAN ACT

The federal government finally assumed control of the regulation of immigration in 1882. Before that, Congress had concerned itself with conditions aboard immigrant ships exclusively, leaving to the states with immigrant-receiving ports all responsibility for accepting and rejecting immigrants, for protecting and advising them, and for caring for any who became public charges. Federal supervision came after a period of near-anarchy with respect to immigrant regulation following the Supreme Court's rejection, in 1875, of the state head taxes by which New York had supported its Castle Garden facilities and other states had insured themselves against the potential impoverishment, illness, or crime of immigrants who remained in their jurisdiction. For six years transportation companies successfully fought federal bills to impose a substitute for the state head tax.[1] When the Supreme Court, in 1881, upheld the claims of the steamship lines that the New York "inspection tax," another device for circumventing the earlier decision, was also unconstitutional, the situation became acute.

The general economic condition of the country in 1882 favored a swerve toward restrictionist sentiment as the tremendous cyclical upswing of 1879 and 1880 leveled off. According to the Castle Garden Labor Bureau, the insistent demand for labor which had been characteristic of the years 1879 and 1880 receded in 1882 and 1883. The point-of-view of the *Railroad Gazette* was perhaps as good an index as any to the lessening of the demand for labor, important as railroad construction was in the nation's economy. As late as 1881 the *Gazette* wrote: "With the enormous amount of railroad construction laid out for this year, there would be danger of something like a labor famine if the immigration were not so large . . ."[2] The following year the same paper observed that unless the rate of construction increased, there would be no need to import railroad labor.[3]

Federal intervention was characterized from the outset by the search for a formula of entrance restrictions which would protect the country from "undesirable" immigrants. The first steps in this direction, taken in 1882, prohibited the immigration of convicts, lunatics, idiots, persons suffering from specified diseases, paupers, and the Chinese. The second step, the Foran Act of 1885, forbade the importation of contract labor. More than one critic of American immigration legislation has pointed out an important contradiction in these laws which on the one hand laid upon the immigrant the burden of proving that he was not likely to become a public charge or pauper, and on the other hand, threatened to exclude him if he had fortified himself against such an eventuality by arranging for work in the United States before he left Europe. This anomaly was one of the causes of uncertainty and anxiety among immigrants during the next thirty years.[4]

Restrictions on entry rather than positive measures to assist the rational distribution of immigrants to places where their labor was needed became the foundation of United States immigration policy. Twenty-seven years were to pass, years which witnessed the high-water mark of immigration, before the government made a half-hearted attempt to aid immigrants to find jobs only to have such efforts handicapped by the contract labor laws themselves.

While the traditional view that the American labor movement spearheaded the demand for a law against contract labor is right so far as it goes, confusion still surrounds the precise role which different segments of the labor movement played in formulating and pressing for the Foran Act. Furthermore, the question of why the labor movement focused upon contract labor as a formula for restriction at this time has not been adequately answered.

A good example of the inadequacy of the accepted interpretation is found in the standard history of the American labor movement. Selig Perlman attributed the passage of the anti-contract labor law "almost entirely" to the efforts of the Knights of Labor. While it is undeniable that the Knights participated in the drive for such legislation, Professor Perlman's description of the motivations behind the drive conflicts with the findings of this study. "The trade unions," he wrote, "gave little active support, for to the skilled workingman the importation of contract Italian and Hungarian laborers was a matter of small importance; on the other hand, to the Knights of Labor with their vast contingent of unskilled, it was a strong menace."[5]

It was, however, precisely the skilled workers, whom Perlman denied had any interest in the restriction of contract labor, who alone had anything to fear from the importation of Europeans on contracts. In spite of the efforts of the craft unions to regulate the flow of immigrants, to inform prospective immigrants of conditions in America, and to prevent strikebreaking by immigrant workmen, it was primarily in these skilled trades that the system of contract labor was and had been employed. When a skilled workman was needed, employers took the risk of advancing transportation money in the expectation that it would eventually be repaid by the immigrant from his earnings.

In those industries, and branches of industries, in which machinery could be used to reduce the number of skilled workmen required, the threat of contract labor was negligible. Corporations and employers were unwilling to make large investments in unskilled labor. They were able to depend upon recruitment abroad by railroads, steamship lines, and labor agencies to bring immigrants who were novices to industry swarming into the labor agencies of the large cities when demand for such labor was high. When immigrants were sent by these agencies to break strikes in the mines or the steelworks they might indeed be used to menace or destroy labor organization among the unskilled workers, but the prohibition of contract labor was not an appropriate weapon with which to deal with that problem.

Both skilled and unskilled workers had reason to criticize the ways in which immigrants were distributed to American industry during this period. Only skilled workers in unmechanized or not fully mechanized industries had objective reasons to oppose the importation of contract labor by industry. Were any efforts made by the labor movement to deal with the larger problem of the distribution of unskilled workers to industry?

A growing fear and opposition to immigration was evident among both skilled and unskilled workers during the early eighties. Some said that immigration should be stopped altogether for a while.[6] All branches of organized labor agreed that they did not want to compete with either the "pauper labor of Europe or the cheap labor of America."[7] The *Iron Age* noted in 1881 that no one could read the labor papers during the recent elections and not see in them a latent intention of making immigration an issue in the future.[8] As yet the precise aims of such agitation were not clear.

Many elements in the labor movement of the early eighties sought to find some method of coping with the problem of the distribution of immigrants to industry quite apart from the question of contract labor. The Grand Master Workman of the Knights of Labor, T. V. Powderly, stressed the importance of organizing all workmen, regardless of nationality, and also for publicizing information about conditions in American industry through European unions. To gain these ends the Knights tried to spread their organization to Europe. "We must gain a foothold in all of the European countries," Powderly told the Knights of Labor delegates to the convention of 1884, "and, by organization, teach the people of these lands that there is no truth in the representations of those who would lure them from their homes."[9] Powderly had several years earlier begun correspondence with Alexander MacDonald of the British miners with a view toward furthering coöperation between the Knights and the British union, but MacDonald's death cut short negotiations.[10]

Similar suggestions from other labor groups harked back to the attempts of the National Labor Union to publicize abroad American labor's views of the demand for labor. At the second convention of the Federation of Organized Trades and Labor Union in 1882, P. J. Maguire of the carpenters expressed the hope that friendly relations and mutual correspondence between workmen of all countries would "place a check on the transportation of labor from one country in order to cheapen it in another at the behest of capital."[11] Even after the act to forbid the importation of labor on contract was certain of passing, the New York Central Labor Union distrusted its effectiveness sufficiently to pass the following resolution:

That a committee be appointed to draw up a circular, to be sent to newspapers in all countries in Europe and all sections of America, setting forth that the conditions of life among the working classes in the new world have changed within the past ten years; that all the public land has been given away; showing the conditions of the miners of

Pennsylvania, Illinois and Ohio, and also that there are many thousands of idle men and women in all the cities of the [United States . . .].[12]

At least a few unions whose membership included unskilled workers recognized the importance of the urban labor exchanges in distributing immigrant labor. The Cincinnati Trades and Labor Assembly wrote to the Amalgamated Trades and Labor Union in New York City in 1883 asking for information about a "New York Labor Bureau." Cincinnati workers sought some way of coöperating with the New York Union to "destroy this body" by placing information as to true conditions into immigrants' hands before they signed contracts in New York.[13] An investigation begun by the New York Trades and Labor Union came to nothing for want of any public interest in it.[14] Miners in Knights of Labor locals in the Pittsburgh area and in the Hocking Valley also asked New York unions to warn immigrants at Castle Garden against going to mines where there were strikes.[15] Similarly, the City Federation of Labor in Washington, D. C. wrote to the city commissioners complaining against the use of emigrant agencies to obtain labor for the city water-works extension, but without success. The first thousand immigrants, the latter replied, ought not to exclude the thousands who desire to follow even though their wages be lowered.[16]

Craft unionists as well as unskilled workmen were discussing the possibilities of setting up some kind of disinterested labor exchanges in America to counteract the work of the private labor bureaus. Some proposed, as had the National Labor Union before them, that the unions themselves should organize distributing agencies. In 1884 the delegates to the Federated Organization of Trades and Labor Unions passed a resolution in favor of opening a labor exchange "in every city and district which has a trade assembly for the purpose of acting as an intelligence office between employers and employed and guarding against the confidence games of certain employment agencies. . . ."[17] Other workingmen suggested in state and federal hearings that public immigration bureaus should be established to help immigrants get to places where they were legitimately needed.[18]

The publicity devoted to the anti-contract labor movement eclipsed all other labor ideas on immigration during 1883 and 1884 and perhaps even sidetracked the maturing of suggestions for more disinterested distributing agencies on this side of the water. The pressure for an anti-contract labor law was begun and organized by a group of craft unionists, not all of whom were affiliated with the Knights of Labor, who were able to capitalize upon the growing opposition to immigration in the balance of the labor movement whose proposals for dealing with the question were less clearly formulated.

After 1878, when the Knights of Labor incorporated a resolution against the importation of Chinese labor on contracts in its statement of principles, the Knights' conventions took no notice of the question of contract labor again until 1883.[19] In that year the Knights were asked to place their strength and resources behind a drive for which the groundwork had already been laid and specific demands articulated.

Two years before the Knights of Labor began agitating against the importation of European workers on contracts, the Federation of Organized Trades and Labor Unions placed the prevention of the importation of foreign contract labor in its Declaration of Principles.[20] The leaders in founding this organization, which the American Federation of Labor later claimed as its parent, reluctantly accepted an amendment from the floor adding "Labor Unions" to the "Federation of Organized Trades Unions" proposed by the Committee on Organization as the name of the new organization.[21] The narrow craft-union viewpoint had important exponents at this convention, among them Samuel Gompers. The printers, carpenters, cigar-makers, and iron-molders, as well as the Amalgamated Association of Iron and Steel Workers and the Window Glass Workers of America all sent delegates.[22] In December 1881, four months after the Pittsburgh convention, the Federation of Organized Trades and Labor Unions circularized trades unions noting the importance of prohibiting the importation of foreign contract labor.[23]

The second and third meetings of this federation were less well attended than the first had been, with most of the Knights of Labor locals dropping out by 1882. Only 27 delegates came to the third convention, held in New York City in 1883, as compared with the 107 who appeared at Pittsburgh in 1881.

After the 1883 Convention, however, the delegates remained in New York to testify at hearings of the Senate Committee on Education and Labor. All of them impressed upon the committee the desire of the trades-unions for an anti-contract labor law.

Among those who testified were P. J. Maguire, General Secretary of the Brotherhood of Carpenters and Joiners; P. H. Logan, representing the Chicago Trades Assembly; Louis F. Post of the New York Central Labor Union; Robert Blissit, New York City tailor and Secretary of the Workingman's Union of New York City; Hugh T. Elmer, Boston trade unionist. Later William Weihe, President of the Amalgamated Association of Iron and Steel Workers, which had withdrawn from the Federation, also testified in favor of the prohibition of contract labor.[24] Samuel Gompers later elaborated that the purpose of the Federation in favoring an anti-contract labor law was that "we hoped to prevent employers from importing strikebreakers or workers to lower the standards. . . ."[25] The cigar-makers had been threatened during the Milwaukee strike of 1881 and other strikes in New York and Cleveland in 1883 and 1884 by both importation of skilled cigar-makers from Bohemia and the introduction of new machinery.[26] The outlawing of contract labor might at least save the cigar-makers' union the expense and difficulties of having to cope with imported skilled cigar-makers. In January and July 1883, the circularized platform of the Federation again included the contract labor issue.[27]

Meanwhile the Knights of Labor began to take up the question of contract labor. The impetus came from Local Assembly 300, the Window Glass Workers, who had been represented by four delegates at the first meeting of the Federation. Following the negotiations which ended its eastern strike, the Window Glass Workers began, in March 1883, to prepare a bill on the subject of contract labor.[28] According to the Secretary of the Amalgamated Association of Iron and Steel Workers, "A bill, such as was thought would meet the exigencies of the occasion, was drafted and taken to Washington, by a member, Mr. John G. Schlicker, of the Window Glass Blowers Association."[29]

After these initial steps had been taken, according to Powderly, "all labor organizations agreed in backing" this bill.[30] The Executive Board of the Knights of Labor called the attention of delegates at the convention of 1883 to the evil of contract labor, but still did not make any specific recommendations such as the Window Glass Workers had prepared. The Board merely "urged" upon members of the Order the need for "unremitting and vigilant efforts looking toward its check."[31]

The Knights of Labor began organizing mass meetings and

petition drives against contract labor in December 1883.[32] At the same time the craft unions, both inside and outside the Knights of Labor, continued to agitate the question.[33]

Much of the preparatory work [reported William Martin of the Amalgamated Association of Iron and Steel Workers which was not affiliated with the Knights of Labor] was done in our General office by joint committees of the Unions in this city, the result of which was the issuing of circulars and petitions calling on all who favored *free labor* to sign the same and send them to their Representatives in Washington in favor of the passage of a bill prohibiting the importation of foreign labor under contract.[34]

The man who introduced the bill to prohibit the importation of contract labor in the House of Representatives at the moment when these mass meetings and the petition drives had reached a climax, was intimately acquainted with the aims and problems of craft unionists. Probably one of the first former trade unionists to sit in the American Congress, Martin Foran had been president of the Coopers International Union and editor of their journal from 1870 until 1874 when he was admitted to the Ohio bar.[35] Like his closest associates in the trade-union movement during those years, Saffin of the Molders and Fehrenbatch of the Machinists and Blacksmiths, Foran had advocated pressing for immediate and specific trade-union gains such as the eight-hour day and a national labor bureau as the basis of political action and criticized "independent political action" and efforts to coöperate with any but "bona fide representatives of bona fide organizations" in working for such measures.[36] In 1874 he had deplored the fact that some employers "at the first appearance of trouble with their employees send to Europe for 'decent workmen.' "[37] Thus Foran's background qualified him by inclination and experience as a spokesman of the views of craft unionists. Shortly after his election to Congress in 1882 Foran spoke at the second meeting of the Federation of Organized Trades and Labor Unions, held in the city of Cleveland where he had once worked at his trade, and was warmly received as "one man on the floor of Congress who would not betray the workingman."[38]

In January 1884 Foran introduced in the House a bill which was referred to the newly created labor committee. Powderly first saw its text a few days later when Foran sent it to him with a covering letter asking for "information" on the subject of contract labor.[39] In reply, Powderly forwarded a copy of the petition the Knights were circulating adding that he had asked parties who could furnish complete statistics to send them to Foran.[40] A week later Foran was again begging Powderly for "all the facts you run across on the importation of laborers."[41] Throughout the committee hearings which followed there was a remarkable absence of facts about contract labor in spite of Foran's efforts to get information on the importation of unskilled workers from the Knights of Labor. All of the actual facts submitted on the nature and extent of contract labor related to the window glass industry.

The Window Glass Workers also dominated the arrangements for sending spokesmen for the bill to the committee hearings. Powderly was merely informed by the Secretary of the Knights of Labor:

> Brother Campbell [of Local 300] writes me that the "Foreign Contract Labor" bill will come up before the Committee in Washington this week and your presence will be required. At the last meeting of the Executive Board it was decided that yourself, the Ex Board and the G.S. should appear before the committee in defense of that bill. You will be wired when to go . . .[42]

Three spokesmen for the Knights appeared in the House hearings, in keeping with this decision. In addition to these national officers, other affiliates of the Knights of Labor who sent delegates were the Pennsylvania and Ohio bituminous miners, the telegraphers, and the cotton-mill operatives.

The testimony of these Knights as to the prevalence of contract labor was remarkably weak. Powderly made reference to strikebreakers "engaged . . . at Castle Garden." William Barclay, for the miners of the Pennsylvania coke region, reported that there was an agency in Pittsburgh and one in New York for the employment of Slavonians. The president of the Pittsburgh Miners Association noted that operators "sometimes go to Castle Garden and engage men to work in the mines." A spokesman for the New England cotton-mill operatives admitted, with reference to strikebreakers, "whether under contract or not we are not able to prove . . . ," while the telegraph operator postulated that during their late strike "the telegraph companies would have imported foreign telegraphers if they could have gotten them. . . ."[43]

The only solid evidence of contract labor submitted to the House Committee came from the Window Glass Workers who sent a strong delegation of eight of their officers, from Pittsburgh, New Jersey, Baltimore, and Philadelphia. The Window Glass Workers not only brought certified copies of actual contracts but also included in their delegation glassworkers who had come as contract laborers.[44] The only important amendment to the original bill made at the committee stage was one suggested by one of the glassmakers' spokesmen who recommended permitting manufacturers to import foreigners for new industries.[45] Other craft unionists heard from were three representatives sent by the Amalgamated Association of Iron and Steel Workers.[46] The Federation of Organized Trades and Labor Unions also claimed that it was represented before the House Committee in favor of the Foran Bill.[47]

After the hearings the Knights again circulated petitions; one of these, forwarded to Congress, contained over thirty thousand signatures of "mechanics."[48] In 1884 the Knights of Labor Convention definitely declared itself in favor of an act to prohibit contract labor.[49] Powderly circularized every lodge, sending sample post cards and letters to Congress which favored, in addition to the bill against contract labor, an eight-hour day, regulation of lake and marine shipping, enlarged postal facilities, and a labor bureau.[50] The week before the Foran Bill was scheduled to come up in the House a labor demonstration, said to be the largest yet held in New York City, with perhaps thirty thousand people present (did that figure have a mysterious attraction for the Knights?), was staged in favor of the contract labor bill and other labor demands.[51] At another demonstration in Buffalo, precipitated by the use of carefully guarded Italians in a longshoreman's strike, Martin Foran spoke.[52]

The bill finally came up for debate in the House on 19 June. It would be interesting to know who decided the line of argument to be used by its proponents. In spite of the fact that every piece of evidence of contract labor was drawn from the glass industry, the traffic suddenly emerged in the House debates as a variation of the Chinese coolie trade. Without exception, the Congressmen who spoke for the bill rested their case on the degradation of the "new immigration" from Italy and Hungary, quoting statements by Powderly and the miners on the food, dress, and habits of these people, as well as their "unpatriotic" views of America.[53] These accounts made more lurid reading and carried a broader appeal to racial prejudice than did the complaints of craftsmen against the importation at most of a few hundred skilled workmen.

Foran himself set the pattern of exposition. After noting briefly that skilled workers such as the glassworkers had been replaced by contract laborers during a recent strike, he went on to claim that Italian and Hungarian workers were being imported in great droves by capitalists; he devoted the balance of his time to denouncing the races of Southern and Eastern Europe. When asked how many contract laborers were being brought in, Foran gave figures for the glass industry, compiled by the union, and then the bare immigration figures for Italians and Hungarians, resting his proof that most of them were contract laborers on the fact that males greatly outnumbered females.[54]

The House passed the bill by a voice vote after making three amendments. The first of these, which exempted new industries from its provisions, came from the labor committee. An amendment from the floor was adopted which stipulated that assisting relatives was not to be prohibited, thus leaving open one important avenue of recruitment of both skilled and unskilled workers. Finally, it was agreed that the act should not cover contracts made with aliens after they arrived in the United States. This last exception left both steamship and other private labor agencies untouched by the act in all important respects.[55]

The Foran Bill failed to become law during the first session of the 48th Congress. It was allowed to die in the Senate during the closing days of the session even though the Labor and Education Committee reported it without amendment.[56] The Senate did not finally pass the bill until 18 February 1885. If there was to be any organized opposition to it, plenty of time was allowed for it to mature. The delay, in spite of the flood of petitions and demonstrations from labor, leads one to question whether the pressure of the labor movement was the only factor bringing about the acceptance of the measure.

No opposition to the bill developed among industrialists. Although several of the Congressmen, both Senators and Representatives, who praised it, maintained that mine operators and railroad corporations were the principal importers of contract labor,[57] the *Railroad Gazette,* which frequently commented on the state of labor supply for construction, did not even mention the Foran Bill in its columns. Nor did the *Engineering and Mining Journal.*

The chief explanation for the quiescence of industry lies in the evidence of this volume that industry was not deeply involved in importing European labor and was certainly not importing unskilled workers on contracts in any numbers, if at all.

The Foran Bill actually received positive support from some of industry's watchdogs of the tariffs, who had for years used the protection of American labor as one of the chief weapons in their battle to retain tariffs. Protectionist interests took notice when labor spokesmen threatened to reject this type of benevolence from industry.

Labor journals were becoming restive on the tariff question during the early eighties. They pointed out that wages in protected industries were not higher than those in unprotected industries. When workingmen in protected industries struck for higher wages, the manufacturers imported labor from Europe, free of duty, to take their places. "Do the manufacturers of the country imagine the workingman will help them vote high tariff for their benefit and then permit them to flood the country with cheap foreign labor to break down prices?" threatened one editor.[58] When Hungarian and Swedish immigrants were being imported into the Pittsburgh region in 1882, the editor of the *Labor Tribune* in that city noted that: "This wholesale importation of cheap labor into this district is going to modify the opinions of the workingmen voters on the tariff."[59] The New York correspondent of the Birmingham *Post* in England reported, perhaps a bit wishfully, that a demonstration organized among miners and ironworkers of Pennsylvania in favor of the tariff had broken down because workingmen refused to carry the "approved banners."[60]

The relationship between tariffs and immigrant restrictions was discussed at the first meeting of the Federation of Organized Trades and Labor Unions in 1881. At this session were union leaders, like John Jarrett of the Amalgamated Association of Iron and Steel Workers, who had long coöperated with manufacturers in urging protective tariffs.[61] Other delegates agreed that "protective tariff means protection to the American manufacturer against the importation of foreign cheap goods, but it does not mean protection to the American laborer against the importation of foreign cheap laborers."[62] Although a compromise was reached at this first meeting by including both anti-contract labor and pro-tariff planks, the next year, after long debate, the arguments of Jarrett failed to persuade the convention: the protective tariff plank was dropped, with but one negative vote.[63] Craft unionists placed the argument of labor's right to protection before the Senate Committee on Education and Labor in 1883 when they advocated a law against contract labor.[64]

Some protectionists answered these arguments, first by calling them illogical and irrelevant, and then by pointing out that each new immigrant was a consumer as well as a laborer, and that his more important function was that of increasing the market for skilled labor.[65] This was roughly the Carey position of twenty years before when the Act to Encourage Immigration was passed. Far from objecting to wage-cutting by immigrants and the lack of protection to American labor, the editor of the Philadelphia *Times* saw immigration as a necessary and inevitable deterrent to "artificial" wage advances. "If wages here are advanced too far out of proportion to wages in other countries, the result must be an increased competition, caused by immigration which will necessarily bring wages down again."[66]

The American Iron and Steel Association, however, paid attention to labor's anti-protectionist arguments. John Jarrett had been a "prize exhibit" of the protectionist manufacturers in his consistent support of high tariffs. In keeping with his views, Jarrett had pulled the Amalgamated Association out of the Federation of Organized Trades and Labor Unions because it rejected a tariff plank. During the same summer of 1883, when labor's right to protection from foreign workmen was being argued before the Senate Committee, Jarrett reported on a circular sent out by the Executive Board of the Amalgamated Association urging pro-tariff meetings and pressure from local unions: "Judging from indications generally, I am under the impression that the response to this circular was of a rather plethoric nature."[67]

In the autumn of 1883 the American Iron and Steel *Bulletin* contained an article which marked a new approach to immigration. The editor noted:

We have a large minority of people among us who receive low wages and are always poor because of the very prosperity of our country, which tempts large numbers of foreigners to come here, or tempts some of our capitalists to bring them here, to overload the labor market. This is the trouble to-day in almost all our coal-mining districts, in our iron-ore mining districts. . . . It is a cause of trouble wherever unskilled or but poorly skilled labor is employed. We not only have to find employment for our own helpless classes, but for the shiploads of helpless people who are sent to us by other countries or whom we unwisely bring here.[68]

As recession became more pronounced in 1884, almost half the iron furnaces of the country were idle. The situation sharpened the Association's position to outright advocation of restriction. In October 1884, the *Bulletin* announced: "The right thing to do with all Italian and Hungarian laborers is not to import them. Congress should prohibit the traffic at its very first session. . . ."[69]

The desire to find a scapegoat for recession and unemploy-ment probably entered into the Association's position.[70] Equally important was the effort to retain a labor vote for protectionist policies. The old advocate of free immigration, Abram Hewitt, re-marked in a speech on the Morrison tariff in 1884 that importa-tions of foreign labor appeared to follow the attempts of trade unions to get a share in the profits from tariffs.[71] The president of the Iron and Steel Association, James Swank, had expressed the opinion as early as 1877 that a new approach was needed to immi-gration because of "evidence of poverty and growing discontent."[72] As the years went on Swank became keenly aware of the potential strength in votes of the argument that labor was not getting a pro-portionate benefit from protection.

We cannot as a party [he wrote to Senator William Chandler in 1892] hope to live with only one plank in our platform, Protection and home industry. We must promptly meet the criticism of all classes, workingmen included, that our Protection policy helps only the manu-facturer. . . . Let us have a plank which workingmen can see plainly keeps out of our country the competition of cheap foreign labor. . . .[73]

Protection to labor was an important political slogan. Labor had apparently tossed to the politicians, both Democratic and Republican, a request for reciprocal protection which would hurt no important business interest to grant. Both Republicans and Democrats condemned contract labor in their 1884 election plat-forms, and the Republicans were particularly careful to remind voters that they traditionally opposed all forms of "servile labor."[74] If the argument of tariffs as a gift to workers was wearing a bit thin, here was an opportunity to fortify it without sacrifice. And the more ominous the danger of contract labor could be made to appear, the more grateful the workers should be.

The most persistently recurring theme, employed by Demo-crats and Republicans alike, by opponents and proponents of the

Foran Bill, in both the House and the Senate, was this one of protecting American labor. Republicans announced that the bill was thoroughly consistent with the party's protectionist stand—that the protection of free labor had ever been its avowed policy.[75] Democrats who favored the bill accused the Republicans of applying for a "copyright" on "the protection of American labor" and reminded them of the Act of 1864 which had legalized contract labor.[76] Even the southern Democrats who opposed the bill argued that it did not really aid American labor. Senator Butler of South Carolina characterized it as a "stone," a sham, requested by some Knight of Labor, while Senator Blair of New Hampshire wondered how Butler had the affrontery to pose as a friend of labor.[77] The parties vied with each other as champions of the workingman and in so doing wrote a number of politically useful speeches into the *Record*.

When Senator Blair of the Committee on Education and Labor was finally able to get an occasion for debate on the Foran Bill in mid-February 1885, most of the senators who spoke in the debate assumed that the bill would be passed. Nevertheless, the discussion spread over three days before the bill was adopted on 18 February without substantial amendment.

Several attempts were made during the debates to make important changes. At the outset, Senator Bayard of Delaware tried to enlist the support of Senator Frye of Maine, whom he described as "one of the most persistent Congressmen in efforts to restore American shipping," in a move to strike out one of the penal sections of the bill which threatened with a fine any captain of a vessel who "knowingly" landed contract labor. Frye replied that he would agree to join such a move "if we had any immigrant ships," but fortunately the punishment would fall on Englishmen who could "use a little disadvantage."[78] Bayard's amendment was defeated.

A similar fate befell amendments from southern senators and others to get agricultural labor and mechanics or artisans excluded from the prohibitory clauses of the bill, as well as the activities of state agents in inducing immigration.[79] The group favoring this type of amendment denied to a man that contract labor was employed, but maintained that the bill would "injure the agricultural interest."[80]

The bill was denounced for being "class legislation," for including British emigrants in its terms, and for making the fulfillment of a contract a crime.[81] Both Bayard of Delaware and Hawley of Connecticut endeavored to show that no contract made under duress or for unreasonably low wages could ever be enforced in court.[82] While Bayard did not vote on the bill in the end, Joseph R. Hawley, who had formerly been a close associate of the American Emigrant Company group in Connecticut, a law partner of John Hooker, and the editor of the Hartford *Evening Press* when it came close to being an official organ of the American Emigrant Company, remained to cast his vote against this interference with the "natural right" of employers to import needed labor.[83]

Confronted by these efforts to amend the bill, its pilot in the Senate, Blair of New Hampshire, attempted to introduce new evidence of the enormity of the contract labor evil beyond the meager findings of the House Committee which had been read into *Record* in the Senate the previous summer. The Knights of Labor Local in Washington, D. C. submitted two reports on contract labor among unskilled workers which Blair read to the Senate. The first of these was a statement by an investigator sent by the Local to pose as a contractor to the "boss" of a "gang" of workers on a new reservoir. The investigator reported that the boss confessed to importing his men from Italy under contract.[84] The second report came from the same union. It quoted C. C. Moreno, described as an Italian "abolitionist," who, as guest speaker at a meeting of the Washington Federation of Labor, stated that there were eighty thousand Italians in the country under the control of padroni.[85] Whatever the accuracy of these reports, the Washington Federation of Labor was not turning over first-hand, but second-hand, information and made no claims that these were cases of direct competition with them.

Another eleventh-hour petition read out by Blair came from skilled workers, and here the evidence was again first-hand and specific like that submitted by the glassworkers. The Massachusetts goldbeaters forwarded a copy of a contract made by a Philadelphia firm with skilled immigrants in London. After this document was read out, Blair was forced to concede that the bill was designed to exclude contract labor, "not necessarily pauper labor."[86]

Throughout the Senate debates, men who promised to vote for the bill commented upon its "crudities," observing that it was clearly not drawn up by men with legal training.[87] Yet no one offered an amendment which would have provided for enforcement by appropriating money for inspection and investigation. Probably the frankest statement of all was that made by Senator Call of Florida who commented that he did not think the bill would afford the protection to labor expected by its authors. He saw no harm "in gratifying [their] desire and allowing this measure of theirs to be tested," and anticipated that the bill could work hardship on no one.

To affirm that there is any great economic benefit to the people of this country in prohibiting the small number of persons, whether good or bad, who are imported here under contracts, and preventing the competition on the part of that small number of people with the great body of laborers in this country, is in my opinion an unworthy proposition on which to base a great public policy.[88]

The "great public policy," as it was adopted in the Senate by a vote of fifty to nine, declared it a misdemeanor

for any person, company, partnership, or corporation, in any manner whatsoever, to prepay the transportation, or in any way assist or encourage the importation or migration of aliens into the United States, under contract or agreement, parol or special, express or implied, made previous to the importation or migration of such . . . aliens . . . to perform labor or service of any kind in the United States.

It provided for a fine of $1,000 on the importer for each violation and of $500 on the ship's master who "knowingly" brought such an alien to America; the Senate dropped a provision whereby the person bringing the suit, presumably the immigrant himself, was to receive half the fine. The law specifically exempted companies who engaged labor on contract for any new industry not "at present" established in the United States if skilled labor could not otherwise be obtained. Artists, lecturers, singers, actors, and domestic servants were not to come under its provisions, nor was the act to prevent any individual from assisting relatives or personal friends (the "friends" were added by the Senate) to emigrate.[89]

The craft unionists who had framed the original bill and worked so hard to obtain its enactment, carrying the rest of the labor movement with them, did not find that the bill really met their demands. It had, in fact, been badly framed, and among other things, appropriated no funds for enforcement. In spite of its weaknesses, however, the craft unionists continued to hope that, with appropriate amendment, the anti-contract labor law would provide the antidote to the threat which they felt from European contract labor. Consistently enough, it was the Federation of Organized Trades and Labor Unions, not the Knights of Labor, which took up the battle to obtain enforcement provisions. Already in 1885 they requested an amendment to provide for the appointment of special agents at every port of entry.[90] And the American Federation of Labor took up the standard during the nineties and opening years of the twentieth century in a continual effort to get legislative amendments and administrative enforcement which would make the act serve the purpose for which they had intended it, that of excluding skilled contract labor.

One of the main obstacles to realizing this aim lay in the prejudices and necessity for propaganda which had led the crafts leaders to attack the unskilled and to appeal to racist sentiment in trying to achieve their narrower purpose. The bill was conceived by skilled workers to exclude contract labor but urged in terms of the harmful effects of "pauper," "servile," unskilled labor. This dichotomy was bound to confuse the courts in interpreting the statute and government officials in enforcing it, even if they had had the best will in the world. As was to be expected, for many years the persons deported under the act were chiefly unskilled workers suspected of being contract laborers, although the charge could not be proven. One had only to read the newspapers and debates of 1884 and 1885 to gain the undeniable impression that these were the people the legislators had intended to exclude.

Another difficulty, for which the strategy of the policy's framers could be held to blame only very indirectly, was that the act and its later revisions could not be enforced because the opinion prevailed, as the federal immigration officials declared, that the contract labor laws had been forced on Congress by the labor movement.[91] The willing support of the bill from protectionists and the indifference of American industrialists were forgotten. That the bill had been passed on a wave of nativist sentiment, heightened by depression, from "citizens," merchants, and manufacturers and state boards of charity, was also overlooked.[92]

The central problem of the distribution of the unskilled immigrants to industry was left untouched by the contract labor laws; and the American Federation of Labor, during the next twenty-five years, made no effort to deal with this question which, unlike contract labor, did not affect them. T. V. Powderly, on the other hand, at the 1885 convention of the Knights of Labor, questioned that the bill met the needs of that organization at all. Perhaps what they should have fought for was a bill to prevent the employment and hiring of low-paid foreigners.[93] Powderly also urged the importance of placing a respresentative at Castle Garden to inform immigrants about wage rates paid in the United States before they went to labor bureaus and there agreed to take jobs below those rates.[94] But the Knights of Labor was not to live to continue its search for an answer to this broader problem which lay much closer to the heart of the "immigration question."

Chapter 10

EXPERIMENTS WHICH FAILED

During the last third of the nineteenth century the infant American labor movement proposed two ways of handling immigration to prevent its injuring workers already in America. Both of these methods aimed primarily, so far as labor was concerned, at inhibiting strikebreaking with immigrant labor. Both became the subject of feeble and half-hearted governmental experiments which failed to achieve labor's aims.

The first of these methods, prohibition of contract labor, was, it is contended, originally proposed by skilled craft unionists. The contract labor system, which was being adopted successfully elsewhere in the world to recruit Indian and Chinese labor, failed to take root in the American economic environment of the last half of the nineteenth century. Not gangs of mine workers and railroad laborers but small groups of selected skilled workers came to the United States on work contracts drawn up abroad. Consequently, it was skilled workers who initiated the movement to prohibit its use, gaining support, but at the same time confusing the issue, by arguing that employers were importing great numbers of unskilled workers on contracts. The American Federation of Labor, born in 1886 as heir to the craft union aims of the early eighties, carried on the struggle for effective anti-contract labor laws but was frustrated at every turn.

The second experiment sought to rationalize the immigrant labor market rather than to restrict entry. Public labor exchanges were begun in an endeavor to reform the abuses of private labor exchanges by setting standards for distributing unskilled workers to jobs cheaply and efficiently. The American Federation of Labor remained aloof from these efforts and eventually condemned them outright. Having already developed trade-union labor exchanges the craft unions resisted government interference in the immigrant labor market. Nevertheless, many of the early public employment offices had links with the labor movement, and the idea of forming such institutions was to be found in discussions of immigration at meetings of the old International Workingmen's Association as well as the Knights of Labor.

These two suggestions, the one emanating primarily from craft unions and the other from unions directly concerned with the distribution of unskilled labor, were perhaps the only original and constructive proposals submitted by the American labor movement itself in the great immigration debate. The fact that in practice both types of legislation appeared to the labor movement to raise more problems than they solved perhaps explains in some measure the eventual eagerness of the A. F. of L. to obtain a simple solution to the immigration question, a quest which led to more and more prejudice and racism and less and less constructive thought about appropriate legislative measures.

In a vain search for a formula by which legislation against the recruitment of labor abroad could be made to restrict immigration, Congress rewrote and amended the contract labor laws in 1887, 1888, 1891, 1893, 1903, and 1907. All these efforts were closely followed and often influenced by craft union leaders. The legislators never succeeded in finding a set of definitions which obtained the stated goal of the laws, that of excluding contract labor. As time went on it became increasingly clear that the effect of the contract labor laws on the flow of immigration was negligible. The difficulties encountered can probably best be dealt with by considering the work of the two bodies in whose hands enforcement was centered: the courts, which handled the prosecution of importers; and the port inspectors, who were responsible for detecting cases of contract labor.

During the first three years after the Foran Act was passed, importers of labor had no difficulty whatsoever in evading it. Congress had failed to provide for inspectors at the ports to investigate violations of the law. In 1887, when an amendment was passed stipulating that the Secretary of the Treasury was to make contracts with state officials for inspection, no appropriation was made to pay the states for this service. All that was possible, under its terms, was that the superintendents at the landing depots include in their investigation into pauperism and disease a perfunctory question as to whether or not the immigrant came on a contract.[1] In 1888 a small fund was finally appropriated for contract labor inspection.

In any case, even if administrative staff had been available, the Foran Act made no provision for deporting contract laborers.[2] The A. F. of L. was quick to point out this deficiency in the law, and took the credit for the amendment of 1887 which gave the Secretary of the Treasury the power to deport contract laborers at the expense of the steamship company or the importer.[3] Because of the difficulty of detecting contract laborers at the ports, Congress amended this clause the following year to permit deportation within a year of the immigrant's entry.[4] Although the A. F. of L. convention of 1892 recommended that immigrants be subject to deportation for two years after their arrival, it was not until 1907 that Congress extended the period—to three years.[5]

Port inspectors were responsible for detecting cases of contract labor. After 1891 they were instructed to report suspected cases to a Board of Special Inquiry whose rulings could be appealed to the Secretary of the Treasury, and, after 1903, to the Secretary of Commerce and Labor, whose decisions were final.[6] Port inspection staffs generally handled contract labor along with their questions about pauperism, disease, and crime. Up to 1909 there were only two full-time inspectors for contract labor matters, one at New York, and one at Boston.[7]

The attitude of port inspectors toward the anti-contract labor laws was consequently very important. Samuel Gompers complained to the Ford Committee that

so long as the public opinion of this country does not force the officials of our Government to enforce the law, not only in the letter but in the spirit, so long will the laws be violated . . . the officers of the Government seem to make it their purpose to bring odium and ridicule upon the law by its non-enforcement.[8]

Recognition of the key position of inspectors led the A. F. of L. convention of 1893 to propose that port officials be drawn from the ranks of labor.[9] At least one craft unionist, William Weihe, former president of the Amalgamated Association of Iron and

Steel Workers, obtained an appointment as a contract labor inspector. By 1894, Gompers declared that he was satisfied with the coöperation immigration officials were giving trade-unions which called attention to cases of contract labor.[10]

The numbers of immigrants deported as contract laborers rarely rose above two thousand in any single year, insignificant figures when compared with the total immigration of this period. From 1892 through 1902 only 6,394 immigrants were turned away from American shores as contract laborers. Under the stricter laws of 1903 and 1907, 15,326 were returned during the eleven-year period from 1903 through 1913.[11]

Although the records do not classify deportees by occupation, the nationality classes suggest that by far the greater number of immigrants deported were not skilled industrial workers. Conclusions as to the proportions of skilled and unskilled workers on the basis of nationality or "race," assuming that southern and eastern Europeans were less likely to be skilled workers than people from northern and western Europe, cannot be entirely accurate. Since, however, unskilled workers came in large numbers from the former areas during the nineties and the 1900 decade, the fact that between 1895 and 1902 the proportion of southern and eastern Europeans deported under the contract labor laws was never less than six out of seven indicates that officials interpreted the contract labor laws as measures for excluding unskilled workers from southern and eastern Europe. After the 1903 Act restated clearly the original principle that skilled contract labor as well as unskilled was to be kept out, the proportion of northern Europeans deported climbed. In the next four years more than one in four of those excluded under the contract labor laws came from a northern or western European country.[12]

There were a number of ways in which the anti-contract labor laws could be circumvented to import skilled workers. Contract laborers could be coached to answer questions of inspectors in such a way as to avoid detection. Since inspectors had to depend primarily upon the confession of the immigrant for evidence, coached workers frequently eluded them.[13] Another technique was to bring over contract laborers cabin class. Individual inspection was carried out only among steerage passengers. Cabin class travelers received only a perfunctory inspection before the ship docked, and contract labor coming in that way was rarely detected.[14] Sometimes importers came to the docks where during the confusing bustle and turmoil of landing they asked immigrants to sign affidavits stating that their emigration had been in no way solicited.[15] Another method of evading the law, believed by an immigration inspector at Montreal to be the most important, was to advise immigrants "that the Canadian frontier affords the easiest access to the United States."[16]

Applying the contract labor law to skilled immigrant workers was further hindered by court interpretations. Court rulings undoubtedly guided port inspectors and the Board of Inquiry to some extent in their policy of deporting chiefly unskilled workers. Convictions against importers were very difficult to obtain under the interpretations laid down in the courts. One immigration inspector spoke of the "contempt" which United States judges had for the contract labor law.[17] The slowness of the courts in handling cases sometimes made it impossible for the government to keep necessary witnesses on hand, a situation which led the A. F. of L. in 1894 to request the speedy trial of alleged violators of these laws.[18]

It was not merely the cumbersomeness of court procedure, however, which made the prosecution and conviction of importers difficult. By 1903, after fifteen years of decisions on the anti-contract labor laws, the courts had arrived at certain interpretations which severely limited the cases in which the penal provisions of the acts could be applied.[19] The courts adopted a very strict definition of a contract.[20] To be considered a contract within the meaning of the law for purposes of prosecuting an importer, agreements with foreign workers had to stipulate both the duration of the contract and the exact wages to be paid. Furthermore, the courts refused to recognize a contract unless it had been completed, that is, the immigrant had actually migrated and landed on American soil. Since the law instructed officials to deport all alien contract laborers, the only witnesses for the prosecution were frequently sent back and the importer left unpunished on the grounds that the contract had not been completed.[21] Of the 231 suits begun or pending between 1889 and 1894, 97 had to be dropped, usually because of insufficient evidence and the disappearance of witnesses.[22]

Defense counsels were said by the Commissioner General of Immigration to claim that violations of the law were mere technicalities committed by "citizens whose law abiding disposition is attested by their unquestioned influence in the world of affairs and by their equally unquestioned wealth."[23] One such technicality upheld in the courts was that an importer could not be convicted and fined unless the government could prove that he knew of the existence of the illegal contract. This ruling made it very difficult to fix the blame for illegal contracts. Owners and managers of corporations could deny knowledge of the activities of their foremen or agents abroad, and the latter were not likely to be men of means who could pay the fine if convicted.[24]

William Weihe called attention to one such case in which the manager of a company in Harrisburg, Pennsylvania, wrote to Wales for a roll turner and an annealer on the letterhead of the company, forwarded transportation money, and brought the men over on completed contracts. The president of the company could not be prosecuted because the government could not prove that he had directly authorized the manager to hire these people; and it was impossible to prosecute the company on account of the activities of a manager who was only an employee.[25]

Congress attempted to broaden the terms under which importers could be sued in the Act of 1891 by providing that promises of employment in advertisements abroad, with the exception of such înducements authorized by state immigration bureaus, were to be deemed violations of the law equivalent to contracts.[26] The courts again responded with a narrow and strict interpretation, ruling that the only kind of solicitation abroad recognized as subject to penalty was actual published advertisement.[27]

Contrary to their strict definition of a contract, the courts tended to give a loose interpretation of the law on the question of what classes of immigrants were excludable under its terms. Temporary alien visitors were allowed to come on contracts, and also any aliens who had previously lived in the United States. Although the law was amended in 1894 to include these "birds of passage" under the deportation provisions, no importer bringing in such aliens could be fined.[28]

The clause in the Foran Act which allowed immigrants already in this country to send for relatives and friends enabled employers to continue recruitment through their immigrant work-people. Immigration inspectors pointed out that it remained a common practice for an employer or foreman to mention to immigrant workmen the existence of jobs and to ask them to invite their friends and relatives in the old country to take them.[29]

Congress tried to deal with this type of recruitment in the

Act of 1891. Immigrants whose passage was paid for by another person were prohibited from landing unless they could prove that they were not contract laborers. Individuals living in the United States were still permitted to send for friends and relatives.[30] In 1903 the A. F. of L., still trying to prevent this type of recruitment, asked that assisted immigration be confined to nearest relatives.[31]

Again in 1907 a legislative attempt was made to set up definitive limits within which financial assistance could be given toward the emigration of friends and relatives. The new law prohibited corporations, associations, societies, municipalities, and foreign governments from prepaying passages but excluded states and individuals from the ban.[32] This marked a backward step from labor's point of view by leaving the recruitment of friends and relatives untouched. Moreover it raised an additional problem which the A. F. of L. quickly pointed out. Could states prepay passages from funds to which corporations had contributed? The A. F. of L. objected to the exclusion of state activities from supervision on the grounds that state immigration bureaus could be used as fronts for employers in getting strikebreakers from Europe.[33]

The most significant court interpretations were those which ruled on what types of labor Congress had intended to exclude under the Foran Act. Excellent examples of judicial legislation, these decisions inquired into the original intent of Congress and found (not without evidence) that it had meant to prohibit only the recruitment of cheap, unskilled labor under contract.

The Trinity case, which raised this issue shortly after the Foran Act was passed, was a suit brought by the Attorney General against the congregation of a church for importing a minister. As far as Samuel Gompers was concerned the government prosecuted for the purpose of ridiculing the contract labor law.[34] As a result of this case, Congress added ministers and professional people to the exceptions to the contract labor law in 1891.

The Supreme Court broadened these exceptions considerably in its decision in the case of U. S. *v.* Gay in 1897 when it stated:

The main purpose of the law, no doubt, was to prevent great corporations and business firms from contracting abroad for common, cheap, unskilled laborers to work in our mines, our mills, our factories, our lumber woods, in grading canals and railroads, and to work upon public improvements where a great many manual laborers are required . . . It would be absurd to suppose that Congress intended that persons employed in trade or any business requiring intelligence and skill, or indeed any except those from the lowest social stratum engaged in unintelligent and uncultivated labor, should be sent back to the nations from whence they came.[35]

This decision ran directly counter to the original aim of the anti-contract labor laws. The unskilled rarely had completed contracts within the interpretation of the courts.[36] The trades-unions of skilled workers who had initiated the movement for anti-contract labor legislation were left with virtually no protection against contract labor.

The Foran Act had allowed for the importation of skilled contract labor to establish new industries. This provision proved difficult to apply because it raised the question of how far advanced a particular industry must be before it could no longer be considered new. For example, this rule had been applied in 1893 to allow the entry of skilled lace-makers on the grounds that before the McKinley tariff of 1890 there was no factory lace industry in the United States.[37] Seven years later, in reviewing the Dowie case the Secretary of the Treasury cited the 1893 court decision in permitting the entry of skilled lace-workers in spite of the contention of the Amalgamated Lace Curtain Operatives of America that the industry was no longer new and that unemployed lace operatives could be obtained from among locked-out workers at a Wilkes-Barre mill.[38] In fact, it appeared that such cases were being decided, not on the 'newness of the industry, but rather on the basis of whether or not skilled labor could be obtained in the United States without raising wages.

The Immigration Act of 1903 sought to clarify the law on the question of the importation of skilled workers by stating that both skilled and unskilled workers under contract were to be excluded. Recognizing also the failure of the courts to apply strictly the "new industry" criterion in cases involving the importation of skill, Congress substituted for it the proviso that immigrants could be imported on contract if "labor of like kind" could not be found in America.[39]

Under the 1903 and 1907 acts more skilled workers were deported as contract laborers than previously, but the exception in cases in which "labor of like kind" could not be obtained proved no less ambiguous a guide for the courts and executive officials than the "new industry" criterion. Frequently conditions prevailed in which labor of like kind could be found in this country only by raising wages. Employers interpreted this circumstance as proving that labor was not available; trade-unions, as the fulfillment of the aims of the contract labor laws.[40]

The "Lithographers' Case" in 1907 illustrated the difficulties of getting the revised law applied to the satisfaction of craft unionists. In this case the A. F. of L. officers took to the Secretary of War (in the absence of the Secretary of Commerce and Labor) the objections of the Lithographic Artists, Engravers and Designers League of North America, even though the latter was not affiliated with the A. F. of L., because the principle involved was so important from the craft viewpoint. The Special Board of Inquiry, in a decision upheld by the Attorney General, had allowed the entry on contract of two German lithographers at a time when 240 lithographers had been out of work for eleven months in the United States because of a lockout. The union maintained, but without success, that at least one hundred lithographic stipplers in the United States were unemployed at the time the German craftsmen had been sent for.[41] If the contract labor law did not even prevent the importation of skilled European workmen during strikes and lockouts, its benefits to crafts unionists were negligible.

After more than twenty years of operation the contract labor laws had failed to deter the occasional recruitment of skilled European workers by American industry and had fallen far short of satisfying the growing opposition of craft unionists to immigration. The United States Industrial Commission had declared as early as 1898 that the laws were "practically a nullity."[42] Loopholes in the terms of the laws combined with successive court interpretations enabled American industry to carry on its traditional policy of nourishing infant industries with European skills by means of contract labor. The relatively new American tin-making,[43] silk,[44] hosiery,[45] and lace[46] industries all received importations of skilled workers from abroad. On the other hand, though many agricultural immigrants were deported as contract laborers, railroads, mining companies, and steel firms who were assumed to be importing them were rarely investigated or prosecuted.[47] When the government sought to prove that unskilled workers were coming in as contract laborers it was usually the labor agency or the labor agent who became entangled in legal proceedings. Sometimes such defendants left immediately for Europe. Many such cases could not be prosecuted for want of sufficient evidence of contracts or even of active solicitation of immigrants.[48]

In spite of the fact that most of the deportees under these laws were probably unskilled workers, the anti-contract labor laws had little effect on the recruitment and distribution of common labor for American industry. The private labor agency and agent continued to hold a central position as suppliers of immigrant labor to industry. Congress finally took some cognizance of this fact in 1907 when, in addition to trying again to define contract labor effectively, it provided for the establishment of a Division of Information in the Bureau of Immigration. This division was to furnish newly arrived immigrants with up-to-date and disinterested information on jobs and thus assist in the rational distribution of immigrant labor. This was the first attempt made by the central government to help the immigrant find a job since 1864. One important difference between this experiment and the earlier one was that whereas the Act of 1864 envisaged government supervision of the recruitment of skilled immigrants, the new Federal Division of Information was frankly an effort, however feeble, to distribute unskilled workers.

This public employment bureau for immigrants came after nearly twenty years of experimentation with such agencies in a number of states and a few cities. It was peculiarly appropriate that T. V. Powderly, who had led America's first federation of both skilled and unskilled workers, should have headed the new agency. The Knights of Labor had, in the eighties, toyed with the idea of distributing unskilled immigrant labor through more disinterested channels than private labor agencies. In 1892 the Knights of Labor convention at St. Louis endorsed the movement for state free employment bureaus.[49] Powderly recommended the establishment of employment agencies in all the large cities of the United States to the immigration investigating commission in 1894 and envisaged regulating the flow of immigrants according to the demand for labor reported by such agencies.[50] A few years later, when he was serving as Commissioner General of Immigration, Powderly had outlined a plan whereby the federal government should designate the heads of state bureaus of labor statistics as its agents, to collect through local post offices information on where jobs were to be had, which should in turn be made available to the immigrant by the federal immigration authorities.[51]

The American Federation of Labor, on the other hand, never endorsed as a body the project of state free employment offices. While some state affiliates gave support to the idea,[52] the craft unions as a whole never backed the movement. They saw little gain in it for themselves. Strong trade-unions handled the distribution of labor within their crafts through their own local union employment bureaus, and weaker unions aimed at controlling its distribution themselves. Even when not hostile to the state agencies, which were set up to assist the unskilled, the craft unions opposed any suggestions that such agencies broaden their scope to serve skilled workers.[53]

The aim of the first state free employment bureaus was to wipe out the abuses of private labor agencies and railroad labor agents by establishing offices in which the unskilled industrial worker could obtain a job without paying the fees of one to fifteen dollars charged by private bureaus and without running the risk of placing himself in the hands of dishonest or sharp operators.[54] Although the state offices were not set up to deal with immigrant labor in particular, one of the conditions of their success had to be the capture of an important segment of the immigrant labor supply, since much of the work of the private agencies in large immigrant reservoir cities like New York and Chicago was among the foreign born.

Furnishing gangs of immigrant workmen for railroads, mines, lumbering, and brickyards continued to be a specialty of many private labor agencies during the decade prior to the First World War.[55] Actually intelligence bureaus supplying domestic and farm help outnumbered the labor agencies dealing in industrial labor in both New York and Chicago. Yet most of the agencies which handled immigrant workers were furnishing labor to industry.[56] A survey made in 1908 which covered 178 of the 289 licensed private labor agencies in Chicago found that 110 of them handled foreigners. Forty-nine of the 56 agencies which handled only male immigrant laborers offered them jobs in industry.[57] The Illinois superintendent of licensing these agencies estimated that a quarter million foreigners were sent out to railroad and similar gang work from Chicago in 1910.[58]

Employers were usually indifferent to the movement to control

and reform private labor agencies whether by licensing and supervision or by establishing competing state agencies. Trade-unions
were involved in these experiments in some places. In Ohio, where
the first state-supported labor exchanges in the country were
started in 1890, the Municipal Labor Congress of Cincinnati began the agitation and drafted a bill for setting up state offices
which was crippled by the legislature.[59] In a good many states in
the far west and the midwest labor was active, in urging either the
formation or the extension of the state system.[60] Three out of four
of the officials of state employment offices were said to come from
the labor movement.[61] In Iowa and Illinois where labor was
closely associated with the movement, employer hostility was out-
spoken.[62]

Labor support for free employment offices was rarely wholehearted and often merely nominal. In two states, Massachusetts in
1895 and New Jersey in 1907, the direct opposition of organized
labor figured in the defeat of bills for the establishment of state
employment offices. The chief architects of the movement, in fact,
were officers of state bureaus of labor statistics.[63] Nevertheless,
since state bureaus were frequently tagged as sops to the labor
movement, this stigma was partly responsible for the niggardly
support given them by state legislatures.[64]

By 1914 there were fifty-one state offices in operation in seventeen states. While they varied widely in efficiency, they were, almost without exception, failures from the standpoint of influencing significantly the distribution of industrial labor. Most state
offices served primarily as the familiar type of intelligence office,
providing domestic help and farm workers.[65] Apart from those in
one or two Ohio cities and in Wheeling, West Virginia, state employment offices had not succeeded in driving private agencies from
the business of supplying industrial labor. After over ten years of
operation in Illinois there were more private labor agencies than
when the state entered the business.[66]

Partly because of the inadequate appropriations they received,
state offices were unable to break into the market handling unskilled immigrant labor for industry. Labor agencies and the so-
called padroni provided services to industry which state officials
could not undertake. None of the state offices could support a program of sending out interpreters, forwarding transportation
money, lodging and feeding men on the way to distant jobs.[67]
The West Side Chicago office of the state of Illinois boasted of a

real coup when it obtained the contract for furnishing the Chicago and Northwestern Railway with laborers.[68] For the most part the railroads did not patronize the state bureaus. One sympathetic railroad superintendent, interviewed in 1907, said that whenever state offices could bring as good a proposition to them as did the Italian contractors he would be willing to come to an agreement.[69] Reformers concluded that state employment offices would have to duplicate the methods and facilities of "padroni" before the railroads would patronize them.

State free employment agencies encountered another seemingly insurmountable problem also related to the distribution of immigrant labor. The Illinois Act of 1899 and the Wisconsin Act of 1901 establishing state labor exchanges contained clauses forbidding state officers from supplying strikebreakers to industry.[70] In 1903 the Supreme Court ruled the Illinois Act unconstitutional because of the clause forbidding strikebreaking on the grounds that such legislation discriminated among employers.[71] Thereafter states could give no legal guarantee that their employment bureaus would not be used as strikebreaking agencies. Two state legislatures, New York and Wisconsin, tried to cope with this ruling by requiring that applicants for jobs be told of the existence of strikes before they were sent to such areas.[72] Other state officials followed a similar policy without specific legislative authorization.

Although the practice of leaving the decision as to whether or not to serve as a strikebreaker to the individual applicant was generally described as "impartial" or neutral, to unions it was little better than organized strikebreaking since it reduced such decisions to individual rather than collective bargaining.[73] In Wheeling, West Virginia, where the state employment exchange had the cordial support of the trade unions, impartiality was interpreted to mean refusing to furnish strikebreakers at all, but assisting strikers to find work.[74] This viewpoint was exceptional. The ambiguous position of state employment offices with respect to industrial disputes was an added reason why unions opposed any extension of their work to the trades and why employers in some cities organized their own employment exchanges to furnish strikebreakers.[75] Impartiality could be interpreted to the satisfaction of neither the trade-unions nor employers.[76]

All observers agreed that the state free employment offices were not making a significant contribution to the organization of the labor market during the period before World War I. Doubts were also being expressed about the usefulness of the institutions which were more specifically designed to serve the immigrant, those run by immigrant groups in the United States. As time went on the "newer" immigrant nationalities developed societies which included in their activities some assistance to immigrants in finding work.

The Italian Information Office, incorporated in 1906, supported in part by the Italian government, actually sent out only 3,705 Italian immigrants from April through October 1907, to railroads, mines, and factories, although it received applications from employers for 37,058 men.[77] Another similar institution, the Immigrants Home and Free Employment Office, financed by the Hungarian Society of New York with aid from the Austrian government, found jobs out of the city for 1,407 Hungarians during the year ending November 1906; 612 of these were sent out as farm laborers and domestic servants.[78] Compared with private labor agencies these efforts were very small. In addition to these new societies, the German and Irish Emigrant Societies continued to support an employment office at the Barge Office in New York after the federal government took over the supervision of immigrants; but, as was the case earlier, it served immigrants from Northern Europe almost entirely.[79]

Most of these philanthropic organizations which placed immigrants in jobs suffered from insufficient funds. They had another major problem as potential rationalizers of the distribution of immigrant labor. Since these institutions were charitable undertakings, immigrants usually came to them as a last resort, when all other efforts to find jobs had failed, often when they were penniless or too sick, too weak, or too old to work. Knowing the desperate straits of some of the applicants for work at such immigrant homes, employers hesitated to accept these people for ordinary jobs and came to expect to obtain strikebreakers or workers at low wages from immigrant homes.[80] Because of the difficulties of combining relief work with an employment exchange, the United Hebrew Charities in 1903 closed its labor bureau which had placed a few immigrants every year since 1875.[81]

The Federal Division of Information was similar to these national organizations in that it was established to serve the immigrant primarily, rather than the native-born worker. In outlook and mode of operation, the Division was more closely related to state employment offices. As head of the division, T. V. Powderly repeated the arguments used so often by state labor commissioners in advocating this particular cause—the fact that the government already provided businessmen and farmers with marketing and weather reports, and the hope that through government labor bureaus the private labor agent would be displaced.[82] The new agency also encountered and failed to solve the same problems which baffled the state bureaus.

Lack of funds prevented the Federal Division of Information from carrying on any significant work in distributing immigrant labor. The section of the Act of 1907 which authorized the formation of the division envisaged not a labor exchange but an information office, to be devoted largely to correspondence with state officials and publication of a brochure containing advice for immigrants.[83] Thus, while under Powderly, the Division of Information did undertake to place immigrants in jobs, no funds had been provided to carry out this project on a large scale, and the immigrants directed to work formed an insignificant proportion of those applying for jobs at the Division.[84] In working among the unskilled, the Division suffered from the same inability to forward transportation money and supervise immigrant labor which state bureaus experienced in their efforts to compete with the private labor agency.[85] Moreover, the Federal Division had no agents in the field to gather information about jobs or to verify reports which came to it. It had no offices in the principal cities from which labor was distributed, other than New York.[86]

Like the state bureaus, the Federal Division of Information came to handle only unskilled labor. After the first two experimental years, Powderly admitted that the Division served farm labor, common labor, and domestic servants exclusively.[87] Skilled workers who applied at the New York office were sent to trade-unions for assistance.[88] The emphasis upon finding farm work reflected the view, with which Powderly agreed, that the cause of the "immigration problem" was that too many immigrants were going into industry when opportunities existed in farming. The Division's outlook reflected the common misconception that the farm population was more expandable than the industrial working force. As time went on, Powderly began to doubt the wisdom of this approach. "The great drawback to venturing on the land by many of small means," he wrote, "has been the size of the American farm as compared with that held in the countries of Europe. European farmers are accustomed to tilling small holdings and lack the funds to pay for large farms. . . ."[89] A program of farm-credit and training as well as reclamation was needed to carry out this dream.[90]

Ironically enough, the contract labor laws themselves and the other restrictions on immigration were among the most important obstacles to the functioning of the Federal Division. In fact, any plan for the distribution of immigrant labor ran counter to the principle of the anti-contract labor laws. These laws prevented the Division of Information from contacting immigrants before they landed in the United States, even when they were on board ships bound for America. The Division was not placed at Ellis Island because immigrants would then hesitate to come to its office for fear of being deported as persons likely to become public charges. After its second year of operation, Powderly remarked that up to that time no immigrant had stated that he had a knowledge of the Division or its work prior to his arrival in America, a statement which was given as evidence that the Division was not violating the contract labor law but which equally illuminated the very limited nature of its activities.[91]

The new Division of Information soon ran into direct opposition from organized labor. When the Division was started Powderly took pains to try to enlist the support of trade-unions by writing to all national officers calling attention to the fact that in all its requests for information on the demand for labor, the Division asked about the existence of strikes and about prevailing wages. The Division failed in its efforts to get the addresses of local labor unions to keep itself posted on labor's view of the local situation in towns and cities from which orders for workmen arrived.[92] Gompers' first reply was sympathetic; he expressed satisfaction that the "right spirit" was back of the bureau.[93] Powderly's reports continued to claim that every precaution was taken not to send workers to regions in which there were labor disturbances.[94] While it is doubtful that the Division ever did provide strike-breakers, there were some grounds for labor's fear of it as such, in that government agencies, according to the courts, could not legally discriminate between employers whose workers were on strike and those with "bona fide" labor needs.[95] Moreover, the information on industry available to the Division was by no means complete, and the possibility of making errors existed even if the "right spirit" prevailed.

The Executive Board of the United Garment Workers had

condemned the idea before it was even made law. In 1905 they had declared:

We call on American trade unionists to oppose emphatically the proposed scheme of government distribution of immigrants since it would be an obvious means of directly and cheaply furnishing strike-breakers to the combined capitalists now seeking the destruction of trade unions. . . .[96]

In 1909 the A. F. of L. asked for the abolition of the Federal Division of Information.[97] While the A. F. of L. during the years just before World War I criticized severely all plans for distributing labor through philanthropic or public labor exchanges, the Federal Division of Information and the philanthropic organizations assisting immigrants came in for particularly strong denunciation. Gompers' position was that all schemes for aiding the distribution of immigrants had the effect of encouraging emigration. Throughout the 1910 decade the A. F. of L. officers regarded any such proposals as something approaching a "plot" on the part of the steamship companies and industrial employers to keep the level of immigration high and wages low; and Gompers castigated the well-meaning reformers, "patriots," and "philanthropists," as the willing tools of these interests. Frankly stating his belief that only those immigrants who spoke English or an allied tongue were desirable, Gompers held that existing means for such workers to find jobs—including trade unions, newspaper want ads, and licensed labor bureaus—were entirely satisfactory, though they had to be supplemented by "individual hustle, horse-sense, courage and independence of character," qualities which he clearly assigned only to individuals of Northern European extraction.[98]

The attitude of the A. F. of L. led reformers who sympathized with the immigrant to observe that the skilled worker had abandoned the unskilled worker to the private labor agent.[99] The craft-union attitude toward the job was undoubtedly an important factor in the A. F. of L.'s opposition to public agencies for the distribution of immigrant labor. They regarded their own labor bureaus as of foremost importance in the struggle for the closed shop. Only through the union could they hope to monopolize labor in the craft. This thinking was transferred into the field of unskilled labor in which it was not appropriate. The A. F. of L. objected to government placement of unskilled immigrants because such institutions threatened to remove the one most important service trade-unionism, as they understood it, might afford. Thus the A. F. of L. organized in 1913 its own Department of Migratory labor through which it hoped to organize the unskilled under its control by means of a system of labor exchanges.[100]

The prohibition of contract labor and the establishment of public labor exchanges were the only specific legislative suggestions about immigration contributed by the American labor movement. Both plans turned out to be abortive and ineffectual experiments. The anti-contract labor laws failed to achieve the original objectives of their craft-union planners in part because those objectives were not clearly stated but camouflaged during the debates in Congress. Constant vigilance on the part of the A. F. of L. over a period of more than fifteen years to secure their application against skilled workers met constant frustration at the hand of courts and immigration officials who were not only confused as to the law's intent but as often determined to emasculate a labor measure. As the A. F. of L. leadership moved toward a general restrictionist position about immigration, the contract labor laws clearly could not be made to serve such a purpose, based as they were upon a false assumption that the bulk of European emigration was "involuntary" or "forced."

The attempt to transform the Federal Division of Information into an immigrant labor bureau under Powderly was doomed from the start by niggardly appropriations. The fierce opposition of the only national federation of labor to its work and the apparent conflict with the principles of the anti-contract labor laws obliterated any possibility of expansion and growth.

The years during which these two experiments were being tested in a half-hearted fashion marked the hardening of the position of the A. F. of L. leadership to one of favoring restriction of immigration on a broad front. Although during the first ten years of its life, up to 1896, the A. F. of L. limited its proposals on immigration to recommendations for strengthening the contract labor laws, the Cigar Makers asked vaguely for "more restriction" of immigration in 1893.[101] The convention of 1896 marked the turning point for the national federation. After long and bitter debate a small majority of the delegates that year voted support to the Lodge-Corliss bill which embodied the principle of the literacy test, a device for excluding southern and eastern European agricultural immigrants. At every convention from 1902 to 1914 the

A. F. of L., following the lead of its officers, placed itself with ever increasing majorities behind the literacy test as a simple method of restricting immigration.[102] Three times Congress passed, and Presidents vetoed, such measures.

Just as the literacy test technique did not originate in the labor movement but was accepted and supported by it, so the recommendations of the Dillingham Commission in 1911, one of which embodied the idea of a quota system to restrict southern and eastern European immigration, were welcomed by the labor movement though not formulated by it. After the war the A. F. of L. demanded a complete stop to immigration for a period of two years. Failing that, they supported the quota scheme adopted in 1921.

Important as the organized restrictionist lobby outside the labor movement and the postwar political hysteria undoubtedly were in bringing about the acceptance of a racialist basis for American immigration legislation, the persistent backing given by organized labor to such ideas has long been accepted as a significant factor in American immigration policy. Labor leaders castigated unskilled workers for competing with American labor by taking jobs which the craftsmen who formed the bulk of the A. F. of L. membership would have scorned. When they argued in more general terms of their fears of a dilution of Anglo-Saxon culture through the "new immigrants" they spoke less as labor leaders than as middle-class Americans who became prey to irrational fears and racial prejudices. The A. F. of L., in its fight for the restriction of new immigration, was no longer speaking in terms of specific craft-union interests. It took over the programs of restrictionist propagandists, printed their articles in trade-union papers, listened to their speeches at conventions, but it made no specific contribution of its own on the immigration question either by legislative proposals or by organizing unskilled immigrants.

It is possible that frustration and disappointment with the anti-contract labor laws helped to attract America's skilled workers to simpler, more direct, methods for limiting immigration. Perhaps the increased desire to cut off the supply of new labor resulted in part from the snags encountered in trying to define such terms as "new industries" and "labor of like kind." In so far as such motives were behind labor's shift in position, narrow trade-union interests were involved. Since no direct evidence has been found on this point, it is impossible to estimate what weight such considerations carried.

In any case, the movement for the contract labor laws themselves marked the beginning of confused and unrealistic thinking about immigration on the part of the American labor movement. The shift in argument from a practical to a racialist basis which took place during the fight for the Foran Act marked the virtual end of the practical and critical discussions of the immigration question which had been so frequent in the infant labor movement of the previous twenty years. The prejudices which were called in to aid the movement against contract labor, to obtain a limited end, later dominated the views of American labor leadership on the immigration question. If the American labor movement had continued on a broader basis than it in fact did after 1885, perhaps the more constructive policy of regulating immigration according to the nation's needs might have gained stronger support. But such suppositions are both logically and historically unsound. Instead, the American labor movement allowed itself to share the nation's hysterical fears of certain foreigners as causing the problems of American industrial society and has never remodeled or reformed its views on immigration.

APPENDICES

APPENDIX I

STATEMENTS OF WAGES AND PRICES
PUBLISHED BY THE AMERICAN EMIGRANT COMPANY IN EUROPE

TABLE I

Wages in the United States in 1865

Occupation	A. E. C. statements	Bureau of Labor Statistics estimate			
		State	Average	Minimum	Maximum
Cotton	$5.00–	Mass.	$4.08	$2.70	$4.98
spinners	8.00/week	N. Y.	3.00	3.00	3.00
(female)					
Coal miners	$4.00–	Penn.	$2.00	$2.00	$2.00
	5.00/day				
Iron molders	$3.00/day	Conn.	$2.28	$1.67	$3.25
	Sweden:	Ill.	5.00	5.00	5.00
	$2.00–	Md.	2.50	2.33	2.67
	3.00/day	Mass.	2.18	1.25	2.76
		Penn.	2.50	1.84	2.77
		N. Y.	2.27	1.50	3.75
Puddlers	$3.00–				
	4.00/day	Penn.	$3.99	$3.85	$4.14
Iron rollers	$4.00–				
	6.00/day	N. Y.	$4.14	$4.00	$4.25
		Penn.	4.40	4.40	4.40

Notes: The minimum for cotton spinners in Massachusetts was calculated on the basis of a six-day week, 11-hour days; the maximum, on a 6-day week, 12-hour days; and the average, on a 6-day week, 11½-hour days.

Sources: *Iron Age*, 24 Aug. 1865, p. 4. *Bihang till Göteborgs Handels-och Sjöfarts-Tidning*, 31 March 1866, p. 3. The Bureau of Labor Statistics estimates are taken from Bureau of Labor Statistics, *Bulletin*, no. 604, *History of Wages*, pp. 246, 241–242, 311–313, 330–331, 386–388.

TABLE 2
Wages in the United States in 1866

Occupation	A. E. C. statements	Bureau of Labor Statistics estimate			
		State	Average	Minimum	Maximum
Coal miners	$4.00– 6.00/day	Penn.	$2.00	$2.00	$2.00
Iron molders	$2.00– 4.50/day	Conn.	$2.24	$1.50	$3.25
		Mass.	2.64	2.50	3.00
		Md.	2.36	1.35	2.75
		N. Y.	2.35	1.38	3.95
		Penn.	2.86	2.50	3.00
Boilermakers	$2.50– 4.50/day	Conn.	$2.66	$2.00	$4.00
		Md.	2.57	2.25	3.33
		N. Y.	2.06	1.25	2.63

Sources: *Iron Age*, 29 March 1866, p. 2. Bureau of Labor Statistics, *History of Wages*, pp. 283, 311, 330.

TABLE 3

Statements of Prices of Certain Foods Published by the American Emigrant Company Compared with Prices at the New York Produce Exchange, 1865

Product	A. E. C. statement	New York price
Butter, per lb.	$ .12– .14	$ .36
Wheat, per bu.	1.12–1.30	1.69 1/4
Oats, per bu.	.48– .50	.74 13/24
Corn, per bu.	1.10–1.15	1.19 1/12

Sources: American Emigrant Company prices taken from Chicago *Republican*. published in *Bihang till Göteborgs Handels-och Sjöfarts-Tidning*, 31 March 1866, p. 3. "Yearly Average of Prices at New York," by E. H. Walker, Statistician, New York Produce Exchange, *Senate Committee on Education and Labor*, III (1885), 683.

APPENDIX II

TABLE I

Percentage of Total Labor Force of Total Foreign Born and Selected
Foreign-Born Nationalities in Selected Occupations in the United
States, 1870, 1880, 1890

Year	Total Labor force	Per cent f. b.	Per cent born in				
			Germ.	Ire.	G. B.	Scan.	Italy
1. All Occupations							
1870	12,505,923	21.6	6.7	7.6	3.0	0.9	0.1
1880	17,392,099	20.1	5.9	5.6	2.7	1.2	n. g.[a]
1890	22,735,661	23.0	6.6	4.7	3.1	2.5	0.5
2. Agriculture							
All agriculture							
1870	5,922,471	10.4	3.8	2.3	0.2	0.1	0.002
1880	7,670,493	10.6	3.8	1.8	1.4	1.2	n. g.
1890	8,663,744	13.3	4.6	1.6	1.5	2.3	0.2
Agricultural labor							
1870	2,885,996	6.4	2.0	1.5	0.1	0.1	0.001
1880	3,323,876	4.9	1.5	0.7	0.5	0.7	n. g.
1890	3,004,061	8.6	2.7	0.8	0.7	1.8	0.02
3. Other Common Labor[b]							
Domestic servants							
1870	1,031,666	41.6	9.4	22.2	2.1	1.5	0.1
1880	1,859,223	28.1	6.2	12.1	1.7	1.5	n. g.
1890	1,913,373	36.1	8.2	10.6	2.3	3.7	2.1
Railroad employees, not clerks							
1870	154,027	38.6	5.1	24.6	3.1	2.6	0.004
1880	236,058	28.2	4.1	13.7	2.8	1.9	n. g.
1890	382,750	27.2	4.9	8.7	2.2	3.2	2.7

Year	Total Labor force	Per cent f. b.	Per cent born in				
			Germ.	Ire.	G. B.	Scan.	Italy

4. All Mining, Mechanical and Manufacturing Industries[c]

Year	Total Labor force	Per cent f. b.	Germ.	Ire.	G. B.	Scan.	Italy
1870	2,707,421	34.3	11.4	9.8	6.5	0.8	0.001
1880	3,837,112	31.9	9.6	6.5	5.9	1.2	n. g.
1890	5,440,885	31.8	9.7	5.4	5.9	2.6	0.6

5. Mining

Year	Total Labor force	Per cent f. b.	Germ.	Ire.	G. B.	Scan.	Italy
1870	152,107	63.3	5.6	15.0	22.6	1.0	0.006
1880	234,228	53.9	4.3	10.9	20.3	2.1	n. g.
1890	349,592	49.1	4.7	6.8	16.8	3.6	0.02

6. Branches of the Iron and Steel Industry

Year	Total Labor force	Per cent f. b.	Germ.	Ire.	G. B.	Scan.	Italy
1870[d]	82,630	43.4	10.2	19.4	10.5	0.3	0.00
1880[e]	117,880	36.2	8.2	14.6	8.7	0.9	n. g.
1890[f]	220,142	37.9	9.5	10.5	8.6	2.6	0.02

7. Branches of the Textile Industry

Year	Total Labor force	Per cent f. b.	Germ.	Ire.	G. B.	Scan.	Italy
1870[g]	215,789	37.6	3.3	16.6	10.5	0.2	0.00
1880[h]	294,036	40.9	2.6	12.1	10.0	0.4	n. g.
1890	357,584	42.8	3.6	9.8	10.7	0.9	0.02

[a]Not given.

[b]The category "domestic servants" is based on "laborers, not stated," under "professional and personal services" in the 1870 and 1880 Censuses; and on "laborers, not stated," under "domestic and personal services" in the 1890 Census.

The category "Railroad Employees, not clerks" is based on "Employees of Railway Companies, not clerks" in the 1870 and 1880 Censuses; and on "Steam Railway Employees, not otherwise stated" in the 1890 Census. Both of these appear under the "Trade and Transport" division. A cross reference to "locomotive engineers and firemen" suggests that these categories may not be comprised exclusively of common laborers.

[c]In the 1890 Census "Mining" is calculated with Agriculture and Fisheries. In the above figures "Mining" has been subtracted from Agriculture and added to "Mechanical and Manufacturing Industry."

[d]1870 includes iron and steel works operatives, not otherwise specified; iron and steel rolling mill operatives; stove, furnace and grate-makers; iron furnace operatives; iron foundry operatives.

[e]1880 includes iron and steel works and shops operatives and foundries and furnaces and rolling mills operatives; stove, furnace and grate-makers.

[f]1890 includes iron and steel workers, including employees of foundries, furnaces, and rolling mills; molders; stove, furnace and grate-makers.

[g]1870 includes cotton-mill operatives; mill and factory operatives, not otherwise specified; print works operatives; woolen mill operatives.

[h]1880 and 1890 include identical classes.

Sources: *Ninth Census*, 1870, I, *Population and Social Statistics*, Table xxix, p. 703. *Tenth Census*, 1880, *Compendium*, Pt. 2, Table, ciii. *Eleventh Census*, 1890, *Compendium*, Pt. 3, Table 90; Table 74.

APPENDIX III

TABLE I

Total Immigrants Placed in Jobs Through the Castle Garden Labor Bureau with Percentages of Selected Nationalities Placed, 1868–1886 and 1905

Year	Total number immigrants placed	Per cent German	Per cent Irish	Per cent Scandinavian	Per cent Italian
1868	32,646	27.4	65.1	1.5	n. g.
1869	46,293	23.1	49.8	1.2	n. g.
1870	29,290	25.1	67.6	1.2	n. g.
1873	25,325	31.1	62.8	1.5	1.3
1874	16,910	25.3	67.7	1.7	0.4
1875	12,440	27.9	65.6	1.1	0.1
1876	10,215	31.0	65.1	0.6	0.1
1877	10,314	30.3	65.4	0.5	0.1
1878	10,568	32.4	61.6	1.0	0.0
1879	16,533	40.2	49.1	n. g.	n. g.
1880	39,311	41.8	48.0	2.7	0.9
1881	49,745	49.1	40.2	2.2	0.7
1882	37,516	45.3	36.1	2.0	0.1
1883	27,903	51.5	39.6	1.6	0.7
1884	23,687	51.2	40.1	1.8	0.4
1885	15,539	41.9	49.2	1.1	0.6
1886	14,257	39.7	49.8	0.8	0.1
1905	9,837	53.7	25.7	16.3	n. g.

Notes: The percentages given for Germans obtaining employment, 1868–1874 are based on figures which include Austrians. The Irish figures for the same years include British immigrants.

The 1905 figures are for the labor bureau at the Battery run by the German and Irish Emigration Societies.

Sources: 1868–1886, New York, Commissioners of Immigration, *Annual Reports 1868–1886*. 1905, J. E. Conner, "Free Public Employment Offices in the United States," U. S. Bureau of Labor, *Bulletin*, XIV, no. 68, Jan. 1907, pp. 104–105.

TABLE 2

Proportions of Males Placed by the Castle Garden Labor Bureau in
Skilled and Unskilled Jobs, 1868–1886 and 1905

Year	Total men placed	Per cent placed in agriculture or common labor	Per cent, placed as mechanics
1868	18,114	76.2	23.8
1869	22,844	75.5	24.5
1870	17,857	82.2	17.8
1873	17,821	80.5	19.5
1874	10,148	79.5	20.5
1875	7,008	82.4	17.6
1876	5,394	84.1	15.9
1877	5,362	86.6	13.4
1878	5,623	85.9	14.1
1880	28,806	84.7	15.3
1881	38,606	82.9	17.1
1882	29,419	82.2	17.8
1883	19,519	77.9	22.1
1884	15,302	76.9	23.1
1885	8,643	78.5	21.5
1886	6,894	82.6	17.4
1905	9,837	89.6	10.4

Sources: See Table 1.

TABLE 3

Location of Jobs in Which Immigrants Were Placed by the Castle
Garden Labor Bureau, 1868–1886 and 1905

Year	New York	New Jersey	Connecti- cut	Pennsyl- vania	Per cent of total placed in 4 states
1868	22,270	5,688	1,146	730	95.8
1869	23,896	7,575	1,712	1,262	98.5
1870	19,479	5,850	1,128	206	95.5
1873	15,340	7,466	1,077	496	96.3
1874	10,883	4,745	913	86	98.3
1875	7,754	3,574	1,033	21	99.5
1876	6,747	2,740	643	47	99.6
1877	6,721	2,919	612	22	99.6
1878	7,082	2,687	728	36	99.7
1880	20,645	7,995	3,844	4,262	93.5
1881	21,547	7,517	3,973	9,328	85.2
1882	17,954	6,096	3,731	5,854	89.7
1883	15,284	4,327	2,429	3,724	92.3
1884	14,387	3,922	2,256	1,725	89.9
1885	10,951	1,348	1,021	532	89.1
1886	9,897	2,259	1,022	573	96.4
1905	n. g.[a]	n. g.	n. g.	n. g.	93.9[b]

[a]Not given.
[b]Per cent employed in New York and New Jersey.

Sources: See Table 1.

APPENDIX IV

TABLE I

Total Contract Laborers Deported to All Places and to Europe from the United States with Percentages of Deportees to Northwestern Europe and Southeastern Europe, 1889–1914

Fiscal year ending June 30	Number of contract laborers deported		Per cent of Europeans deported	
	To all places	To Europe	To north & west Europe	To south & east Europe
1889	3	3	n. g.	n. g.
1890	40	40	n. g.	n. g.
1891	123	123	n. g.	n. g.
1892	1,763	932	n. g.	n. g.
1893	766	518	n. g.	n. g.
1894	640	553	n. g.	n. g.
1895	694	692	16.0	84.0
1896	776	772	12.2	87.8
1897	328	324	15.1	84.9
1898	417	408	6.6	93.4
1899	741	641	7.6	92.4
1900	833	481	10.9	89.1
1901	327	150	10.7	89.3
1902	275	203	20.7	79.3
1903	1,086	988	12.4	87.6
1904	1,501	1,323	17.7	82.3
1905	1,164	1,057	19.8	80.2
1906	2,314	2,150	9.2	90.8
1907	1,434	1,155	23.7	76.3
1908	1,932	1,724	28.9	71.1
1909	1,172	913	46.2	53.8
1910	1,786	1,447	25.5	74.5
1911	1,336	1,077	29.0	71.0
1912	1,333	1,021	22.7	77.3
1913	1,624	1,366	16.2	83.8
1914	2,793	2,502	31.9	68.1

Notes: Before 1899, immigrants were classified in United States immigration figures by nationality. The following countries have been included in the esti-

195

mates made in this table of contract laborers deported to north and west European countries: Belgium, Netherlands, England, Scotland, Wales, Ireland, Sweden, Norway, Denmark, France, Germany, and Switzerland.

Those classed as deported to south and east European countries were: Austria-Hungary, Italy, Greece, Roumania, Russia, Poland, Finland, Portugal, Spain.

After 1898, immigrants were grouped, in the official figures, according to "race." For purposes of the above estimates, the following racial groups were classed as northern and western European: Dutch and Flemish, English, Irish, Scottish, Welsh, Scandinavian, German, French; as southern and eastern European: Bohemian, Moravian, Croatian, Slovakian, Dalmatian, Herzogovenian, Bosnian, Finnish, Greek, Hebrew, Hungarian, Italian, Lithuanian, Magyar, Montenegran, Polish, Portuguese, Spanish, Roumanian, Ruthenian, Servian, Slovenian.

Sources: Figures for 1888–1891, *Senate Executive Documents* (1893–94), IV, 53c., 2s., no. 102, p. 9. Figures for 1892–1894, U. S. Superintendent of Immigration, *Annual Reports* (1892–1894). Figures for 1895–1914, calculated from U. S. Commissioner General of Immigration, *Annual Reports* (1895–1914).

APPENDIX V

FEDERAL DIVISION OF INFORMATION

TABLE I

Total Applicants and Total Persons Placed in Certain Occupations by the Federal Division of Information, 1908–1914

Fiscal year ending June 30	Number of applicants	Number placed in jobs	Number placed as			Per cent placed in 3 types of work
			Common laborers	Farm workers	Domestic servants	
1908[a]	n. g.[b]	840	421	250	116	93.6
1909	26,477	4,168	794	2,315	122	78.3
1910	18,239	4,283	1,047	2,747	314	95.9
1911	30,657	5,176	1,215	3,083	360	90.0
1912	26,213	5,807	2,167	2,813	245	90.0
1913	19,981	5,025	2,482	1,920	90	89.4
1914	19,303	3,368	1,022	1,870	73	88.0

[a]Covers February to July only.
[b]Not given.

Sources: U. S. Commissioner General of Immigration, *Annual Reports* (1908–1914).

NOTES

ABBREVIATIONS USED IN NOTES

A. A. Z.	*Allgemeine Auswanderungs Zeitung*
A. A. I. S. W.	Amalgamated Association of Iron and Steel Workers
B. B. H. S.	*Bulletin of The Business Historical Society*
B. M. R.	Burlington and Missouri Railroad
B. H. R.	*Business History Review*
B. P. P.	*British Parliamentary Papers*
D. M. A.	Durham Miners Association
F. B. I.	Federal Bureau of Immigration
F. O. T. L. U.	Federation of Organized Trades and Labor Unions
G. O. I. C.	General Offices, Illinois Central Railroad
I. M. I. J.	*Iron Molders International Journal*
I. M. J.	*Iron Molders Journal*
I. W. A.	International Workingmen's Association
J. E. H.	*Journal of Economic History*
N. A. W. M.	National Association of Wool Manufacturers
N. E. C. M. A.	New England Cotton Manufacturers Association
P. A. P. S.	*Proceedings of the American Philosophical Society*
P. R. O.	Public Records Office
W. G. W. A.	Window Glass Workers of America

NOTES

1. ORGANIZED EFFORTS TO PROMOTE IMMIGRATION

1. "Report on Manufactures," 5 Dec. 1791, *American State Papers, Finance*, I, 123.

2. Theodore F. Marburg, "Aspects of Labor Administration in the Early Nineteenth Century," *Bulletin of the Business Historical Society*, XV (Feb. 1948), 2-4; William G. Lathrop, *The Brass Industry in the United States* (Mount Carmel, Conn., 1926), pp. 91–92; Norris G. Osborn, *History of Connecticut* (New York, 1925), IV, 65–66; Herbert Heaton, "The Industrial Immigrant in the United States," *Proceedings of the American Philosophical Society*, XCV (1951), 526–527.

3. In addition to books and articles cited elsewhere in this section, see David Creamer, "Recruiting Contract Laborers for the Amoskeag Mills," *Journal of Economic History*, I (1941), 48; H. H. Earl, *A Centennial History of Fall River* (New York, 1877), p. 28; Rowland T. Berthoff, *British Immigrants in Industrial America* (Harvard, 1953), pp. 48, 62-63; Ebenezer Edwards, *Welshmen as Factors in the Formation and Development of the United States Republic* (Utica, 1899), pp. 199–200.

4. Caroline F. Ware, *Early New England Cotton Manufacture* (Boston, 1931), p. 206.

5. Ware, *Early New England Cotton Manufacture*, pp. 205–207; Heaton, *P.A.P.S.*, XCV, 524; Arthur H. Cole, *American Wool Manufacture* (Cambridge, Mass., 1926), I, 234; letter from Horace Capron, 22 May 1871, National Association of Wool Manufacturers, *Bulletin*, XI (1881), 126–127.

6. Nancy P. Norton, "Labor in the Early New England Carpet Industry," *Bulletin of Business Historical Society*, XXVI (1952), 19, 20; Samuel Foy, "Carpetweaving and the Lowell Manufacturing Company," N. A. W. M., *Bulletin*, V (1874), 18.

7. Ray Ginger, "Labor in a Massachusetts Cotton Mill, 1853–1860," *Business History Review*, XXVIII (March, 1954), 73.

8. Ware, *Early New England Cotton Manufacture*, p. 205; Norton, *B. B. H. S.*, XXVI, 20; Marburg, *B. B. H. S.*, XV, 5.

199

9. "Memorandum of agreement between Erskine Hazard for the Lehigh Crane Iron Company and David Thomas of Castel DDu, 31 Dec. 1838," Swank Papers, Historical Society of Pennsylvania.

10. *Exportation of Machinery,* United Kingdom, *British Parliamentary Papers* (1841), VII, 124–125; Heaton, *P. A. P. S.,* XCV, 524.

11. Harriet Robinson, *Loom and Spindle* (New York, 1898), p. 11; George F. Kenngott, *The Record of a City: a Social Survey of Lowell* (New York, 1912), p. 26; Jack Rohan, *Yankee Arms Maker* (New York, 1935), pp. 190–194.

12. John Wilson, Lowell, Mass., to his father, 21 April 1849; Wilson to his parents, 23 July 1849, Wilson Letters, Cornell Collection of Regional History.

13. Ware, *Early New England Cotton Manufacture,* p. 207; Cole, *American Wool Manufacture,* I, 234n; Lathrop, *Brass Industry,* p. 94.

14. Lathrop, p. 94; Osborn, *History of Connecticut,* IV, 65; Marburg, *B. B. H. S.,* XV, 5–6.

15. Norton, *B. B. H. S.,* XXVI, 21, 22, 24–25.

16. N. A. W. M., *Bulletin,* XI (1881). 127; U. K., *B. P. P.* (1841), VII, p. 23, 205; Ware, *Early New England Cotton Manufacture,* p. 206; Ginger, *B. H. R.,* XXVIII, 83–85.

17. James Roberts and others, Waterville, Conn., to John and Mary Ann Loxley, 30 Sept. 1849; James Roberts, Waterville, 6 Feb. 1852, Preston Papers, Cornell Collection of Regional History.

18. Representative Washburne estimated in 1864 that one and a quarter million laboring men had gone into the army; Fite minimized the decimation of the ranks of labor by the Union Army on the grounds that two million of the northern soldiers were under 21 years of age. *House Reports,* 38c., 1s., no. 56, 16 April 1864; David E. Fite, *Social and Industrial Conditions in the North During the Civil War* (New York, 1910), p. 198.

19. Pittsburgh and Boston Mining Company, *Annual Report,* (1864), p. 8; Belmont Coal Mining Company, *Report* (1863), p. 12; Mount Pleasant Coal Company, *Report* (April 1864), p. 4; Lehigh Valley Coal Company, *Annual Report* (1864), p. 16; Bear Valley Coal Company, *First Report of Directors* (Oct. 1864), p. 23; Harewood Iron and Mining Company, *Report of Directors* (Boston, 1864); Atlantic and Great Western, *Annual Report* (1864), pp. 5–6; Cleveland and Pittsburgh Railway, *Annual Report* (1863), p. 10; *Hardware Reporter,* Oct. 1863, p. 3.

20. Chicago and Alton Railway, *Annual Report* (1863), p. 20; (1864), p. 24; (1865), p. 19; Carlton C. Qualey, *Norwegian Settlement in the United States* (Northfield, 1938), p. 138; Fite, *Social and Industrial Conditions,* p. 55.

21. Resolution of Convention of Illinois Coal Operators, St. Louis, 20 May 1863, U. S. State Department, *Miscellaneous Letters* (June 1863); John Jones, agent of the Hannibal and St. Joseph Railroad, to W. H. Seward, 3 June 1863, State Dept., *Misc. Letters,* National Archives; J. Osborn to W. T. Mali, Belgian Consul in N. Y., 27 Oct. 1863, Illinois Central Papers, 63rd St., Chicago, Box 48, p. 420, copy lent by Paul W. Gates.

22. Henry Carey, *Essay on the Rate of Wages* (1835), pp. 18, 245; *Idem. The Past, the Present and the Future* (1848), pp. 13, 15, 56, 260–261; Henry Carey, Philadelphia, to John Williams, 27 Aug. 1864. This letter was printed in the Circular distributed by the American Emigrant Company to employers. See, for example, the copy in the Burlington Railroad Papers, Newberry Library, Chicago.

23. Carey had large investments in coal, and was involved in business enterprises

ranging from paper mills to a gas company. In 1855 he had become an honorary member of the Iron Association (Joseph Dorfman, *The Economic Mind in American Civilization*, London, 1949, II, 789, 803).

24. Eber B. Ward, Detroit, to Henry Carey, 26 Dec. 1862, Edward Carey Gardiner Collection, Historical Society of Pennsylvania.

25. "American Emigrant Company," p. 21, Burlington Archives.

26. E. Peshine Smith to Henry Carey, 2 Sept. 1862, Gardiner Collection. In 1863 Smith wrote a *Manual of Political Economy* designed as a readable summary of Carey's teachings. (Dorfman, *Economic Mind,* II, 808.)

27. W. H. Seward, Washington, to New York Chamber of Commerce, 24 Sept. 1862, New York Chamber of Commerce, *Annual Report* (1862–63), p. 47.

28. See, for example, letter from Thomas Birtwistle on behalf of the East Lancashire Power Loom Weavers Friendly Association, 6 Jan. 1864; Abel Schofield on behalf of the Lancashire cotton operatives, 15 Jan. 1864, State Dept., *Misc. Letters Index* (1864); Letter from Frederick Jepson, Secretary of the Manchester Operatives Emigration Fund, 31 March 1863, London *Times,* 4 April 1863, p. 9; B. O. Duncan to Seward, 11 June 1863, *Consular Despatches,* Carlsruhe, vol. I; J. H. Anderson to Seward, 12 Feb. 1863, *Cons. Desp.,* Hamburg, vol. XVI; Charles D. Cleveland to Seward, 13 May 1863, *Cons. Desp.,* Cardiff, vol. I, no. 10; William B. West to Seward, 2 April 1864, *Cons. Desp.,* Dublin, vol. IV, no. 54; John Hynes, Lancashire, to William B. West, 28 Jan. 1864, enclosures in *Cons. Desp.,* Dublin, vol. IV, no. 54, enclosure. O. E. Dreutzer forwarded a petition from 185 Norwegian laborers asking for aid, *Cons. Desp.,* Bergen, vol. II, no. 34, National Archives.

29. William B. West to Seward, 18 April 1863, *Cons. Desp.,* Galway, vol. I, no. 32; West to Seward, 6 May 1864, *Cons. Desp.,* Dublin, vol. IV, no. 6; C. D. Cleveland to Seward, 10 March 1864, *Cons. Desp.,* Cardiff, vol. I, no. 11; W. W. Thomas to Seward, 12 Feb. 1864, 8 March 1864, 6 July 1864, *Cons. Desp.,* Gothenberg, vols. IV and V; E. P. Hanson to Seward, 18 July 1863, *Cons. Desp.,* Elsinore, vol. V, no. 9; August Glaeser to Seward, 23 Feb. 1864, *Cons. Desp.,* Frankfurt, vol. XIV.

30. B. O. Duncan to Seward, 24 May 1864, *Cons. Desp.,* Carlsruhe, vol. II; Duncan to Seward, 11 June 1864, *Cons. Desp.,* Carlsruhe, vol. I.

31. Peter Sinclair, *Freedom or Slavery in the United States* (London, 1862), particularly pp. 154–155. When Sinclair visited the United States again in 1864 in the interests of raising money from manufacturers for loans to emigrants, he was described as "Secretary of the Union and Emancipation Society" (Boston *Daily Advertiser,* 18 Jan. 1864, p. 1). On the "secret service fund," see F. H. Morse to Seward, 13 March 1863, *Cons. Desp.,* London, vol. XXXI, no. 33.

32. W. H. Seward to Lorenzo Sabine, 1 April 1863, Boston Board of Trade, *Annual Report* (1864), p. 16.

33. Seward to Sabine, *loc. cit.,* p. 17.

34. William Bray, Boston, to Seward, 7 Jan. 1864, State Dept., *Misc. Letters;* New York *Evening Post,* 9 Jan. 1864, quoted in *Hardware Reporter,* Jan. 1864, p. 2; New York *Tribune,* 31 March 1864; London *Cooperator,* May 1864, p. 282; Boston *Daily Advertiser,* 18 Jan. 1864, p. 2; 6 Jan. 1864, p. 2; *D. A. B.*

35. Boston *Daily Advertiser,* 2 May 1864, p. 2.

36. Connecticut, *Private Laws,* V (1857–1865), 528.

37. For a discussion of the Hartford group, see the author's Ph.D. thesis at the Cornell University Library, pp. 68–69.

38. *Hardware Reporter,* Sept. 1863, p. 2. Williams responded with the suggestion that an agent be sent to England, backed by a fund of twenty million dollars (*Iron Age,* 24 Nov. 1864, p. 2). For evidence that Morris was acquainted with Carey, see John Williams to Carey, 26 Nov. 1864, Gardiner Collection. For advertisements of Morris, Wheeler and Co., see *Hardware Reporter,* May 1864, p. 1.

39. *Senate Petitions,* 38c., 1s., recd. 18 May 1864, National Archives; *Hardware Reporter,* Oct. 1863, p. 1.

40. *Iron Age,* 24 Nov. 1864, p. 2.

41. The American Emigrant Company was first mentioned in the *Hardware Reporter* in March 1864.

42. John Williams to Seward, 6 April 1864, State Dept., *Misc. Letters.* That the American Emigrant Company was already having difficulty getting manufacturers to contribute is indicated in *Hardware Reporter,* March 1864, p. 3.

43. Petition from Manufacturers and Citizens of Hartford; Petition of Manufacturers of the United States; Petition from companies in Sturbridge, Massachusetts; Petition of Citizens of Massachusetts; Petition from Miners, Agriculturalists, and Manufacturers of Pennsylvania; Petition from Citizens of Philadelphia; Petition from Pittsburgh Companies. All in *Senate Petitions,* 38c., 1s., National Archives.

44. *Fincher's Trades Review,* 19 Dec. 1863, p. 10; Abraham Lincoln, *Complete Works,* ed. Nicolay and Hay (New York, 1904), II, 447.

45. U. S. *Statutes at Large,* XIII (1863–1865), pp. 385–387. For a discussion of the Congressional debates, see George M. Stephenson, *A History of American Immigration* (Boston, 1926), pp. 135–138.

46. James Bowen to John P. Cumming, 12 Aug. 1864, Federal Bureau of Immigration, *Letters Sent,* National Archives. The Senate bill had provided for the establishment of a federal superintendent at New Orleans (*Congressional Globe,* 38c., 1s., p. 865). After 1847 the New York legislature required immigrant agents to obtain licenses. In 1855 Castle Garden was established as the immigrant landing depot; there immigrants could buy inland railway tickets from authorized agents at a special third-class rate fixed by the railroads and posted for the information of immigrants. Immigrants could also exchange money, obtain refreshment, and see to the forwarding of luggage at Castle Garden (New York, *Annual Report of the Commissioners of Emigration* (1882), pp. 11–12. U. S. Immigration Commission, *Report,* XXXIX (1911), 768–799).

47. John P. Cumming to J. H. Anderson, *Cons. Desp.,* Hamburg, vol. XVII; E. P. Jacobson to Charles Page, Consul at Zurich, 18 Nov. 1865, no. 508; Jacobson to Henry Toomy, Consul at Munich, 18 Nov. 1865, no. 512, F. B. I., *Letters Sent.*

48. E. P. Smith to J. H. Anderson, Consul at Hamburg, 3 April 1866, F. B. I., *Letters Sent,* no. 561.

49. Jacobson to Governor Anderson of Ohio, 11 Nov. 1865, no. 493; H. N. Congar to Governor Brownlow of Tennessee, 25 Oct. 1865, no. 479; Congar to Governor Bramlotte of Kentucky, 25 Oct. 1865, no. 476; Congar to Isador Bush, Secretary of the Missouri Board of Immigration, 14 July 1865; Congar to D. Blakely, Secretary of Minnesota Commission of Immigration, 14 July 1865, F. B. I., *Letters Sent.*

50. Albert H. Leisinger, "The Federal Act to Encourage Immigration" (M.A. thesis, Cornell, 1938), p. 47.

51. Congar to Cumming, 1 Sept. 1865, F. B. I., *Letters Sent*.

52. C. C. Cutting, New York, to Webster Woollen Mills, 23 June 1865, Webster Woolen Mills, *In-Letters*, vol. 125, Baker Library, Harvard University.

53. Williams to Carey, 10 March 1866, Gardiner Collection, Historical Society of Pennsylvania. Smith held office for only a few months in 1866. His first letter as Commissioner was dated 22 March, and his last 7 August 1866.

54. E. Peshine Smith to Carey, 4 May 1866, Gardiner Collection.

55. Smith to Charles Leas, 5 April 1866, F. B. I., *Letters Sent*, no. 674.

56. Charles Leas, Consul at Funchal, 23 Feb. 1866, F. B. I., *Letters Recd.*, no. 8; Smith to Gibbons, San Francisco wine-grower, 18 July 1863, no. 711; Smith to Leas, 18 July 1866, no. 712; Smith to Cumming, 18 July 1866, no. 713; Smith to Leas, 2 Aug. 1866, no. 714, F. B. I., *Letters Sent*.

57. Smith to G. Harrington, U. S. Minister Resident, Berne, Switzerland, 6 April 1866, F. B. I., *Letters Sent*, no. 673.

58. Smith to Nicholas Wehr, Paris, 7 April 1866, no. 670; Smith to G. Harrington, 6 April 1866, no. 673; Smith to Cumming, 28 May 1866, no. 701; Smith to Defosse, 9 June 1866, no. 706, F. B. I., *Letters Sent*.

59. John Williams, New York, 25 Aug. 1863, F. B. I., *Letters Recd.*, W. no. 6; Congar to Williams, 28 Aug. 1865, F. B. I., *Letters Sent*, no. 426. Circular of the American Emigrant Company, Burlington Archives.

60. Congar to George Van Horne, 21 Nov. 1865, F. B. I., *Letters Sent*, no. 515.

61. *Iron Age*, 8 Dec. 1864, p. 2; 12 Jan. 1865, p. 1; 2 Feb. 1865, p. 2; 15 June 1865, p. 1; 9 Nov. 1865, p. 2.

62. John Hooker to Senator Sherman, 31 Jan. 1865, *Senate Misc. Doc.*, 38c., 2s., no. 13, p. 2. The Amoskeag Mills forwarded $56.03 for each of 18 weavers imported in 1865, although they were later able to negotiate a refund of a part of this because several of the persons sent were not skilled weavers (David Creamer, "Recruiting Contract Laborers," *J. E. H.*, I, 52).

63. "Order to Import Workmen," and "Form of Contract," *Hardware Reporter*, Aug. 1864.

64. *Hardware Reporter*, July 1864, p. 2.

65. *Iron Age*, 9 Nov. 1865, p. 2. *Fincher's Trades Review*, 23 Dec. 1865, p. 23.

66. Williams to Carey, 2 March 1865, Gardiner Collection.

67. Williams to Carey, 26 Nov. 1864, Gardiner Collection.

68. Newcastle *Chronicle*, 22 March 1865, p. 3, *Iron Age*, 2 March 1865, p. 2.

69. Resolution passed at the quarterly meeting of the American Iron and Steel Association, Washington, 28 Feb. 1866, printed in *Iron Age*, 8 March 1866, p. 1. See also *Ryland's Iron Trade Circular*, 6 May 1865, p. 4; 25 Feb. 1865, p. 6; 24 June 1865, p. 17; *Fincher's Trades Review*, 4 March 1865, p. 54.

70. Williams to Carey, 25 May 1866; Williams to Carey, 31 Dec. 1867, Gardiner Collection.

71. George S. Harris to Eli Thayer, 25 March 1864, Hannibal and St. Joseph Land

Commissioner Papers, Newberry Library. Compare price list in *Hardware Reporter*, Feb. 1864, p. 2.

72. Springfield *Republican*, 24 Dec. 1864, p. 2.

73. John Hooker, *Account Book, 1857–1876*, Connecticut State Library, Hartford.

74. American Emigrant Company, "Annual Statement," filed 1 Feb. 1869, State Capitol, Hartford.

75. Letter from Edward Williams, Bilston, Staffordshire, 2 Feb. 1864, *Hardware Reporter*, March 1864, p. 2.

76. *Hardware Reporter*, March 1864, p. 2; London *Star*, 16 March 1865; *Beehive*, 20 Feb. 1864, p. 4. Advertisements of the American Emigrant Company appeared in almost every issue of the *Beehive* from 29 Oct. 1864 until 18 Feb. 1865, and again in the spring of 1865 and of 1866. Nothing about labor contracts appeared in these advertisements.

77. Oldham *Chronicle*, 11 June 1865, p. 5. The American Emigrant Company was not alone in recruiting operatives in Lancashire during the famine. There is no direct evidence that the Boston Society was working in Lancashire, but at least one textile firm, the Webster Woollen Mills, sought workers in Lancashire towns at this time (S. Slater & Sons to Messrs. Jn. L. Bowes and Bros., Liverpool, 22 Aug. 1865, Webster Woollen Mills, *Letter Book*, vol. 124, p. 374. See also Oldham *Chronicle*, 18 June 1864, p. 6).

78. Charlotte Erickson, "British Trade Unions and Emigration," *Population Studies*, III (Dec. 1949), 254.

79. Oldham *Chronicle*, 15 March 1864, p. 3; 11 June 1864, p. 5.

80. Edward Williams to Peter Cooper, 24 Feb. 1864, *Hardware Reporter*, April 1864, p. 1.

81. See testimony of Daniel Guile, *Reports of the Trade Union Commissioners*, *B. P. P.*, XXXIX (1867–68), 16–17. The Webbs stated that the first strong organization among South Wales miners was the Lancashire Amalgamated Association of Miners whose origins they placed in 1869 (Sidney and Beatrice Webb, *The History of Trade Unionism*, 1920 edition, London, 1950, p. 306). Ness Edwards maintained, however, that locals of this union had appeared as early as 1864 (*The History of the South Wales Miners*, Labour Publishing Co. Ltd., 1926, p. 39).

82. Letter from Edward Williams, *Miner and Workman's Advocate*, 6 Feb. 1864, p. 8.

83. Letter from "Scotchman, P. S.," New York, 14 March 1864 *Miner and Workman's Advocate*, 7 May 1864, p. 8.

84. Erickson, *Population Studies*, III, 253–263.

85. *North British Daily Mail*, 24 April 1865, p. 2; Alexander MacDonald, Holytown, to Alexander Campbell, 13 Feb. 1865, *Ryland's Iron Trade Circular*, 25 Feb. 1865, p. 13; *Miner and Workman's Advocate*, 27 May 1865, pp. 4, 5; Thomas Gemmel to Alexander MacDonald, 26 Jan. 1865, *Ryland's Iron Trade Circular*, 25 Feb. 1865, p. 13. Advertisements appeared in *Mining Journal*, 13 Dec. 1864, p. 889; 19 Nov. 1864, p. 806.

86. For example, *Iron Age*, 13 Feb. 1865, p. 2; 30 March 1865, p. 2; 6 April 1865, p. 2.

87. Newcastle *Daily Chronicle,* 21 March 1865, p. 3; 22 March 1865, p. 3; 25 March 1865, p. 3; 30 March 1865, p. 3; 3 April 1865, p. 3.

88. Seward to Cumming, 8 Dec. 1864–24 March 1865, *passim;* W. Hunter to Cumming, 17 April 1865–10 June 1865, *passim;* H. N. Congar to Cumming, 11 Aug. 1865–19 March 1866, *passim;* E. P. Smith to Cumming, 11 April 1866–7 June 1866, *passim;* F. B. I., *Letters Sent.*

89. Aberdare *Times,* 6 May 1865, p. 4; *Miner and Workman's Advocate,* 20 May 1865, p. 6; London *Times,* 23 May 1865, p. 12; *Ryland's Iron Trade Circular,* 3 June 1865, p. 12.

90. *Iron Age,* 11 May 1865, p. 2.

91. T. Wolcott to J. Frederick Elliot, 27 Aug. 1864, CO/386. LXXXV, 319–322, Public Records Office, London; *Twenty-fifth Report of the Commissioners of Emigration, B. P. P.,* XVIII (1865), 14.

92. Preston *Guardian,* 19 Nov. 1864, p. 2; 30 Nov. 1864, p. 4; Liverpool *Mercury,* 16 Nov. 1864, p. 6; E. M. Archibald to Lord Russell, 16 Dec. 1864, Foreign Office, *Cons. Desp.,* New York, P. R. O.

93. Liverpool *Mercury,* 16 Nov. 1864, p. 6; 18 Nov. 1864, p. 7; Preston *Guardian,* 19 Nov. 1864, p. 3.

94. Liverpool *Mercury,* 3 Feb. 1865, p. 7; E. M. Archibald to Secy. of State, 3 Feb. 1865, *Despatches to and from Consuls,* New York, FO5/1023, P. R. O.

95. For example, Preston *Guardian,* 3 Dec. 1864, p. 8; 10 Dec. 1864, p. 7; Oldham *Chronicle,* 11 June 1864, p. 5; London *Times,* 26 April 1865, p. 11; Aberdare *Times,* 25 March 1865, p. 4; Merthyr *Telegraph,* 25 March 1865, p. 3; Cardiff and Merthyr *Guardian,* 17 Feb. 1865, p. 8.

96. Part of a letter from Andrew Leighton to the Liverpool *Mercury,* quoted in *Iron Age,* 16 March 1865, p. 2.

97. Letter from G. R. Haywood, Manchester, Manchester *Guardian,* 6 Feb. 1863, p. 4.

98. R. Arthur Arnold, *History of the Cotton Famine,* (2nd ed.; London, 1865), p. 219. Arnold was a government inspector of public works in Lancashire. Thomas Birtwistle to Lincoln, 6 Feb. 1864, State Dept. *Misc. Letters,* National Archives. London *Times,* 24 March 1863, p. 12.

99. *Economist,* 31 Jan. 1865, pp. 117–118. This article was reprinted in the *British Miner and General Newsman,* 14 Feb. 1863, p. 5.

100. See, for example, article by George Shepherd, mining engineer, *Mining Journal,* 10 Sept. 1864, p. 647; *Mining Journal Supplement,* 1 Oct. 1864; *Mining Journal,* 8 Oct. 1864, p. 720.

101. Testimony of George T. Clarke, trustee, Dowlais Works, *Reports of the Trade Union Commissioners, B. P. P.* (1867–68), XXXIX, 92; *Mining Journal,* 23 June 1865, p. 400.

102. *Ryland's Iron Trade Circular,* 17 June 1865, p. 12. For Williams' reply, see *Iron Age,* 13 July 1865, p. 2.

103. *Ryland's Iron Trade Circular,* 29 April 1865, p. 12; 6 May 1865, p. 4; 10 June 1865, p. 15; 1 July 1865, p. 17; 22 April 1865, p. 12; 13 May 1865, p. 13; 1 April 1865, p. 12; 20 May 1865, p. 16; 15 July 1865, p. 16; 9 Sept. 1865, p. 13.

104. Letter printed in *Fincher's Trades Review,* 16 Dec. 1865, p. 20.

105. *Workman's Advocate,* 9 Sept. 1865, p. 6; *Miner and Workman's Advocate,* 8 April 1865, p. 6; John Watson to the editor, Durham *Chronicle,* 31 March 1865, p. 3; Merthyr *Telegraph,* 20 May 1865; article from Glasgow *Sentinel,* reprinted in *Ryland's Iron Trade Circular,* 21 Oct. 1865, p. 11; Sheffield *Independent,* 29 March 1865, p. 2.

106. *Bihang till Göteborgs Handels-och Sjöfartstidning,* 31 March 1866, p. 3.

107. *Fincher's Trades Review,* 23 Dec. 1865, p. 30.

108. See Appendix I.

109. *Iron Age,* 29 March 1866, p. 2. For fuller details, see author's thesis at Cornell University Library, pp. 166–167.

110. *Beehive,* 20 Feb. 1864, p. 4; *Fincher's Trades Review,* 23 Dec. 1865, p. 30. Address to the Iron Workers of Great Britain by the United Sons of Vulcan, 1 March 1866, Aberdare *Times,* 16 June 1866, p. 4.

111. John Fleming, Philadelphia, to Robert Humphreys, 23 March 1866, private collection of letters seen through the courtesy of Mrs. D'Arcy, Dauphin's Barn, Dublin.

112. London *Times,* 17 April 1865, p. 9; Belfast *Morning News,* 17 Oct. 1864, p. 3; *Irish Farmer's Gazette,* 25 March 1865, p. 105; William B. West to Seward, 11 June 1864, *Cons. Desp.,* Dublin, vol. IV, National Archives.

113. Clipping from Cork *Daily Herald,* 8 Oct. 1864, quoted in *Iron Age,* 10 Nov. 1864, p. 1.

114. *Hardware Reporter,* May 1864, p. 2; letter from Dublin, 21 April 1864, *Hardware Reporter,* April 1864, p. 2.

115. Drouhn de Lhuys to John Bigelow, 11 Nov. 1865, *House Exec. Doc., Diplomatic Correspondence,* 39c., 2s. (1866–67), vol. I, part 1, no. 213, p. 269. For licensing of the Le Havre agent, see Leisinger, "The Federal Act to Encourage Immigration," pp. 101–102.

116. Bigelow to de Lhuys, *House Exec. Doc.,* 39c., 2s., I, 291.

117. Bigelow to Seward, 11 Dec. 1865, *House Exec. Doc.,* 39c., 2s., I, 291. In 1866 the French Minister of Internal Affairs directed prefects to oppose emigration with all their might (*Allgemeine Auswanderungs Zeitung,* Rudolstadt, 26 April 1866, p. 69).

118. *Hardware Reporter,* July 1864, p. 2.

119. See, for example, copy of law of 16 May 1847 for the regulation of emigrant agents in the Grand Duchy of Hesse, enclosure in *Cons. Desp.,* Frankfort, vol. XVII, no. 701; P. Sidney Post to Seward, 28 Feb. 1867, *Cons. Desp.,* Vienna, vol. IV, no. 16; W. W. Murphy to Seward, 17 March 1868, *Cons. Desp.,* Frankfort, vol. XVII, no. 701; Prussian laws of 7 May and 8 Sept. 1853, *Zeitschrift des Preussischen Statistische Bureau, Jahrgang XIII* (1873), Heft I and II, pp. 18–23.

120. *Hardware Reporter,* July 1864, p. 2. See also, *Hardware Reporter,* May 1864, p. 2; *Iron Age,* 10 Nov. 1864, p. 2.

121. *Allgemeine Auswanderungs Zeitung,* 22 Sept. 1864, p. 155.

122. Article in Berlin *Volks-Zeitung,* 10 May 1864, reprinted in *Allgemeine Auswanderungs Zeitung,* 19 May 1864, p. 84. See also 18 Aug. 1864, p. 135; 6 Oct. 1864, p. 163; 5 Jan. 1865, p. 3; letter from Dis Debar, West Virginia Commissioner of Emigration, 9 June 1864, State Dept., *Misc. Letters.*

123. *Der Ansiedler im Westen,* Berlin, II (May 1864), 60. Compare statement by the Consul at Carlsruhe that "strong opposition in all the governing and employing classes" was expressed toward the Government's plans to encourage emigration (B. O. Duncan to Seward, 24 May 1864, *Cons. Desp.,* Carlsruhe, vol. II).

124. *Deutsche Auswanderer-Zeitung,* 13 June 1864. See also *Allgemeine Auswanderungs Zeitung,* 19 May 1864, pp. 82–83.

125. *A. A. Z.,* 12 Jan. 1865, p. 8; 22 Feb. 1866, p. 33; 1 March 1866, p. 35.

126. *A. A. Z.,* 30 Jan. 1863, p. 19; 17 March 1864, p. 47; 24 March 1864, p. 51; 8 Sept. 1864, p. 147; 28 July 1864, p. 123. For cases of arrests of emigrant agents in Hamburg and Antwerp, see *A. A. Z.,* 4 Aug. 1864, p. 127; 18 Aug. 1864, pp. 135–136.

127. *A. A. Z.,* 1 June 1865, p. 87; 10 Aug. 1865, p. 127; letter from Prussian Consul in Chicago, *A. A. Z.,* 24 Aug. 1865, p. 135.

128. For example, *A. A. Z.,* 13 April 1865, p. 57; 20 April 1865, p. 63; 22 June 1865, p. 99.

129. John Williams to J. H. Anderson, 24 Sept. 1864, *Cons. Desp.,* Hamburg, vol. XVII.

130. Frederick Sommerschu to J. H. Anderson, Karlsruhe, Baden, 19 Sept. 1864, *Cons. Desp.,* Hamburg, vol. XVII (copy).

131. Anderson to Seward, 9 Feb. 1866, *Cons. Desp.,* Hamburg, vol. XVIII.

132. William Marsh to Seward, 15 April 1865, *Despatches from Altona;* Marsh to Aug. Batton, Hamburg Steamship Co., 29 Jan. 1866; Anderson to Seward, 9 Feb. 1866, *Cons. Desp.,* Hamburg, vol. XVIII.

133. *Iron Age,* 11 May 1865, p. 2.

134. *A. A. Z.,* 30 Nov. 1865–15 Feb. 1866, *passim.*

135. I am indebted to Mrs. Ingrid G. Semmigsen, of Oslo, for information relating to the activities of Consul Kraby at Porrsgrund.

136. Edward Habicht to Stats Ministern för Utrikes Ärendena, 23 Jan. 1865, *Svenska Konsulars Skrivelser,* New York, 1865, Utrikes Departmentet, Riksarkivet, Stockholm.

137. Applications were received from 68 miners, 28 ironworkers, 13 machinists, 36 quarrymen, 3 foundrymen, and 133 common laborers (*Iron Age,* 11 May 1865, p. 2). See also *Iron Age,* 27 April 1865, p. 2.

138. Count Edward Piper to Stats Ministern för Utrikes Ärendena, 12 July 1864, *Amerika, Depescher från Beskickningen i Förenta Staterna,* vol. I (1864), Riksarkivet, Stockholm.

139. Habicht to Stats Ministern för Utrikes Ärendena, 23 Jan. 1865, 2 Feb. 1865, *Svenska Konsulars Skrivelser,* New York, 1865.

140. *Post Tidningen,* 27 April 1865, quoted in *Iron Age,* 27 July 1865, p. 2.

141. *Iron Age,* 22 July 1865, p. 2; 27 July 1865, p. 2.

142. *Hemlandet,* 5 July 1865, p. 1; 12 July 1865, p. 1.

143. Hawkinson was connected with several emigrant recruiting enterprises (*Beskickningen in Archiv i Washington, Avgående och Inkomna,* 1866, Riksarkivet. *Hemlandet,* 23 Jan. 1866, p. 3; 8 Oct. 1867, p. 2).

144. For examples, see Hudiksvalla *Posten,* 2 Sept. 1865, p. 2; *Hemlandet,* 27 Dec. 1865, p. 2.

145. *Hemlandet,* 26 March 1867, p. 1; Hudiksvalla *Posten,* 7 July 1866, p. 2; *Skånska Posten,* Kristianstad, 19 June 1867, p. 2; *Drammens Blad, Upphold,* 20 Oct. 1866, p. 2.

146. Advertisements signed by A. W. Möller appeared in Jönköpings *Tidning,* Feb.–Aug. 1866, *passim.* J. B. Westenius was appointed agent for Skåne (*Skånska Posten,* 21 April 1866, p. 4). Skåne is the prosperous agricultural region in southern Sweden. Compare Florence E. Janson, *The Background of Swedish Immigration* (Philadelphia, 1931), p. 235, where she states that the American Emigrant Company did not advertise in southern Sweden until 1867. A. G. Throlson opened an office in Hudiksvalla in northern Sweden in 1866 (Hudiksvalla *Posten,* 21 July 1866, p. 2). The newspaper accepted his advertisements while opposing his activities in its editorials (Hudiksvalla *Posten,* 28 July 1866, p. 3).

147. See advertisement signed by C. G. Hammond, agent in Illinois for the American Emigrant Company: "Needed: a large number of Scandinavians to go South. Transportation forwarded" (*Hemlandet,* 6 Feb. 1866, p. 4). See also *Bihang till Göteborgs Handels-och Sjöfarts-Tidning,* 31 March 1866.

148. Jönköpings *Tidning,* 21 Feb. 1866, p. 1.

149. Jönköpings *Tidning,* 13 May 1868, p. 3.

150. Kristianstads *Bladet,* 8 June 1868; *Skånska Posten,* 6 Feb. 1869, p. 4; *Amerika-Bladet,* 2 Nov. 1869, p. 4. For other evidence of competition, see *Hemlandet* 23 April 1867, p. 1. David Lyon, agent of the Montreal Steamship Company and the Inman Line, in a pamphlet, "Några Wälmenta Råd," warned emigrants that the American Emigrant Company sold land at five dollars an acre while government land could be purchased for $1.25 an acre. An article in *Amerika-Bladet* (12 April 1870, p. 3) defended the American Emigrant Company against the Inman Line's criticisms of its steamers.

151. John Hooker to Senator Sherman, 21 Jan. 1865, *Senate Misc. Doc.,* 38c., 2s., no. 13, p. 5; *Iron Age,* 16 Feb. 1865, p. 2.

152. Connecticut, *House Journal* (1865), XX, 117, 187; *Senate Journal* (1865), XIX, 79, 154, 185, 193, 199–200, 210.

153. *Public Acts of Connecticut* (1865), pp. 8–9.

154. *Iron Age,* 19 April 1866, p. 2.

155. E. P. Smith to E. Washburne, 27 March 1866, *House Reports,* 39c., 1s., no. 48, p. 2.

156. *Report of Committee on Foreign Affairs,* H. R., 40c., 2s., no. 76, pp. 1, 4.

157. London *Times,* 21 Feb. 1872, p. 6. See Edward Young, *Information for Emigrants* (London, 1873), prepared by the United States Bureau of Statistics, translated into German, French, and Swedish, for distribution in those countries.

158. Hamilton A. Hill, "Immigration and Pauperism," American Social Science Association, *Proceedings of Conference of Public Charities* (Detroit, 1875), p. 92. During the sixties, Hill had been promoting the Boston and Liverpool Steamship Line (Boston *Daily Advertiser,* 9 March 1864, p. 1).

159. Memorial signed by Peter Cooper and Richard M. Henry, President and Secre-

tary of the Citizens Association of New York, *Senate Misc. Doc.*, 41c., 1s. (1870), no. 134, p. 1408.

160. Resolutions of Governors Meeting, 5 Dec. 1870, quoted in Boston Board of Trade, *Annual Report* (1871), p. 64. See also Stephenson, *History of Immigration*, p. 140, and Carl Wittke, *We Who Built America* (New York, 1939), p. 107.

161. Boston Board of Trade, *Annual Report* (1871), pp. 37, 67–69. Steamship and railroad companies successfully advocated the abolition of the head tax in Massachusetts—a tax which had been customarily used to care for immigrants who later became public charges and which was devoted largely to that purpose in New York State (Boston Board of Trade, *Annual Report*, 1873, pp. 29, 75; 1871, pp. 35–36, 48; *Evidence for Freedom of the Port*, 1871, p. 29; *Evidence for Modification of Tax on Aliens*, 1870, pp. 34, 47). In 1873 the National Board of Trade passed unanimously resolutions opposing all head taxes (Boston Board of Trade, *Annual Report*, 1873, pp. 28, 74–75). For rivalry of Philadelphia, see Pennsylvania, Bureau of Labor Statistics, *Second Annual Report*, 1873–74, pp. 347–348.

162. New York, Commissioners of Emigration, *Annual Report* (1872), pp. 2, 11. Memorial of Chamber of Commerce against Bill to Promote Immigration to the United States, *ibid.*, p. 12.

2. PATTERNS OF PRIVATE RECRUITMENT, 1860–1885

1. *Iron Age*, 22 Oct. 1868, p. 4; National Association of Wool Manufacturers, *Bulletin*, VII (1877), 171. For statements of these views, see *Iron Age*, 23 Dec. 1875, p. 15; N. A. W. M. *Bulletin*, XX (1882), 246; New England Cotton Manufacturers Association, *Proceedings*, April 1885, p. 83; Boston, *Report of Committee on Public Instruction* (1879), pp. 13, 30; Springfield *Republican*, 5 May 1869, p. 4; remarks of Gideon Welles, *Senate Executive Documents*, 39c., 2s. (1866–67), I, 23; Henry Carey, Philadelphia, to James Swank, 6 May 1879, Gardiner Collection.

2. N. A. W. M. *Bulletin*, II (1870), 550.

3. E. R. Mudge, Schuyler Colfax, Horace Greeley, and Peter Cooper at the woolen trade banquet, 14 Dec. 1870, N. A. W. M. *Bulletin*, II (1870), 278, 281, 285, 313; George Geddes at the Second Joint Convention of Wool Growers and Wool Manufacturers, 20 Dec. 1871, N. A. W. M. *Bulletin*, III (1871), 42.

4. James Swank in his annual report to the American Iron and Steel Association, quoted in N. A. W. M. *Bulletin*, VI (March 1875), 281–282. See also Statistical Report of the Secretary to the American Iron and Steel Association, 20 Nov. 1873, *Iron and Coal Trades Review*, 10 Dec. 1873, p. 1235.

5. Edward Young, *Special Report on Immigration*, United States Bureau of Statistics, Department of Treasury (Washington, 1872); *idem. Special Report on Labor in Europe and America . . . in 1874* (Washington: G. P. O., 1875); *idem. Information for Emigrants to the United States of America . . .* (London, 1873); Stephenson, *History of Immigration*, pp. 141, 150; *Congressional Globe*, 42c., 2s. (1871–72), pp. 3817, 4181.

6. See remarks of Francis Clare Ford, a British observer: "The system of apprenticeship, moreover, has almost entirely disappeared, and Americans in general appear to begrudge the time necessary to make themselves thoroughly acquainted with the details of a business. . . . The consequence has been that foreign is every day replacing native skilled labor" ("Report on the Condition of the Industrial Classes in the United States," 31 Dec. 1869, *Reports from Her*

Majesty's Diplomatic and Consular Agents Abroad Respecting the Condition of the Industrial Classes in Foreign Countries, London, 1870, pp. 317–318). It was generally admitted that the foreign iron molder was more skilled than the American because of the seven-year apprenticeship common in both Britain and Germany. Employers blamed union apprentice rules for the situation while the union maintained that American employers were not willing to invest the money necessary for training Americans, but preferred to import foreigners (*Iron Molders Journal,* 10 Jan. 1874, pp. 176, 177–179; 10 Nov. 1874, pp. 105, 108–109; 10 Dec. 1874, pp. 144–145; *Iron Age,* 13 Jan. 1881, p. 15; *Coopers Journal,* Nov. 1871, p. 141; 1 Jan. 1873, p. 11).

7. N. E. C. M. A. *Proceedings,* 21 April 1869, p. 5.

8. Address by Edward Atkinson, N. E. C. M. A., *Proceedings,* 1876, p. 45.

9. N. E. C. M. A., *Proceedings,* 20 April 1870, p. 16. The Castle Garden Labor Bureau reported in 1870 that it was unable to fill the orders for female weavers which came from New England (N. Y. Commissioners of Emigration, *Annual Report,* 1870, p. 88). The Massachusetts Bureau of Labor Statistics stated that thirty-eight cotton textile establishments in nine counties were employing 18,830 persons in 1870 but needed a total labor force of 20,668 (*Annual Report,* 1870–71, p. 261).

10. American Social Science Association, *Handbook for Immigrants to the United States* (New York, 1871), p. 48.

11. Gideon Welles, "Cotton Culture in the United States," March 1870, N. A. W. M., *Bulletin,* IV (1873), 61.

12. N. E. C. M. A., *Proceedings,* 17 July 1867, p. 208. For a similar case with knitting machinery, see N. A. W. M., *Bulletin,* I (1869), 335.

13. Remarks of Johnston of Harmony Mills, Cohoes, and of Lockwood, N. E. C. M. A., *Proceedings,* 21 April 1869, pp. 6, 19.

14. N. E. C. M. A., *Proceedings,* 21 April 1869, pp. 5, 19.

15. T. H. Dudley, 28 May 1869, *Cons. Desp.,* Liverpool vol. XXXVIII, no. 972, National Archives. John Kirk, *Social Politics in Great Britain and Ireland* (London, 1870), quoted in Edith Abbott, *Historical Aspects of the Immigration Problem* (Chicago, 1926), p. 160.

16. *Beehive,* 8 May 1869, p. 5; 29 May 1869, p. 6; 5 June 1869, p. 6; 12 June 1869, p. 6; Erickson, *Population Studies,* III, 257.

17. *Beehive* reported that the Preston spinners were sending eight people a week during May and June. Fifty-one spinners and minders left Blackburn the first week in June, and similar assistance was being given in other towns of west Lancashire (*Beehive,* 5 June 1869, p. 6).

18. The U. K. figures for emigration of textile workers to the U..S.A. (including Irish) were 658 in 1869, 408 in 1870, dropping to 223 in 1871. The comparable U. S. immigration figures for the same years give 376 in 1869, 595 in 1870, falling to 224 in 1871 (U. S. Dept. of Treas., *Arrivals of Alien Passengers and Immigrants,* 1869–1871. U. K., *General Reports of the Colonial Land and Emigration Commissioners, B. P. P.,* 1868–69, vol. XVII; 1870, vol. XVII; 1871, vol. XX. The two sets of figures were based upon different fiscal years).

19. *Beehive,* 29 May 1869, p. 6; 22 May 1869, p. 4.

20. One agent, Mr. Henry Davis, was reported as being in England to engage operatives for several firms in New York state in various branches of the cotton industry (*Iron Age,* 3 June 1869, p. 6).

21. Clipping from Liverpool *Times*, 17 June 1869, in *Cons. Desp.*, Liverpool, vol. XXIX, no. 980.

22. U. S., *Letters from Secretary of the Treasury Transmitting a Report of the Commissioners of Immigration upon the Causes Which Incite Immigration . . .* (Washington: G. P. O., 1892), I, 187.

23. *Report of the Select Committee of the House of Representatives to Inquire into Alleged Violations of Laws Prohibiting Importation of Contract Laborers . . .* (Washington: G. P. O., 1889), pp. 587ff.

24. Creamer, *J. E. H.*, I, 48–49.

25. George Dexter, Boston, to James Houston, Glasgow, 12 July 1881, vol. 647, p. 471; Dexter to Houston, 9 Jan. 1882, vol. 648, p. 187; Pepperell Manufacturing Company, *Letter Books*, Baker Library, Harvard University.

26. Evelyn H. Knowlton, *Pepperell's Progress* (Harvard University Press, 1948), pp. 163–164.

27. See letters quoted in Creamer, *J. E. H.*, I, 49–51, 53.

28. Dexter to Houston, 18 Aug. 1881, *Letter Books*, vol. 647, p. 23; Dexter to H. S. Howe, 7 Nov. 1881; Dexter to Houston, 8 Nov. 1881, *Letter Books*, vol. 648, pp. 122, 124; Pepperell Papers.

29. Pepperell's worked through the Allan Line, and later, Cunard (Dexter to Messrs. H. and A. Allan, 14 July 1881; Dexter to Houston, 18 August 1881, *Letter Books*, vol. 647, pp. 475, 23; Dexter to H. and A. Allan, 18 Aug. 1881, *Letter Books*, vol. 648, p. 25; Pepperell Papers).

30. Copy of contract printed in Creamer, *J. E. H.*, I, 52–53; Dexter to Houston, 12 July 1881, *Letter Books*, vol. 647, p. 471; 22 Sept. 1881, *Letter Books*, vol. 648, p. 74; Pepperell Papers. Compare importations made by the Lyman Mills in Holyoke, in the 1850's, discussed by Ray Ginger, for which passage loans were repaid in two to four months ("Labor in a Massachusetts Cotton Mill, 1853–1860," *Business History Review*, XXVIII, March 1954, 75).

31. Dexter to Houston, 9 Jan. 1882, Pepperell Mfg. Co., *Letter Books*, vol. 648, p. 187.

32. Creamer, *J. E. H.*, I, 53–54.

33. Creamer, p. 51.

34. Letter quoted, Creamer, pp. 49–50.

35. Letter quoted, Creamer, p. 53.

36. Dexter to Houston, 17 Sept. 1881; Dexter to Howe, 17 Sept. 1881, Pepperell Mfg Co., *Letter Books*, vol. 648, pp. 67, 69.

37. Dexter to Howe, 7 Nov. 1881, *Letter Books*, vol. 648, p. 124.

38. Dexter to Houston, 17 Jan. 1882, *Letter Books*, vol. 648, p. 199.

39. Dexter to Agent, Cunard Steamship Co., Queenstown, Ireland, 16 March 1882; Dexter to Cunard Agent, Boston, 24 April 1882, *Letter Books*, vol. 648, p. 324.

40. For example, see letter from Joseph Simpson at the Waltham Cotton Mills to Thomas Banks, Secretary of the Preston Spinners and Minders Association, 16 March 1864, Preston *Guardian*, 1 June 1864, p. 2. See also Pepperell Mfg. Co., *Invoices*, vol. 127, no. 136.

41. Harry James Brown, "The National Association of Wool Manufacturers," Ph.D. Thesis (Cornell University, 1949), pp. 127, 263.

42. Special Report of Commissioner of Revenue on Wool and Woollens, 1869, printed in N. A. W. M., *Bulletin,* II (1870), 12. Compare, Cole, *American Wool Manufacture,* I, 308.

43. H. N. Slater to C. H. Cutting, 21 June 1865, *Letter Books,* vol. 124, p. 269; Cutting, New York City, to Webster Mills, 24 June 1865, *In-Letters,* vol. 125; J. J. Osborn, New York City, to Webster Mills, 24 June 1865, *In-Letters,* vol. 125, Webster Woolen Mills Papers, Baker Library.

44. H. N. Slater to J. J. Robinson, American Mill, Lockville, Conn., 25 May 1865, *Letter Books,* 124, p. 230, Webster Mills Papers.

45. J. J. Osborn to Webster Mills, 3 July 1865, *In-Letters,* vol. 125; A. Bartlett to Osborn, 3 July 1865, *Letter Books,* vol. 124. p. 299; Osborn to Webster Mills, 1 Aug. 1865; Osborn to Webster Mills, 12 Aug. 1865; John Osborn, 17 Aug. 1865, *In-Letters,* vol. 125, Webster Mills Papers.

46. S. Slater and Sons to John L. Bowes and Bros., Liverpool, 22 Aug. 1865, *Letter Book,* vol. 124, p. 374, Webster Mills Papers.

47. Pages 48–49. This guide to emigrants, edited by Henry Villard, was recommended to the English working-class by Goldwin Smith as "wholly disinterested" (*Beehive,* 25 Sept. 1869, p. 5). For a discussion of the emigration of Yorkshire woolen operatives to the United States during this period, see Rowland T. Berthoff, *British Immigrants in Industrial America* (Harvard University Press, 1953), pp. 38–39.

48. *Reports of the Trade Union Commissioners, B. P. P.* (1867), XXXII, 6. Ford "Report on . . . Industrial Classes," in Abbott, *Historical Aspects,* p. 383. English, Scottish, and Swedish workmen, in addition to natives, were employed at the hot blast charcoal iron furnaces in Georgia and Alabama (*Iron Molders Journal,* 10 Dec. 1875, p. 536). For further discussion of the labor force in the iron industry, see Allan Nevins, *Abram Hewitt* (New York, 1935), p. 430.

49. Berthoff, *British Immigrants,* pp. 64–65.

50. Isaac Jones to John Williams, *Hardware Reporter,* 3 Dec. 1863, p. 2; *Scientific American,* 14 March 1863; Victor S. Clark, *History of Manufactures in the United States* (N. Y., 1929), p. 39. *Ryland's Iron Trade Circular* (11 Nov. 1871, p. 317) referred to a similar type of recruitment in the iron shipbuilding industry: "The contractor for the new line of iron steamships visited the leading shipyards in the Clyde and elsewhere during the summer, and the visit has been followed by an influx of labour of the best kind."

51. *Beehive,* 4 Jan. 1868, p. 6; *The Mining Journal,* 4 Jan. 1868, p. 11.

52. Sheffield *Independent,* 21 April 1868, p. 7; *The Mining Journal,* 25 Jan. 1868, p. 66; *Ryland's Iron Trade Circular,* 11 Sept. 1869, p. 164.

53. Page 49.

54. *Workingman's Advocate,* 24 Aug. 1867; 31 Aug. 1867, quoted in John R. Commons and J. B. Andrews, *Documents in American Industrial History* (Cleveland, 1910–11), IX, 335; *Workingman's Advocate,* 3 Aug. 1867, p. 2; Leland D. Baldwin, *Pittsburgh* (Pittsburgh, 1937), p. 330; James H. Bridge, *The Inside History of the Carnegie Steel Company* (New York, 1903), p. 32.

55. Contract between Mr. Filley and twenty-five Prussian molders, printed in *Iron Molders Journal,* 10 May 1864, p. 16.

56. *Ryland's Iron Trade Circular,* 13 Jan. 1866, p. 32; 16 Dec. 1865, p. 8; 29 July

1865, p. 9. Compare G. I. H. Lloyd, *The Cutlery Trades* (N. Y., 1913), pp. 187, 315.

57. Conversation with Mr. Councillor Slack, General Secretary of the National Cutlers' Union, Sheffield, 15 Jan. 1949.

58. Letter from West Meriden, Conn., in *Ryland's Iron Trade Circular*, 11 Feb. 1865, p. 16.

59. Sheffield *Independent*, 2 May 1866, p. 2; 8 May 1866, p. 6; 14 May 1866, p. 4; 22 May 1866, p. 6.

60. *Ryland's Iron Trade Circular*, 30 Dec. 1865, p. 16.

61. Letter from eight immigrants in Union City, Naugatuck, Conn., 21 March 1870, in Sheffield *Independent*, 5 April 1870, p. 6; Frank Woestenholm to William Abbott and Ned Armitage, 21 March 1870, Sheffield *Independent*, 6 April 1870, p. 4.

62. Berthoff, *British Immigrants*, p. 65.

63. Thomas Bradley, Walden, N. Y., to James Roberts, 30 Aug. 1869, Preston Collection, Cornell Collection of Regional History.

64. William Dorsheimer, 26 Dec. 1864, State Dept., *Misc. Letters*, National Archives.

65. Berthoff, *British Immigrants*, pp. 49–51.

66. Francis Walker, "Our Foreign Population," *The Advance*, VIII (10 Dec. 1874), 262; *Iron Age*, 10 June 1869, p. 6; *Workingman's Advocate*, 19 June 1869, p. 2.

67. Thomas Middleton, a former Durham miner, wrote on behalf of West Virginia coal fields, but the editor of the *Chronicle* charged that Middleton was on the state committee for "ways and means" of filling its army quota (Durham *Chronicle*, 13 March 1865, p. 5; 24 March 1865, p. 5).

68. Clipping from *American Mining Journal*, in *The Commonwealth*, 25 Aug. 1866, p. 8.

69. J. Kirkland to Lincoln, 13 June 1863, State Dept., *Misc. Letters*, National Archives.

70. J. H. Anderson to Seward, 1 Oct. 1864, *Cons. Desp.*, Hamburg, vol. XVII, no. 329.

71. For criticisms of Dreutzer's work, see Bergens *Posten*, 25 Aug. 1864, p. 3; Tromsø *Stiftstidende*, 11 Sept. 1864, p. 1. Dreutzer's defense was published in Bergens *Posten*, 28 Aug. 1864, p. 2. For further discussion, see Qualey, *Norwegian Settlement in the United States*, p. 183.

72. *Aftonbladet*, 4 June 1864, p. 1. Axel Silverspar was at the same time advertising in Chicago's *Hemlandet* for miners, lumbermen, and smiths, as well as day laborers, to go to the Lake Superior mining region (*Hemlandet*, 8 June 1864, p. 4; 7 Sept. 1864, p. 4).

73. See contracts made by Henry F. Tefft on behalf of the Quincy Mining Company, the Pewabic Mining Company, and others, 25 Jan. 1864, Enclosure in O. E. Dreutzer to W. B. Hunter, 27 June 1865, *Cons. Desp.*, Bergen, II (*Adressebladet*, 10 July 1864, p. 3).

74. *Aftonbladet*, 9 July 1864, p. 2; 13 July 1864, p. 3; *Hemlandet*, 27 July 1864, p. 1; Quebec *Morning Chronicle*, 18 Aug. 1864; letter from passenger on the

Ernest Merck describing runners who boarded the ship in Falmouth, *Aftonbladet,* 4 Aug. 1864, p. 4.

75. Dreutzer to Hunter, 27 June 1865, *Cons. Desp.,* Bergen, vol. II.

77. Tromsø *Stiftstidende,* 29 June 1865, p. 3; Ingrid G. Semmigsen, "Utvanringsagentene," unpublished manuscript lent by the author; Theodore C. Blegen, *Norwegian Migration to America* (Northfield, 1931–1940), II, 146–147.

78. Qualey, *Norwegian Settlements,* p. 184. For examples of newspaper opposition, see *Adressebladet,* 2 Aug. 1865, p. 3; 23 Aug. 1865, p. 3.

79. Ulvestad, *Nordemaend i Amerika,* p. 193, quoted in Qualey, *Norwegian Settlements,* p. 184. A contemporary source stated that one hundred persons from Badsø and Alten" in the far north of Norway were in the party (*Adressebladet,* 9 Aug. 1865, p. 3).

80. R. V. Clements, "English Trade Unions and the Problem of Emigration," Oxford B. Litt. Thesis, Nov. 1953, p. 154; Berthoff, *British Immigrants,* p. 50.

81. *Workingman's Advocate,* 25 Dec. 1869, p. 2.

82. *The Trades,* 20 Sept. 1879, p. 2; *Labor Standard,* 8 July 1882, p. 2.

83. Evan Roland Jones, *The Emigrant's Friend* (London, 1882).

84. *Annual Report of the Commissioner General of Immigration* (1904), pp 38–39 (Ellsworth Coal Co. case). Also *ibid.* (1906), pp. 65–66.

85. *Miner and Workman's Advocate,* 30 July 1864, p. 7. See also 5 March 1864, p. 7; 29 Oct. 1864, p. 7; 4 March 1865, p. 6; 24 Sept. 1865, p. 5.

86. Testimony of J. Quinlan, New York Contract Labor Inspector, 25 July 1899, U. S. *Reports of the Industrial Commission,* XV, *Immigration* (1901), 123–124.

3. UNCERTAINTIES OF THE CONTRACT LABOR SYSTEM

1. John Hooker, Hartford, to Senator Sherman, 21 Jan. 1865, *Senate Misc. Doc.,* 38c., 2s., no. 13, p. 3; *Iron Age,* 19 April 1866, p. 2.

2. Edward Winslow, Boston agent of the Foreign Emigrant Association, 8 Dec. 1864, State Department, *Misc. Letters,* National Archives.

3. Vera Shlakman, *The Economic History of a Factory Town,* Smith College Studies in History, 1934–35, pp. 148–149.

4. Creamer, *J. E. H.,* I, 55.

5. Letter from Webster, Mass., 10 June 1864, first published in the Ashton *Reporter,* reprinted in Manchester *Guardian,* 5 July 1864, p. 4. Another emigrant to the Webster Mills wrote back: "Lots of our people have gone away; some will never come back. He [the master] wanted us to work for very low wages" (letter from Providence, R. I., 2 May 1864, Oldham *Chronicle,* 18 June 1864, p. 6).

6. Oldham *Chronicle,* 18 June 1864, p. 6; Manchester *Guardian,* 5 July 1864, p. 4.

7. Dexter to Houston, 7 Nov. 1881, Pepperell Mfg. Co., *Letter Books,* vol. 648, p. 123. Dexter to Howe, 19 Nov. 1881; Dexter to Houston, 19 Nov. 1881, *Letter Books,* vol. 648, p. 136. "That lot of men are nearly all gone from the mill & we are out several hundred dollars" (Dexter to Houston, 14 Feb. 1882, *Letter Books,* vol. 648, p. 236).

8. Dexter to Houston, 9 Jan. 1882; Dexter to Houston, 17 Jan. 1882; Dexter to Howe, 10 Feb. 1882; Dexter to Allan, 6 Nov. 1881; 8 Nov. 1881; Dexter to

Houston, 6 Nov. 1881; 8 Nov. 1881; *ibid.,* vol. 648, pp. 187, 200, 232, 509, 510, 511.

9. Dexter to Houston, 22 Sept. 1881; 8 Nov. 1881; *ibid.,* vol. 648, pp. 74, 511.

10. Thomas Bradley, Walden, N. Y., to James Roberts, 16 May 1870, Preston Collection, Cornell Collection of Regional History.

11. Letter from an agent who guided a company of Norwegian emigrants from Chicago to the Ontonagon mine, *Hemlandet,* 31 Aug. 1864, p. 3. For other reports on conditions at the mines, see letter from Z. M. to his brother, 27 Feb. 1866, in *Adressebladet,* 14 March 1866, pp. 3–4; *Workingman's Advocate,* 2 Nov. 1867, p. 2; letter from Johann C. Walöen, reprinted from *Faedrelandet* in *Hemlandet,* 16 Aug. 1865, p. 2.

12. *Adressebladet,* 14 March 1866, pp. 3–4.

13. *Hemlandet,* 31 Aug. 1864, p. 3.

14. Johann Schröder, *Skandinaverne i den Forenede Stater og Canada* (La Crosse, Wis., 1867), pp. 63–64.

15. Consul Edward Habicht thought that most of them joined the army (14 Nov. 1864, *Svenska Konsulars Skrivelser,* New York, 1864, no. 18, Riksarkivet, Stockholm).

16. Axel Silverspar to S. S. Robinson, agent for the Quincy Mines, 11 Sept. 1864, in *Hemlandet,* 9 Nov. 1864, p. 1. This plan for emigrant associations, or in effect, company unions, was advertised in Scandinavian-American and Swedish newspapers as an inducement to immigration (*Workingman's Advocate,* 2 Nov. 1867, p. 2; *Adressebladet,* 14 March 1866, pp. 3–4).

17. Oldham *Chronicle,* 16 July 1864, p. 7; Preston *Guardian,* 26 Nov. 1864, p. 3.

18. *Ryland's Iron Trade Circular,* 26 Aug. 1865, p. 12; Merthyr *Telegraph,* 2 Sept. 1865, p. 4.

19. London *Times,* 7 Nov. 1866, p. 6.

20. Associated Iron Moulders of Scotland, *Minutes,* 14 May 1867, 28 May 1867, 2 July 1867, 20 August 1867, Papers at the National Founders Union Headquarters, Manchester, England.

21. Testimony of George T. Clark, *B. P. P.* (1867–68), XXXIX, 92–93. "Occasionally a good English mechanic finds his way to our shores, but his stay is not long" (*Workingman's Advocate,* 4 July 1868, p. 2).

22. *Economist,* 10 April 1869, p. 416.

23. *Iron Molders Journal* (10 Dec. 1874, p. 137) noted the departure of six steamers for Europe carrying 1600 mechanics and laborers. Another account said that 500 skilled mechanics obtained free passages to England in 1874 from various steamship companies (London *Times,* 3 Aug. 1874, p. 8). For mention of machine establishment employees leaving for England, see Ohio Bureau of Labor Statistics, *Report* (1877), p. 115. Another note of skilled carpenters and joiners returning to England, *Iron Molders Journal,* 10 Dec. 1877, pp. 563–564. For miners returning to Scotland see *Workingman's Advocate,* 20 Feb. 1875, p. 2. The return of miners from America in 1874 was reported to have relieved a labor shortage in Cornwall (*Labor News,* 10 Jan. 1874). Alexander Hill, "Immigration and Pauperism," American Social Science Association, *Proceedings of Charities Conference* (1875), p. 86.

24. Report of Prussian manufacturers sending agents to America in *Iron Molders*

Journal, 10 Feb. 1875, p. 204. For cases of recruitment of skilled operatives for Britain, see New York *Tribune,* 1 Aug. 1877, p. 2; Aberdare *Times,* 8 Sept. 1877, p. 3; *Labor Standard,* New York, 2 Nov. 1877, p. 1; 23 June 1878, p. 1.

25. *Labor Standard,* 11 Aug. 1878, p. 4. Notice of emigrant agents from Australia offering inducements to skilled mechanics in New York appeared in American Iron and Steel Association, *Annual Report of Secretary,* 1 Jan. 1877, p. 28.

26. Sheffield *Independent,* 2 Dec. 1871, p. 8. See also return of ironworkers discussed in *Ryland's Iron Trade Circular,* 1 May 1869, p. 282.

27. *Labor Enquirer,* Denver, 17 Nov. 1883, p. 3; 26 Jan. 1884, p. 3.

28. Testimony of James M. McIntosh, 13 Oct. 1883, U. S. Senate Committee on Education and Labor, *Report on Relations Between Capital and Labor,* I (1885), 151.

29. New York Bureau of Labor Statistics, *Annual Report* (1885), pp. 479–495. The British statistician, Robert Griffith, recorded that "thousands" of mechanics crossed to America each year for the boom season (U. K., *Emigration and Immigration, B. P. P.,* 1888, XI, p. 11). Testimony of John Quinland, Inspector of Contract Labor, New York, 25 July 1899, U. S. Industrial Commission, *Immigration,* XV (1901), 122–123. See also testimony of Judson Cross, U. S. Secretary of Treasury, *Causes Inciting Immigration* (1892), I, 187, 209, 210; Report of Commissioner J. Shulteis, 19 Jan. 1892, *ibid.,* p. 282; W. H. Wilkins, "Immigration in the United States," *Nineteenth Century,* CLXXVI (Oct. 1891), 588.

30. George E. McNeill, *Labor Movement* (New York, 1887), p. 258. The Miners National Association was founded in Belleville in 1861 and fared well during the war. British workers who came out to this region at that time were strongly union-minded (Andrew Roy, *A History of the Coal Miners of the United States,* Columbus, 1903, pp. 63–67).

31. Wages were reduced 20 per cent during 1865 in the anthracite mines of Pennsylvania (Peter Roberts, *The Anthracite Coal Industry,* New York, 1901, pp. 109–110). For other mines which reduced wages in spite of strikes, see Manchester Coal Co., *Annual Report* (1866), p. 10; Lehigh Coal Co., *Annual Report* (1866), pp. 8, 9; Pittsburgh and Boston Mining Co., *Annual Report* (March 1866), p. 7; Locust Dale Coal Co., *Report of Directors* (1867), pp. 4–6. Average daily wages in the mines were $2.58 in 1864 and $1.75 in 1865 according to U. S. Bureau of Labor Statistics, Bulletin, no. 604, *History of Wages in the United States* (1934), pp. 300–301.

32. *Workingman's Advocate,* 29 Nov. 1873, p. 1; *Fincher's Trades Review,* 30 Sept. 1865, p. 14.

33. See, for example, letter from Thomas Jordan, Pekin, Tazewell County, Illinois, 17 Feb. 1864, *Miner and Workman's Advocate,* London, 2 April 1864, p. 8; also letter of 22 Jan. 1864, printed *ibid.,* 27 Feb. 1864, p. 7; letters from William Wilson, Pittston, Penn., printed *ibid.,* 19 March 1864, p. 7; 30 July 1864, p. 7; 8 April 1865, p. 6; 9 Sept. 1865, p. 6; letter from William Williamson, Coultersville, Allegheny Co., Penn., on behalf of the Miners Association, Lodge no. 7, printed *ibid.,* 2 April 1864, p. 8; letter from miners, four North of England, one Staffordshire, two Scottish, one Lancashire, and one Welsh, in *The Mining Journal,* London, 25 March 1865, p. 191.

34. *Fincher's Trades Review,* 30 Sept. 1865, p. 14.

35. Samuel Thomas, Plymouth, to Thomas Thomas, Cwndare, 4 July 1865, Aberdare *Times,* 5 Aug. 1865, p. 4.

36. Contract between Mr. Filley and 25 Prussian Molders, *Iron Molders Journal,*

10 May 1864, p. 16. This contract is printed in full in Jonathan Grossman, *William Sylvis* (New York, 1945), pp. 281–282.

37. Clipping from St. Louis *Democrat*, 16 April 1864, in *Fincher's Trades Review*, 30 April 1864, p. 86; *Iron Molders International Journal*, 10 May 1864, p. 15.

38. *Fincher's Trades Review*, 30 April 1864, p. 87; *Workingman's Advocate*, 2 Nov. 1867, p. 2.

39. *Fincher's Trades Review*, 23 Dec. 1865, p. 28.

40. The *Iron Molders International Journal*, edited by Sylvis, suspended publication from 15 Jan. 1865 until Jan. 1867. *Fincher's*, edited by Jonathan Fincher during 1865 and 1866, was the official "voice" of the Sons of Vulcan, but Sylvis became a frequent contributor. *Fincher's Trades Review*, 8 Oct. 1864, p. 74; 16 July 1864, p. 26; 17 June 1865, p. 22; 16 Dec. 1865, p. 20; 15 July 1865, p. 52; 30 Sept. 1865, p. 141; 23 Dec. 1865, pp. 39–40; 1 Jan. 1866, p. 43.

41. *Fincher's Trades Review*, 8 July 1865, p. 45. John Williams to Steele, President of the Scottish Iron Moulders Friendly Society, *Fincher's Trades Review*, 23 June 1866, p. 215.

42. Colin Thomson, Michael M'Laren and David Campbell, Chicago, July 1865, to Scottish Iron Moulders, printed in *Monthly Report* and reprinted in *Fincher's Trades Review*, 23 June 1866, p. 214; *Iron Age*, 18 Jan. 1866, p. 2; Friendly Society of Iron Founders of Scotland, "Minutes," 8 May 1863—Aug. 1866, *passim; Iron Age*, 18 Jan. 1866, p. 2; *Fincher's Trades Review*, 6 Jan. 1866, p. 45.

43. Reports of President Ward to the Regular Quarterly Meeting of the American Iron and Steel Association, Washington, 1866, *Iron Age*, 8 March 1866, p. 1; Address of Sons of Vulcan to Iron Workers of Great Britain, Aberdare *Times*, 16 June 1866, p. 4.

44. Aberdare *Times*, 16 June 1866, p. 4.

45. *Fincher's Trades Review*, 12 May 1866, p. 187.

46. William Hudson, Pittsburgh, 27 Feb. 1866, to wife and friends; John Cherrington, Pittsburgh, 27 Feb. 1866; Benjamin Reynolds, Pittsburgh, 27 Feb. 1866; Thomas Stanton, Pittsburgh, 27 Feb. 1866, all printed in *Beehive*, 24 March 1866.

47. Aberdare *Times*, 16 June 1866, p. 4.

48. *Iron Age*, 8 March 1866, p. 2.

49. George McNeill, *Labor Movement*, p. 406. William Weihe, a puddler, stated before a Senate committee in 1883 that 5,000–6,000 iron workers had been involved in this strike (Senate Committee on Education and Labor, *Report*, 1885, II, 809).

50. *Vulcan Record*, vol. I (1874), no. 13, pp. 35–36. William Weihe estimated that 2,000 Belgian workers were brought in, but this was a later recollection (Senate Committee on Education and Labor, *Report*, II, 809); Pennsylvania, *Annual Report of Secretary of Internal Affairs*, X (1880–81), 283; McNeill, *Labor Movement*, p. 306; Leland Baldwin, *Pittsburgh*, p. 330.

51. *Workingman's Advocate*, 2 Nov. 1867, p. 2. See above, p. 41.

52. *Vulcan Record*, vol. I (1874), no. 13, p. 36.

53. Penn., *Annual Report Secretary of Internal Affairs*, X (1880–81), 283; *Working-*

man's *Advocate,* 10 Aug. 1867, p. 2. Weihe said in 1883 that the Belgians had partly broken the strike since employers took back only the best of the old hands. The union had not been strong enough to stand by all its members. Nevertheless, the Belgians did not remain long in the ironworks (Senate Committee on Education and Labor, II, 809).

54. *Workingman's Advocate,* 2 Nov. 1867, p. 2.

55. *Workingman's Advocate,* 25 Dec. 1869, p. 2. See also *The Life, Speeches, . . . of William Sylvis,* ed. James Sylvis, (Philadelphia, 1872), p. 186.

56. *Fincher's Trades Review,* 26 March 1864, p. 6.

57. Address of Sons of Vulcan to Iron Workers of Great Britain, Aberdare *Times,* 16 June 1866, p. 4. Sylvis also declared war on English "blacklegs" (Grossman, *William Sylvis,* p. 148).

58. Report by Sylvis, 2 Jan. 1867, Boston *Weekly Voice,* 10 Jan. 1867, p. 2; *Beehive,* 21 Sept. 1867; 27 Sept. 1867; letter of three Scottish molders to Scottish Moulders Society, 22 Jan. 1868, *Workingman's Advocate,* 21 March 1868, p. 2; Executive Committee of Friendly Society of Iron Founders of England, Ireland, and Wales, "Minute Book," 29 May 1867, 26 June 1867. The Committee decided on 31 July 1867 to publish letters from America in their *Monthly Journal.*

59. Sylvis to Scottish Moulders Society, 22 Jan. 1868, *Workingman's Advocate,* 21 March 1868, p. 2; Daniel Guile to William Saffin, 13 July 1871, *Iron Molders Journal,* 31 July 1871, pp. 7–8.

60. Saffin to Guile, 20 July 1871, *Iron Molders International Journal,* 31 July 1871, pp. 6–7. See pp. 6–8 for discussion of the plan.

61. *Iron Molders International Journal,* 31 Aug. 1871, p. 16; 30 Sept. 1871, p. 1.

62. *I. M. I. J.,* 30 April 1873, p. 8. Fraser, Secy. of Associated Iron Moulders of Scotland, to Saffin, 12 Oct. 1872, *I. M. I. J.,* 31 Oct. 1872, p. 4; *I. M. I. J.,* 31 Aug. 1872, p. 7.

63. *I. M. I. J.,* 31 Oct. 1872, p. 3; 28 Feb. 1873, p. 7.

64. *I. M. I. J.,* 31 Aug. 1872, pp. 7–8; 30 Sept. 1872, p. 8; 10 Dec. 1875, p. 534.

65. Friendly Society of Iron Founders of England, Ireland and Wales, *Annual Report* for 1874, p. xix; *Iron Molders Journal,* 10 Jan. 1875, p. 183.

66. *I. M. J.,* 10 Jan. 1875, pp. 179–180; 10 March 1875, p. 246.

67. *I. M. J.,* 10 Jan. 1880, p. 2; 10 Jan. 1878, p. 16; 10 Sept. 1882, p. 5; *Iron Workers Journal,* 1 March 1877, p. 4; 1 Feb. 1877, p. 4.

68. Amalgamated Association of Carpenters, *Eighth Annual Report* (1867), p. 5; warning from Chicago Secretary, Manchester *Guardian,* 5 April 1872, p. 7; 23 March 1872, p. 8; Amalgamated Society of Engineers, *Thirtieth Annual Report,* p. xi. See also Steam Engine Makers Society, *Sixteenth Annual Report* (1884), p. ix.

69. Amalgamated Society of Engineers, *Annual Report* (1873), pp. 208–221; *Rules* (1874), p. 174.

70. New York Bureau of Labor Statistics, *Annual Report* (1885), pp. 488–489. Testimony of Judson N. Cross, 20 Jan. 1892, U. S. Secy of Treas., *Causes Inciting Emigration* (1892), I, 183–184.

71. U. S. Ind. Comm., *Immigration,* XV (1901), 310.

72. *Fincher's Trades Review,* 30 Sept. 1865, p. 141. *Beehive,* 7 April 1866, p. 7. *Commonwealth,* 2 June 1866, p. 5.

73. Letter from "Oblique," Cleveland, 7 Sept. 1865, printed in *Workingman's Advocate*, 30 Sept. 1865, pp. 6–7.

74. H. McLaughlin, Chicago, to John O. Edwards, 27 Dec. 1870, *Vulcan Record* for six months ending 31 Dec. 1870, Cincinnati, pp. 31–32.

75. William Martin, Pittsburgh, to E. Trow, 29 Oct. 1879; Report of the Secretary of the National Lodge to the Officers and Representatives of the Fifth Annual Convention, both printed in Amalgamated Association of Iron and Steel Workers, *Journal of Proceedings*, 3–9 Aug. 1880, Pittsburgh, pp. 363 367. See also *The Trades*, Philadelphia, 27 Dec. 1879, p. 2.

76. J. Jarrett and W. Martin to the Iron and Steel Workers of England, Scotland and Wales, A. A. I. S. W., *Journal of Proceedings*, 1–10 Aug. 1882, Chicago, p. 856.

77. E. Trow, Darlington, to W. Martin, 24 Sept. 1881, A. A. I. S. W., 1–10 Aug. 1882, p. 857.

78. *Labor Enquirer*, Denver, 26 Jan. 1883, p. 3.

79. A. A. I. S. W., *Journal of Proceedings*, 5–13 Aug. 1884, Pittsburgh, p. 1374.

80. New York *Sun*, 27 May 1882, p. 1.

81. *Labor Standard*, Patterson, 17 June 1882, p. 1. See also U. S. Ind. Comm., *Immigration*, XV (1901), 424; (1898), p. xxxviii.

82. Andrew Roy, *The Coal Miner* (Cleveland, 1876), pp. 69, 186, 228–231, 241–242, 358–359, 134–135; *Workingman's Advocate*, 29 Nov. 1873, p. 1. For discussion, see Berthoff, *British Immigrants*, pp. 92–93.

83. MacDonald noted, "They have even taken our very name" (Miners National Association, Conference at Barnsley, Yorks., 17–21 Nov. 1874, p. 19). See also *Workingman's Advocate*, 29 Nov. 1873, p. 1; Roy, *The Coal Miners*, pp. 153, 157; Norman J. Ware, *The Labor Movement in the United States, 1860–1885* (New York, 1929), p. 33.

84. MacDonald was in touch with the National Labor Union during his first two trips to America (*Workingman's Advocate*, 14 Sept. 1867, p. 2; 2 Nov. 1867, p. 2; 16 Nov. 1867, p. 2; 18 Dec. 1869, pp. 2–3; 25 Dec. 1869, p. 2).

85. *The Mining Journal*, 8 Jan. 1870, p. 32; *Iron and Coal Trades Review*, 6 April 1877, p. 374; "Report by Alexander MacDonald to the Members of the Miners National Union on the Conditions and Prospects of Labour in the United States," n. d. [c. 1876], Miners Association Headquarters, Durham, England.

86. Leeds *Mercury*, 16 Oct. 1879.

87. Glasgow *Sentinel*, 8 Dec. 1877, p. 5. I have been able to find only a six months' file of this valuable newspaper at the Mitchell Library in Glasgow. Thomas Johnston lost his complete file during the war. See also New York *Tribune*, 26 Aug. 1879. p. 4; *The Trades*, 15 Nov. 1879, p. 3.

88. Durham Miners Association, "Minutes and Balance Sheets," July to Dec. 1877, *passim;* E. Welbourne, *The Miners of Northumberland and Durham* (Cambridge, 1923), p. 181; John Wilson, *A History of the Durham Miners* (Durham, 1908), p. 131.

89. D. M. A., "Minutes of Committee Meeting," 9 Oct. 1879, p. 3; "Minutes of Ordinary Council Meeting," 22 Nov. 1879, pp. 1–2. Crawford took the trip to counteract the influence of articles in the *Pall Mall Gazette* about poor steerage accommodations on Inman Line ships. His trip was probably not altogether

disinterested (William Crawford, "In the Steerage," pamphlet at Miners Association Headquarters, Durham, England); *Iron and Coal Trades Review,* 9 Nov. 1883, p. 583.

90. Welbourne. *The Miners of Northumberland and Durham,* pp. 212–213; Liverpool *Mercury* (11 April 1879) stated during the strike that 400 families had left Durham within a few days for America.

91. D. M. A., "Monthly Report," Oct. 1881, p. 3.

92. Roy, *The Coal Miners,* pp. 260–261, 418–419.

93. Testimony of John Keogh, Fall River, Mass, Senate Comm. on Education and Labor, *Report* (1885), III, 496; letter from Philadelphia, *Textile Manufacturer,* Manchester, 15 July 1881, p. 261; Robert Howard complained that British unions sent men irrespective of the injury done operatives in America (*John Swinton's Paper,* 6 Jan. 1884, p. 1). However the Bolton Operative Cotton Spinners noted depression in the United States cotton trade as a deterrent to emigration (*Fifth Annual Report,* 1885, pp. 14–15).

94. *Iron Molders Journal,* 10 Dec. 1875, p. 524; Carroll D. Wright, "Strikes in Massachusetts," Mass. Bureau of Labor Statistics, *Eleventh Annual Report* (1879), p. 42. See Berthoff, *British Immigrants,* p. 97.

95. W. C. Ford, "Report to the Bureau of Statistics," *House Executive Documents,* 49C., 2S., no. 157, quoted in Abbott, *Historical Aspects,* pp. 383, 389–390; Blanche E. Hazard, *The Organization of the Boot and Shoe Industry in Massachusetts* (Harvard University Press, 1921), p. 144. New York State Workingman's Assembly (*Sixth Annual Session,* pp. 12–14) described German locals in the boot and shoe and tailoring industries. German locals deteriorated considerably between 1870 and 1871 (New York State Workingman's Assembly, *Seventh Annual Session,* p. 14). Compare Wittke, *We Who Built America,* p. 237; Frederic Meyers, "The Economic Philosophy of Organized Labor," Ph.D. Thesis (Univ. of N. C., 1941), p. 135.

96. *Allgemeine Auswanderungs Zeitung,* 13 Nov. 1863, p. 182; 21 Feb. 1867, p. 33; 13 Aug. 1868, p. 141; Wisconsin, *Annual Report of the Commissioner of Immigration* (1882), p. 11.

97. Ware, *Labor Movement,* p. 10.

98 *Workingman's Advocate,* 1 Sept. 1866, p. 1. The Committee called on Johnson 25 Aug. 1866 (*Iron Age,* 30 Aug. 1866).

99. According to the constitution adopted in Geneva in 1866, one of the objects of the I. W. A. was "To counteract the intrigues of capitalists always ready, in cases of strikes and lockouts, to misuse the workman of one country as a tool against the workman of another, is one of the particular functions which our society has hitherto performed with success" (I. W. A., "Resolutions of Congress at Geneva," 1866. Compare Commons *et al., History of Labor,* II, 136). Sylvis, *Life, Speeches,* pp. 186, 211–212.

100. Commons, *et al., Documentary History,* IX, 333–334; *Workingman's Advocate,* 2 Nov. 1867, p. 2. The I. W. A. Council in London noted the proposed visit of an American delegate (*Beehive,* 10 Aug. 1867, p. 1).

101. "Report of the Fourth International Workingman's Assembly," 1869, pp. 34–35; *Workingman's Advocate,* 23 Oct. 1869, p. 2; 25 Dec. 1869, p. 2; *Beehive,* 2 Oct. 1869, p. 6.

102. *Workingman's Advocate,* 27 Aug. 1870, p. 2; 13 Aug. 1870, p. 2.

103. 7 Nov. 1879, p. 4, col. 5.

104. William R. Jones to E. V. McCandless, 25 Feb. 1875, in Bridge, *Inside History of the Carnegie Steel Company*, p. 81.

105. Carroll D. Wright, "Strikes in Massachusetts," Mass. Bureau of Statistics of Labor, *Eleventh Annual Report* (1879), p. 63; M. T. Copeland, *Cotton Manufacturing Industry of the United States* (Harvard University Press, 1912), p. 127

106. New York *Tribune*, 26 June 1879, p. 4.

107. Wright, "Strikes in Massachusetts," p. 60; H. H. Earl, *A Centennial History of Fall River* (New York, 1877), p. 111.

108. See remarks of envoy to the United States sent by English textile manufacturers, *Textile Manufacturer*, Manchester, 15 Nov. 1879, pp. 377, 379. Compare Charles B. Spahr, "Old Factory Towns," *Outlook*, Feb. 1899, p. 292. See also T. M. Young, *The American Cotton Industry* (London, 1902), pp. 4, 18, 45.

4. AGENCIES IN EUROPE FOR RECRUITING UNSKILLED INDUSTRIAL LABOR

1. Harry Jerome, *Migration and the Business Cycle* (National Bureau of Economic Research, 1926), p. 26; Brinley Thomas, *Migration and Economic Growth* (Cambridge University Press, 1954), pp. 83–122; Dorothy S. Thomas, *Social and Economic Aspects of Swedish Population Movements* (New York, 1941), pp. 88–92.

2. *Catholic Encyclopedia*, V, 403.

3. Richard Purcell, "The Irish Emigrant Society of New York," *Studies*, Dublin (Dec. 1938), pp. 588, 590, 591.

4. Massachusetts State Board of Charities, *Second Annual Report* (1866), p. 241.

5. Oscar Handlin, *Boston's Immigrants* (Harvard University Press, 1941), p. 64; Purcell, "The Irish Emigrant Society of New York," pp. 595–596; Robert Ernst, *Immigrant Life in New York City, 1825–1863* (New York, 1949), p. 64.

6. See *Irish-American*, 29 July 1854, p. 3; New Yorker *Staatszeitung*, 13 Feb. 1853, p. 4.

7. Irene Neu, "Erastus Corning, a Business Biography," Ph.D. Thesis (Cornell University, 1949), p. 232.

8. J. N. Brooks, Ste. St. Marie, to John F. Seymour, 30 Sept. 1854, "Memorandum of Agreement between Michigan Central Line and St. Mary Falls Ship Canal Co.," 1854, St. Mary's Falls Ship Canal Co. Papers, Cornell Collection of Regional History.

9. D. C. Whitund, Detroit, to J. F. Seymour, 28 Sept. 1854, *ibid.*

10. Roswell B. Mason, Chicago, to William F. Burrall, 10 Aug. 1853; Mason to Burrall, 4 July 1853, Vault, General Offices of the Illinois Central Railroad, Chicago, cited hereafter as G. O. I. C. See also advertisement reproduced in Paul W. Gates, *The Illinois Central Railroad and Its Colonization Work* (Harvard University Press, 1934), facing p. 96.

11. M. Brayman, Chicago, to Robert Schuyler, 29 Sept. 1852, Letter Box No. 6, Illinois Central Papers, Newberry Library.

12. Mason, Vandalia, Ill., to Robert Schuyler, 22 April 1853, copy from files of C. J. Corliss.

13. Mason to Burrall, 10 Aug. 1853. By July Phelps had arranged transportation for the men (Mason, Chicago, to Burrall, 4 July 1853, Vault, G. O. I. C.).

14. Mason, Chicago, to Schuyler, 14 March 1853, G. O. I. C.

15. Mason to Schuyler, 14 March 1853, G. O. I. C.

16. Mason, Jonesboro, to Schuyler, 3 April 1853, G. O. I. C.

17. Mason, La Salle, to Schuyler, 18 April 1853, copy from files of C. J. Corliss.

18. Mason, Chicago, to Burrall, 4 July 1853, G. O. I. C.

19. Mason to Schuyler, Vandalia, 22 April 1853, copy from files of C. J. Corliss.

20. For laws of Alabama, Georgia, and Arkansas relative to contract labor, see U. S. *Reports of the Immigration Commission, Senate Documents*, 61c., 2s., 1909–10, no. 662, XXI, 513–515, 625–627, 530–532. Virginia and Florida aimed more specifically at getting people with capital to buy land (*ibid.*, pp. 613–614). Notices of contract terms available to immigrants to Alabama, Texas, and other southern states appeared in Malmö *Nya Allehanda*, 18 May 1870, p. 1; *Allgemeine Auswanderungs Zeitung*, 7 Feb. 1867, p. 25; 14 Feb. 1867, p. 28; 16 Sept. 1869, p. 147; 26 July 1866, p. 118; *Adressebladet*, 19 Oct. 1867, p. 1.

21. *Allgemeine Auswanderungs Zeitung*, 20 May 1869, p. 80. See also 2 Aug. 1866, p. 123. Warnings against contracts appeared in Malmö *Nya Allehanda*, 28 May 1870, p. 2.

22. *Hemlandet*, 2 Feb. 1869, p. 2.

23. Missouri Board of Immigration, *Report* (1870), p. 3.

24. Wisconsin Commissioners of Immigration, *First Annual Report* (1871), pp. 9, 156; *Second Annual Report* (1872), pp. 29–30, 39; *Third Annual Report* (1873), p. 157.

25. Wisconsin, "Ein Bericht Über Bevölkerung," pamphlet (1881), p. 20; Wisconsin Board of Immigration, "Soil, Climate, . . . of Wisconsin" (1885), p. 23; "Wisconsin, What it Offers," 1879.

26. Wisconsin Commissioners of Immigration, *Annual Report* (1881), pp. 12, 13; Jönköpings *Tidning*, 30 May 1881, p. 4; Wisconsin Central Railroad, "Wisconsin Central Railroad Lands" (1881), pp. 12, 18, collection of railroad pamphlets lent by Paul W. Gates.

27. K. K. Kennan, "Der Staat Wisconsin, Seine Hülfsquelle und Vorzuge für Auswanderer," Basle, Schweiz, n. d.

28. Qualey, *Norwegian Settlement*, p. 174; M. A. Allardt, Michigan Commissioner of Immigration, "Geographische und Statistische Beschreibung des Staates Michigan" (Hamburg, 1872), p. 21.

29. See, for example, *American Settler*, London, Feb. 1873, p. 8; *Allgemeine Auswanderungs Zeitung*, 15 July 1869, p. 112; extract from Minnesota Board of Immigration, *Report* (1871), pp. 61–69, in Abbott, *Historical Aspects*, p. 171.

30. Advertisement for "New Sweden" in *Amerika*, 5 July 1871, p. 4; 1 Sept. 1870, p. 5; Malmö *Nya Allehanda*, 19 April 1871, p. 3. Compare Janson, *Background*

to *Swedish Immigration,* pp. 255–256; Maine Board and Commissioner of Immigration, *Report* (1870), pp. 5, 7.

31. George S. Harris to John Brown, 9 July 1863. See also Harris to Brown, Roscommon Co., Ireland, 14 Jan. 1864; Harris to Brown, 26 May 1863; Harris to Rev. John Hogan, 6 April 1864, Hannibal and St. Joseph Land Commission Records, Newberry Library.

32. Harris to Wm. Griffiths, Glamorganshire, So. Wales, 11 July 1864; "600,000 Acres of Hannibal and St. Joseph Railroad Lands" (Hannibal, 1859), pp. 18, 31. Compare "Emigration to the U. S. of North America . . . Indiana as a Home for Emigrants," published under Oliver P. Morton, Governor of Indiana, Indianapolis (1864), pp. 14, 19, Gates Collection.

33. *Railroad Gazette,* VIII (14 Jan. 1875), 24; VII (9 Jan. 1875), 14.

34. "Lands of the Central Pacific Company of California" (Sacramento, 1868), Gates Collection.

35. Aberdare *Times,* 9 April 1870, p. 2; *Justitia,* 27 May 1871, p. 2; *Das Auswanderer,* 15 Nov. 1872, p. 4.

36. "Guide to the Lands of the Northern Pacific Railroad in Minnesota," Land Department, Northern Pacific Railroad (New York, 1872), p. 22; "Homes in the New Northwest of America," n. d. p. 13, Gates Collection.

37. Article by Hans Mattson in *Amerika,* 6 Dec. 1871, p. 2. See also offers of work in railroads, building, and mining from Mattson in *Sverige och Amerika,* 26 Jan. 1872, p. 4.

38. *Skandinavisk Post,* New York, 9 March 1870, p. 4. See also California Immigrant Union which offered settlers forty acres of land and railroad jobs at $2.50 to $3.00 a day while the road was under construction (*Skandinavisk Post,* 14 Aug. 1871, p. 3).

39. "Missouri and Kansas! Homes for All," North Missouri Railroad (St. Louis, 1870), p. 22. "Guide to the Lands of the Jackson, Lansing and Saginaw Railroad Company in Michigan" (Mason, Mich., 1875), p. 28; "How and Where to get a Living, a Sketch of the Garden of the West," Atcheson, Topeka and Santa Fe Railroad (Boston, 1876), pp. 5, 7, 30; "Resources of Kansas, It's Development and Future," Atcheson, Topeka, and Santa Fe Railroad (Topeka, n. d. [1884]), Gates Collection.

40. Henry Wilson to William Hockins, Darlington, England, 5 April 1872. See also Wilson to James Gilliland, Bradford, England, 5 April 1872, Burlington Railroad, *Foreign Agency Papers,* Newberry Library.

41. Harris, Form Letter, 1873, Burlington and Missouri Railroad, *Land Department Papers.*

42. See, for example, advertisements in *Beehive,* 20 May 1871, p. 10; 15 April 1871, p. 8.

43. Wilson to Wm. S. Clarke, Ship Broker, Crew Kerne, 5 April 1872, B. M. R., *Foreign Agency Papers.*

44. *Railroad Gazette,* XIII (6 May 1881), 252; (23 Sept. 1881), 526.

45. *Railroad Gazette,* XIV (17 Feb. 1882), 105.

46. *Railroad Gazette,* XIV (1 Dec. 1882), 741; XV (23 Feb. 1883), 122.

47. *Railroad Gazette,* XVI (1 Aug. 1884), 569.

48. *Railroad Gazette,* XIII (28 Jan. 1881), 53.

49. "The People's Guide to Dakota, the Land of Promise," Chicago, Milwaukee and St. Paul Railroad, n. d. [1883], pp. 19, 25.

50. Evan R. Jones, *The Emigrant's Friend for 1883,* Pitt and Scott, London.

51. *Railway Age,* 28 April 1881.

52. Harris to Hollut, 5 March 1870, B. M. R., *Land Department Papers,* quoted in Richard Overton, *Burlington West* (Harvard University Press, 1941), p. 303. However, in 1873 the French were included in the Burlington's foreign advertising (*ibid.,* p. 347). See also letter from K. K. Kennan of the Wisconsin Bureau of Immigration to Albert H. Sanford, writer of an article "The Polish People of Portage County," Wisconsin State Historical Society, *Proceedings* (1907), p. 270n.

53. Contrast with view of William Carlson Smith, *Americans in the Making* (New York, 1939), p. 42: "While the steamship agent operated for many years in Northwestern Europe, he developed his activities very largely in connection with the 'newer' immigration."

54. In 1864, 349 sailing vessels carrying 102,070 steerage passengers arrived at the port of New York while only 197 steamships carrying 78,200 passengers put in at that port. In 1865, steamers were carrying more passengers, with 257 steamers arriving at New York with 131,251 passengers and 302 sailing vessels with only 84,431 passengers (New York State Commissioners of Emigration, *Annual Report* (1864), p. 52; 1865, p. 17). See also 1866, pp. 99–100.

55. Janson, *Background to Swedish Immigration,* pp. 241ff.

56. *Report on Transit of Scandinavian Emigrants, B. P. P.* (1882), LXII, 2, 7. Letter on handling of emigrants forwarded over Hamburg is in *Svenska Konsulars ·Skrivelser,* New York, 1866, no. 8, Edward Habicht, 13 Oct. 1866, Riksarkivet, Stockholm.

57. *Justitia,* Chicago, 11 March 1871, p. 2.

58. *Amerika,* Gothenberg, 16 Dec. 1870. Petitions from H. A. Burger, 2 Jan. 1870, *Avgående Skrivelser, Beskickningen i Washington Archiv,* 1869; 8 Jan. 1870, *ibid.,* 1870. George Stephenson characterized Burger as a "sharp businessman, a good mixer," who was able to get the confidence of men on whose influence he could capitalize (George M. Stephenson, "The Stormy Years of the Swedish Colony in Chicago before the Great Fire," *Transactions of the Illinois Historical Society,* no. 36, 1929, p. 178).

59. Malmö *Nya Allehanda,* 3 July 1869, p. 3; *Skånska Posten,* 14 July 1869. Announcements that Burger himself would meet passengers in New York City and procure work for them appeared in *Skånska Posten,* 23 Feb. 1870, p. 4; Hudiksvalla *Posten,* 5 March 1870, p. 4; *Svenska Amerikanaren,* 19 April 1870, p. 2; *Amerika,* 12 May 1870, p. 7. The Chicago Bureau was run by N. B. Storm, a Swedish-American.

60. *Adressebladet,* Christiana, 1 March 1882, p. 4.

61. *Amerika,* 17 March 1870, p. 5; 29 April 1871, p. 3.

62. Hudiksvalla *Posten,* 2 April 1870, p. 2; *Amerika Bladet,* July 1870, p. 35; *Kristianstadsbladet,* 19 June 1880, p. 4.

63. Montreal Steamship Company, "Några Wälmenta Råd" (1868). *Kristianstads-*

bladet carried State Line and Allan Line labor bureau advertisements (*Kristianstadsbladet,* 24 May 1880, p. 4; 31 May 1880, p. 4; 9 May 1881, p. 4).

64. *Amerika,* 13 April 1872, p. 3. For another case, see *Nya Werlden,* Gothenberg, 17 Feb. 1873, p. 3.

65. *Kristianstadsbladet,* 19 March 1881 p. 4.

66. *Adressebladet,* 24 March 1880, p. 4.

67. U. S. Bureau of Labor Statistics, *History of Wages* (*Bulletin,* no. 604, pp. 330–331), gave average wages for miners in Pennsylvania in 1881 as $2.37 per day.

68. Letter from C. E. Dahlgren and August Bergström, Falun; Anders Pettersson, Aspeboda; Carl Bergström, Filipstad; John Granin, Dannemora, *Kristianstadsbladet,* 20 July 1881, p. 2.

69. Jönköpings *Tidning,* 28 July 1866, p. 1; 15 Aug. 1866, p. 1. *Adressebladet,* 24 Jan. 1866, p. 4; 15 Aug. 1866, p. 4; Malmö *Nya Allehanda,* 28 July 1866, p. 4.

70. Advertisement in Jönköpings *Posten,* 11 Aug. 1866, quoted in Janson, *Background,* p. 238.

71. *Adressebladet,* 26 Sept. 1866, p. 3, quoting *Morgonbladet. Folkstidende,* Mandal, 28 Nov. 1866, pp. 1–3; Jönköpings *Tidning,* 10 Oct. 1866, p. 3.

72. Report from Habicht, 13 Oct. 1866, *Svenska Konsulars Skrivelser,* New York, 1866, Riksarkivet.

73. Missouri Board of Immigration, *Report* (1865–66), cited in Albert H. Leisinger, "The Federal Act to Encourage Immigration," M. A. Thesis (Cornell, 1938), p. 78n.

74. Jönköpings *Tidning,* 10 Oct. 1866, quoted in Janson, *Background,* p. 239; Habicht, 13 Oct. 1866, *loc. cit;* Missouri Board of Immigration, *Report* (1870), p. 12, Appendix C.

75. Stephenson, *Trans. Ill. Hist. Soc.,* no. 36, p. 178; clipping from *Svenska-Amerikanaren* in *Kristianstadsbladet,* 28 July, pp. 2–3; *Amerika-Bladet,* 30 Nov. 1869, p. 3.

76. *Amerika-Bladet,* 15 Feb. 1870, p. 4; 1 May 1870; July 1870, *passim; Amerika,* 16 Dec. 1869.

77. *Amerika,* 12 May 1870, p. 7.

78. *Amerika,* 8 Sept. 1870, p. 8.

79. *Amerika-Bladet,* Örebro, 15 Feb. 1870, p. 4; *Amerika,* 21 April 1870, p. 3.

80. Hudiksvalla *Posten,* 17 June 1871, p. 4; *Amerika,* 19 April 1871, p. 2; 13 Jan. 1871, p. 8.

81. Letter from Thomas Simpson, N. J. and Midland Railroad Company Office, 25 Nassau St., New York City, to Gustaf Akerström, *Amerika,* 5 Jan. 1872, p. 4; 13 April 1872, p. 3.

82. *Amerika,* 5 Jan. 1870.

83. *Sverige och Amerika,* Jönköping, 8 Dec. 1871, p. 4.

84. *Amerika,* 10 Feb. 1871, p. 6; *Justitia,* 27 May 1871, p. 3.

85. Edward Taube to Wetterstedt, 2 June 1868, *Beskickningen i Washington Archiv,* 1868, *Inkomna Skrivelser,* Riksarkivet.

86. Alice Smith, "Caleb Cushing," *Wisconsin Magazine of History* (Sept. 1944),

p. 17. The plight of these emigrants was described in *Amerika-Bladet*, 9 Nov. 1869, p. 2; 22 Feb. 1870, p. 3; and A. Lowenhaupt, 14 Oct. 1870, *Depescher från Beskickningen in Förenta Staterna* (1870), Riksarkivet, Stockholm.

87. Janson, *Background*, p. 241; *Kristianstadsbladet*, 1 April 1868, p. 4; Malmö *Nya Allehanda*, 11 May 1870, p. 4.

88. *Beehive*, 23 April 1870, p. 157; *Free West*, London, Supplement, 8 Oct. 1870, p. 4; *Free West*, 10 Sept. 1870, p. 1. The Company changed its name in 1873 to Anglo-American Land, Labour, and Colonization Agency (*Free West*, April 1873, p. 269).

89. *Free West*, 26 Nov. 1870, p. 188; *Beehive*, 1 April 1871, p. 8.

90. W. R. Dixon, Agent for Royal Mail Steamships, City Emigration and Shipping Offices, London, *Beehive*, 8 April 1871, p. 8; 6 May 1871, p. 8. Advertisement of J. M. McLean and Co., emigration offices, Newcastle-on-Tyne, in Jones, *The Emigrant's Friend* (1882 revision).

91. U. S. Secretary of Treasury, *Causes Inciting Immigration* (1892), I, 250.

92. *Allgemeine Auswanderungs Zeitung*, 1 July 1869, p. 105; former Swiss emigrant asking for two to three hundred workers for Chicago, *ibid.*, 8 April 1869, p. 57. California Labor Exchange in San Francisco offering to provide work and free railroad tickets to jobs, *ibid.*, 28 Oct. 1869, p. 170; *The Exodus of the Nineteenth Century*, German American Association of U. S. (New York, 1872), pp. 5, 7.

93. George Bancroft to Hamilton Fish, Berlin, 21 Nov. 1873, *Foreign Relations* (1873), p. 433, quoted in Merle Curti and Kendall Burr "The Immigrant and the American Image in Europe," *Mississippi Valley Historical Review*, XXXVII (Sept. 1950), 209–210.

94. Extract from Report by Consul Schvenly, U. S. *Consular Reports*, vol. IV (Dec. 1881), no. 14, pp. 625–626, in N. A. W. M., *Bulletin*, XII (1882), 99; testimony of George Jurascheck in Foreign Department of the Equitable, *House Reports, Ford Committee Report* (1889), pp. 351–352.

95. *John Swinton's Paper*, 6 Jan. 1884, p. 1.

96. *House Reports*, 48c., 1s., no. 444, p. 9.

97. Pennsylvania, *Annual Report of Secretary of Internal Affairs, Industrial Statistics*, vol. XII (1884), Pt. 3, p. 71.

98. Report of Consul Starkloff, Bremen, U. S. Dept. of Treas., *Causes Inciting Immigration* (1892), I, 214.

99. New York, Bureau of Labor Statistics (1885), pp. 509, 511; Pennsylvania, *Annual Report of Secretary of Internal Affairs*, vol. XII, Pt. 3, pp. 68, 71.

100. Isaac Hourwich, *Immigration and Labor* (New York, 1913), p. 99; U. S. *Reports of the Industrial Commission, Immigration*, XV (1901), 392.

101. New York *Tribune*, 11 June 1881, p. 5. See also Philadelphia *Times*, 25 May 1882, p. 3; New York *Tribune*, 12 Dec. 1880, p. 6.

102. Testimony of Jules Rosendale, Special Agent of the Department of Agriculture of Pennsylvania, 11 Jan. 1900, U. S. Industrial Commission, XV, 189; testimony of Guiseppe Granozio, 28 July 1888, *House Report, Ford Committee Report* (1889), pp. 120–122; report of Judson Cross, *Causes Inciting Immigration*, I, 215; Broughton Brandenburg, *Imported Americans* (New York, 1904), pp. 37–38.

103. W. H. Wilkins, "Immigration," *Nineteenth Century*, CLXXVI (Oct. 1891), 584–585. Herman J. Schulteis, sometime Commissioner of Immigration, in discussing steamship company lobbying against immigration restriction, pointed out that it was on steerage that companies made their profit. When the steerage was full, all abovedeck passengers were clear profit. They charged $22.50 on the average for steerage passage in the nineties while it cost them only $1.70 to transport the migrant (U. S. Industrial Commission, XV, pp. 24–25). Edward Corsi, *In the Shadow of Liberty* (New York, 1935), p. 51.

104. Senate Committee on Education and Labor, *Report on Relations between Capital and Labor* (1885), I, 337–338.

105. Pennsylvania, *Annual Report of Secretary of Internal Affairs*, vol. XII, Pt. 3, p. 71.

106. Wilkins, *Nineteenth Century*, CLXXVI, 585; H. P. Fairchild, *Greek Immigration to the United States* (New Haven, 1911), pp. 91–92; testimony of Robert Marzo, Manager, Italian Society of Emigration, *Ford Committee Report* (1889), p. 80. See also testimony of five immigrants who had signed such mortgages, *ibid.*, pp. 127–129; 133–135; 156–157; 162–163; 182–183.

107. *John Swinton's Paper*, 6 Jan. 1884, p. 1. He claimed to have $80,000 deposited in a bank in Naples to furnish "guaranteed bonds" of $100 for each individual. For other agencies importing on such contracts, see *John Swinton's Paper*, 27 July 1884, p. 1; *House Reports*, 48c., 1s., vol. II, no. 444; Testimony of Francisco Zapponi, *Ford Committee Report* (1889), pp. 93ff.

108. For list of such agencies, see report of Joseph Powderly, *Causes Inciting Immigration*, I, 251.

109. *John Swinton's Paper*, 18 May 1884, p. 1.

110. Other cases of agents abroad who did not make contracts, *House Reports*, 48c., 1s., vol. II, no. 444, pp. 3, 9.

111. *Labor Enquirer*, Denver, 19 Jan. 1884, p. 2; 9 Feb. 1884, p. 2.

112. See also *John Swinton's Paper*, 17 Aug. 1884, p. 2; 6 Jan. 1884, p. 1.

113. New York *Tribune*, 17 July 1882, p. 8.

114. Testimony of Robert Marzo, Angelo Antonio de Dierro, Gaetano Braccio, Domenico Cingiarella, *House Report, Ford Committee Report* (1889), pp. 5–6, 81, 89, 101, 124–127, 184–185.

115. New York *Tribune*, 3 Dec. 1878, p. 4; 7 Nov. 1878, p. 4; 25 Nov. 1879, p. 2; U. S. Industrial Commission, XV, 431; Robert F. Foerster, *The Italian Emigration of Our Time* (Harvard University Press, 1919), p. 324.

116. John Koren, "The Padrone System," U. S. Bureau of Labor, *Bulletin*, vol. II (March 1897), no. 9, p. 114.

117. *Ford Committee Report* (1889), p. 70.

118. Samuel Koenig, *Immigrant Settlements in Connecticut* (Hartford, 1938), p. 25; T. V. Powderly, *The Path I Trod*, ed. by Harry J. Carmen, Henry David, and Paul N. Guthrie (New York, 1940), p. 409.

119. *Adressebladet*, 2 Feb. 1870, pp. 1–2. See also Hudiksvalla *Posten*, 29 May 1869, p. 3; Axel Bruun, *Breve fra Amerika* (Kristiana, 1870), p. 14.

120. U. S. Industrial Commission, XV, 1x. See also testimony of Charles A. Colcord, Inspector of Immigration in Boston, 2 Aug. 1888, who concluded on the basis of questioning every passenger who came down the gangplank there that when the immigrant says he is going to work in a mill "it always dwindles down to the fact that they are sent for by some friend who is employed by

some corporation, and their fare is usually paid by this friend" (Ford Committee Report, 1889, p. 561). See also Adressebladet, 13 May 1880, p. 3; Emigrationsutredningen, VII, 223.

5. THE DISTRIBUTION OF UNSKILLED IMMIGRANTS TO INDUSTRY

1. 25 May 1882, p. 3. Compare New York Tribune, 12 Dec. 1880, p. 6.

2. See auction notices in Kristianstadsbladet, 1880–81, passim. People going to America sometimes were putting up land for auction, but many notices were from "torpare" who had only copper and ironware, furniture and such property to sell for passage money. Notice appeared in Hemlandet (19 June 1886, p. 1) of the money carried by Norwegian emigrants on two ships. The Eucharis carried 225 adults who took with them 13,840 rdr; but one man had 6,000 of these. This meant that the other 224 had about $2,000 between them. On 3 May, 655 emigrants left Stavanger, few of them, according to the papers, with any more than travel money; and many had borrowed that from relatives.

3. Land and emigration agents said that $40 to $50 was more accurate (Depeschen från Beskickningen i F. S., 1869–70, Lowenhaupt, Års Report, 17 March 1870).

4. Malmö Nya Allehanda, 18 March 1868, p. 1; Hudiksvalla Posten, 28 March 1868. Compare with letter warning Swedes not to expect their countrymen to help them find jobs, Jönköpings Tidning, 11 March 1868, p. 2.

5. E. Habicht, 1 Jan. 1870; 24 Nov. 1866, Svenska Konsulars Skrivelser, New York, 1870, 1866; George H. Garliche, Vice-Consul at Cincinnati, Report, Dec. 1869; Martin Lewis, Vice-Consul at Baltimore, to Wetterstedt, 13 Jan. 1869. Beskickningen i Washington Archiv, 1869; Count Wetterstedt, 7 Jan. 1868, Depescher från Beskickningen i F. S., 1868. For other examples, see Skånska Posten, 25 April 1866, p. 1; Malmö Nya Allehanda, 28 Aug. 1869, p. 2; Kristianstadsbladet, 28 April 1880, p. 2.

6. Lowenhaupt, Års Report, 17 March 1870, Depeschen från Beskickningen i F. S., 1869–70. Compare article on young agricultural workers from Westgotland and Småland who were "sticking in Chicago" in Svenska Posten, 2 Feb. 1870, p. 1.

7. Letter from C. G. Linderborg, Chicago, 24 Dec. 1860, Amerika-Bladet, 22 Feb. 1870, p. 3. See also 15 March 1870, p. 4; Lowenhaupt, 1 July 1870, Depescher från Beskickningen i F. S. (1870).

8. Sverige och Amerika, Jönköping, 8 Sept. 1871, p. 4; Amerika, Gothenberg, 28 April 1870, p. 3.

9. Hemlandet, Chicago, 15 Nov. 1865, p. 1; 23 Oct. 1866, p. 2.

10. In Aug. and Sept. 1866, Frederick Nelson, agent of the society, helped sixty people to find work (Hemlandet, 23 Oct. 1866, p. 2; 16 July 1867, p. 2).

11. Hemlandet, 21 July 1868, p. 3.

12. Amerika-Bladet, Örebro, 28 June 1870, p. 3; 14 June 1870, p. 3.

13. Hemlandet, 30 July 1867, p. 1; 27 Aug. 1867, p. 4; 25 Feb. 1868, p. 4; 28 April 1868, p. 2; 14 June 1870, p. 4; 10 May 1870, p. 3; Amerika, 28 April 1870, p. 3.

14. Svenska Amerikanaren, Chicago, 13 Dec. 1870, p. 3; 22 Sept. 1870, pp. 1–2; 13 Jan. 1871, p. 2.

15. Lowenhaupt, 1 July 1870, *Depescher från Beskickningen i F. S.*, 1870.

16. *Hemlandet*, 3 Oct. 1871, p. 2; *Justitia*, Chicago, 24 June 1871, p. 3.

17. Wisconsin Commissioner of Immigration, *Third Annual Report for 1873*, pp. 6–7.

18. Listed in the author's thesis at Cornell University, pp. 442–443; *Svenska Amerikanaren*, 19 April 1870, p. 1; 21 Sept. 1869, p. 3; 9 Nov. 1869, p. 2; 28 Dec. 1869, p. 2; 11 Jan. 1870, p. 2; 18 Jan. 1870, p. 2; 8 May 1870, p. 3; 29 March 1870, p. 3; *Hemlandet*, 14 May 1867, p. 1; 8 Nov. 1869, p. 3; 22 March 1870, p. 3; *Justitia*, 25 March 1871, p. 2; 27 April 1869, p. 3.

19. *Hemlandet*, 27 Oct. 1868, p. 3; *Svenska Amerikanaren*, 11 April 1871, p. 2.

20. *Railway Age*, Chicago, 10 Feb. 1881, p. 73.

21. *Svenska Amerikanaren*, 28 March 1871, p. 2; *Amerika*, 12 May 1870, p. 7.

22. *Amerika*, 12 May 1870, p. 7; *Svenska Amerikanaren*, 23 Dec. 1870, p. 3; 27 Dec. 1870, p. 3; 24 May 1870, p. 3; 18 Oct. 1870, p. 3; 1 Aug. 1871, p. 2; 15 Aug. 1871, p. 3; *Hemlandet*, 9 Nov. 1869, p. 3; 30 Nov. 1869, p. 3.

23. *Svenska Amerikanaren*, 28 March 1871, p. 2; *Hemlandet*, 15 June 1869, p. 3; 21 Sept. 1869, p. 2.

24. *Svenska Amerikanaren*, 29 March 1870, p. 3.

25. *Railway Age*, 10 Feb. 1881, p. 73; *Svenska Amerikanaren*, 29 March 1870, p. 3; 13 Sept. 1870, p. 3; 29 Nov. 1870, p. 3; 10 Jan. 1871, p. 3; 11 April 1871, p. 3; 18 July 1871, p. 3; 22 Aug. 1871, p. 3.

26. *Hemlandet*, 31 May 1870, p. 3.

27. *Svenska Amerikanaren*, 13 Sept. 1870, p. 3.

28. *Svenska Amerikanaren*, 18 Oct. 1870, p. 3.

29. *Svenska Amerikanaren*, 29 March 1870, p. 3.

30. Letter from C. G. Linderborg, Chicago, 24 Dec. 1869, *Amerika-Bladet*, 22 Feb. 1870, p. 3; *Amerika*, 12 May 1870, p. 7; *Railway Age*, 10 Feb. 1881, p. 73.

31. *Amerika-Bladet*, 22 Feb. 1870, p. 3; *Amerika*, 23 June 1870, p. 3.

32. *Amerika*, 3 March 1871, p. 7; *Hemlandet*, 1 Feb. 1870, p. 3; "Special Circular of Frans Peterson," March 1870, in *Svenska Amerikanaren*, 27 Sept. 1870, p. 2.

33. *Amerika*, 18 May 1870, pp. 2–3; *Hemlandet*, 7 July 1868, p. 2.

34. *Railway Age*, 10 Feb. 1881, p. 73.

35. H. P. Fairchild, *The Greek Immigration to the United States* (New Haven, 1911), p. 163. See also Grace Abbott, "The Chicago Employment Agency and the Immigrant Worker," *American Journal of Sociology*, XIV (Nov. 1908), 293–294.

36. *Railway Age*, 10 Feb. 1881, p. 73.

37. *Amerika*, 10 May 1871, p. 2; 11 April 1871, p. 2; *Justitia*, 11 March 1871, p. 2; 24 June 1871, p. 3; 16 May 1871, p. 2; 23 March 1871, p. 2; 15 April 1871, p. 2; 25 Feb. 1871, p. 1; 29 April 1871, pp. 1–2; *Hemlandet*, 16 March 1871, p. 2; 14 March 1871, p. 2; 23 May 1871, p. 1; *Sverige och Amerika*, 20 Oct. 1871, p. 4. See also George Stephenson, *Trans. Ill. Hist. Soc.*, no. 36, pp. 178, 180, 182.

38. Lowenhaupt, "Official Report on Norwegian and Swedish Immigration, 1870,"

Nowegian American Studies and Records, XIII (1943), 54; *Amerika,* 18 May 1870, pp. 2–3; *Railway Age,* 10 Feb. 1881, p. 73.

39. *Svenska Amerikanaren,* 14 Feb. 1871, p. 2.

40. *Railway Age,* 10 Feb. 1881, p. 73.

41. Letter from Chicago, 10 Jan. 1871, *Amerika,* 17 Feb. 1871, pp. 1–2.

42. *Hemlandet,* 26 May 1868; *Amerika-Bladet,* 22 Feb. 1870, p. 3; 28 Dec. 1869, p. 4; *Illinois Zeitung,* 1 Dec. 1869; *Amerika,* 12 May 1870, p. 7.

43. *Svenska Amerikanaren,* 29 March 1870. For statements of wages, see *Svenska Amerikanaren* and *Hemlandet,* 1868–1871, *passim; Amerika-Bladet,* 30 Nov. 1869, p. 1; *Amerika,* 17 Feb. 1871, pp. 1–2.

44. *Amerika-Bladet,* 30 Nov. 1869, p. 1; Lowenhaupt, *Norwegian American Studies and Records,* XIII, 54; *Svenska Amerikanaren,* 4 Jan. 1870, p. 2.

45. *Svenska Amerikanaren,* 9 Nov. 1869, p. 2; letter from Sun Prairie, Wis., 30 Oct. 1868, *Adressebladet,* 16 Dec. 1868, p. 4. The road from Coal Water, Mich. to Chicago offered only $1.50 a day (*Svenska Amerikanaren,* 5 Jan. 1869, p. 2).

46. Friedrich Kapp, *Immigration and the Commissioners of the State of New York* (1870), pp. 238–240.

47. *Svenska Amerikanaren,* 11 Oct. 1870, p. 2; 22 Nov. 1870, p. 2; 13 Dec. 1870; 28 Dec. 1871, p. 4.

48. Lake Superior Iron Mines, *Agents Report* (Ishpeming, 1 May 1880), p. 6. For lumbering and canal recruitment, see *Svenska Amerikanaren,* 19 July 1870, p. 2; 17 May 1870, p. 2; 25 Oct. 1870, p. 3; 29 March 1870, p. 3.

49. Carlton Qualey, "Gjerdrum's America Letters," *Norwegian American Studies and Records,* XI (1940), 88–89; Wittke, *We Who Built America,* p. 266; Alfred Bergin, *Settlement of the Swedish in Central Kansas* (Topeka? 1910), p. 21. Compare Albert H. Sanford, "The Polish People of Portage County," Wisconsin State Historical Society, *Proceedings* (1907), pp. 265–272.

50. *Report of the Select Committee Appointed by the State Legislature to Examine into Frauds upon Emigrants* (Albany, 1847).

51. Canada, *Annual Report Minister of Agriculture* (1866), p. 78; Kapp, *Immigration and the Commissioners,* pp. 115–116; New York State Commissioners of Emigration, *Annual Report* (1867), pp. 87–88. In four months of 1857, employment had been found for eight thousand through this bureau (Wittke, *We Who Built America,* p. 127).

52. New York, Commissioners of Emigration, *Annual Report* (1868), pp. 83–84; (1869), p. 106; (1870), p. 93; (1873), p. 44; (1875), p. 73; (1876), p. 42.

53. *Annual Report* (1864), p. 6; (1865), p. 4; (1870), p. 101.

54. See Appendix II.

55. See circular letter periodically sent out to employers by the Chief Clerk of the Castle Garden exchange, in Kapp, *Immigration and the Commissioners,* p. 238.

56. See Appendix II.

57. New York, Commissioner of Emigration, *Annual Report* (1875), p. 74. Circular continued to be sent to employers by the commissioners (1873, p. 41; 1879, pp. 12–13).

58. See Appendix II.

59. New York, Commissioners of Emigration, *Annual Reports* (1875–1881), *passim*.

60. See Appendix II. Edward T. Devine, *Report on the Desirability of Establishing an Employment Bureau in the City of New York* (New York, 1909), p. 14.

61. New York, Commissioners of Emigration, *Annual Report* (1867), p. 88.

62. *Annual Report* (1875), p. 6; (1880), p. 7.

63. *John Swinton's Paper,* 1 Feb. 1885, p. 1.

64. *Irish Farmer's Gazette,* 4 Sept. 1852, p. 428.

65. See, for example, Leeds *Mercury,* 29 May 1865, p. 3; John F. Maguire, *The Irish in America* (London, 1867), pp. 207–208; U. K., Colonial Land and Emigration Commissioners, *Thirtieth Report, B. P. P.* (1870), XVII, 14; American Social Science Association, "Handbook" (1871), p. 13; *Irish Farmer's Gazette,* 26 Feb. 1878, p. 34; Aberdare *Times,* 25 March 1882, p. 3.

66. *Allgemeine Auswanderungs Zeitung,* 26 Sept. 1867, p. 157; 19 Nov. 1868, p. 196; 27 Feb. 1868, p. 37; 23 Aug. 1866, p. 137; 9 Jan. 1868, p. 6; 2 Jan. 1868, pp. 2–3; *Der Ansiedler im Westen,* XVII (1879), 122–123; X (1872), 7; Deutsches Gesellschaft, New York City, "Praktische Ratschläge" (1883), p. 24.

67. See, for example, Joseph Pachmayr, *Leben und Treiben der Stadt New York* (Hamburg, 1874), pp. 110–112.

68. *John Swinton's Paper,* 1 Feb. 1885, p. 1.

69. *Amerika,* 14 April 1870, p. 3; *Amerika-Bladet,* 21 June 1870, p. 4; Lowenhaupt, *Norwegian American Studies and Records,* XIII, 51.

70. *Amerika-Bladet,* 9 Nov. 1869, p. 2.

71. A Lowenhaupt, 1 July 1870, *Despescher från Beckickningen i. F. S.,* 1870, Riksarkivet, Stockholm.

72. See Pachmayr, *Leben und Treiben,* p. 112; *Allgemeine Auswanderungs Zeitung,* 11 Feb. 1864, p. 27; 18 Feb. 1864, pp. 20–21; 7 Aug. 1863, pp. 126–127; 17 Nov. 1864, p. 188; 10 Feb. 1866, p. 25.

73. *Allgemeine Auswanderungs Zeitung,* 2 March 1865, p. 35; 15 Feb. 1866, p. 28.

74. *Der Ansiedler im Westen,* XI (1873), 160.

75. *Der Ansiedler im Westen,* VI (1868), 103.

76. *Der Ansiedler im Westen,* V (1867), 54–55, 106; VIII (1870), 57–60.

77. *Catholic Encyclopedia,* V, 403.

78. *Catholic Encyclopedia,* V, 404.

79. Devine, *Report on Establishing an Employment Bureau in New York,* pp. 113–116; Frances Kellor, *Out of Work* (New York, 1915), 2nd ed., p. 274.

80. New York City, Commission on Public Charity, *Report* (1868); Citizen's Association Report, *Iron Age,* 2 July 1868, p. 4; Copy of Resolution for a Labor Bureau adopted by Department of Public Charities and Corrections, New York, 24 June 1868, *Iron Age,* 2 July 1868, p. 4.

81. *Amerika-Bladet,* 15 Feb. 1870, p. 1.

82. *Amerika-Bladet,* 15 Feb. 1870, p. 1; *Svenska-Amerikanaren,* 30 Nov. 1869, p. 2; *Iron Molders Journal,* 10 Dec. 1874, pp. 132–133, 153.

83. New Yorker *Staats-Zeitung,* 13 Feb. 1853, p. 4; see also Ernst, *Immigrant Life in New York City,* p. 64.

84. New Yorker *Staats-Zeitung*, 10 March 1864, p. 2; Zauder, Mayer and Curtis, 4 Greenwich Street, advertised for 5,000 workers for the Chicago and Great Eastern Railroad, 22 April 1864, p. 2; 23 April 1864, p. 2. See also 30 April 1864, p. 2; 11 June 1864, p. 2; 22 June 1864, p. 2.

85. *Skandinavisk Post*, 24 May 1871, p. 2; 29 Aug. 1871, p. 1; 21 March 1873, p. 1; 16 March 1871, p. 2.

86. Habicht, 14 March 1867, *Svenska Konsular Skrivelser*, New York, 1867, no. 2, Riksarkivet.

87. *Amerika-Bladet*, 15 Feb. 1870, p. 1.

88. New York *Tribune*, 11 June 1881, p. 5; *John Swinton's Paper*, 18 May 1884, p. 1.

89. *John Swinton's Paper*, 1 Feb. 1885, p. 1; 6 Jan. 1884, p. 1.

90. Testimony of Robert Marzo, 27 July 1888, *House Report, Ford Committee Report* (1889), p. 85.

91. U. S. *Reports of the Industrial Commission, Immigration*, XV (1901), 30–31.

92. Frank J. Sheridan, "Italian, Slavic and Hungarian Immigrant Laborers," U. S. Bureau of Labor, *Bulletin*, vol. XV (Sept. 1907), no. 72, p. 415.

93. Kellor, *Out of Work*, p. 150; Edwin Hardin Sutherland, *Unemployed and Public Employment Agencies* (Chicago, 1914), p. 111.

94. New Jersey, Bureau of Industry and Labor, *Seventh Annual Report* (1884), p. 278; findings of John Fallon, Knights of Labor investigator, *Congressional Globe*, vol. XVI, Pt. 2, p. 1633.

95. *John Swinton's Paper*, 1 Feb. 1885, p. 1.

96. *John Swinton's Paper*, 31 Aug. 1884, p. 1.

97. *John Swinton's Paper*, 31 Aug. 1884, p. 1.

98. Sheridan, U. S. Bureau of Labor, *Bulletin*, XV, 403, 413; New York, *Third Annual Report of Commissioners of Labor* (1903), I, 195–196; *Fourth Annual Report* (1904), I, 47–50; Sutherland, *Unemployed and Public Employment Agencies*, p. 112.

99. *John Swinton's Paper*, 1 Feb. 1885, p. 1.

100. New York, Bureau of Labor Statistics, *Report* (1885), pp. 495–498.

101. Sheridan, U. S. Bureau of Labor, *Bulletin*, XV, 415.

102. *John Swinton's Paper*, 31 Aug. 1884, p. 1; New York, Bureau of Labor Statistics, *Report* (1885), pp. 495–498, 506.

103. Testimony of Charles T. Parsons, labor recruiter for New England farms, factories, and sawmills, 2 Aug. 1888, *House Reports, Ford Committee Report* (1889), pp. 562–570.

104. U. S. Ind. Comm., *Immigration*, XV, 434.

105. *John Swinton's Paper*, 31 Aug. 1884, p. 1; New Jersey, Bureau of Industry and Labor, *Seventh Annual Report* (1884), p. 278.

106. Haverhill *Laborer*, 8 Nov. 1884, p. 4.

107. *John Swinton's Paper*, 6 Jan. 1884, p. 1; 3 Aug. 1884, p. 1; 10 Aug. 1884, p. 1.

108. Pennsylvania, *Annual Report of Secretary of Internal Affairs, Industrial Statistics*, vol. XII (1884), Pt. 3, p. 66. New York, Bureau of Labor Statistics,

Report (1885), p. 509. Polish immigrants were brought to Pennsylvania on contracts to work at sixty cents a day until transportation was repaid at the rate of three dollars a month (*John Swinton's Paper,* 10 Aug. 1884, p. 1. Boston *Pilot,* 25 April 1885, p. 8).

109. *John Swinton's Paper,* 21 Aug. 1884, p. 1; 6 Jan. 1884, p. 1; New York, Bureau of Labor Statistics, *Report* (1885), pp. 497–498; *House Reports, Ford Committee Report* (1889), p. 67; *Congressional Globe,* vol. XVI, Pt. 2, p. 1633.

110. New York, Bureau of Labor Statistics, *Report* (1885), pp. 496, 498–500, 505, 506; *John Swinton's Paper,* 18 May 1884, p. 1.

111. Hudiksvalla *Posten,* 2 Sept. 1865, p. 2; *Hemlandet,* 27 Dec. 1865, p. 2; 13 Sept. 1865, p. 2; 14 May 1867, p. 1; *Skånska Posten,* 14 Feb. 1866, p. 3; *Allgemeine Auswanderungs Zeitung,* 12 April 1866, pp. 59–60; 19 April 1866, pp. 63–64; 26 April 1866, pp. 67–68; 3 May 1866, pp. 71–72.

112. *Iron Age,* 30 Nov. 1865, p. 2.

113. *House Reports, Ford Committee Report* (1889), pp. 92, 97, 104, 115, 117, 119, 123, 129.

114. See U. S. Ind. Comm., *Immigration,* XV, xli, for definition similar to mine.

115. *Immigration,* XV, 434; New York, Bureau of Labor Statistics, *Report* (1885), p. 497.

116. U. S. *Ind. Comm., Immigration,* XV, 8, 434; *John Swinton's Paper,* 7 Sept. 1884, p. 1.

117. U. S. Ind. Comm., *Capital and Labour,* VII (1901), 212; *Immigration,* XV, 432; Philadelphia *Times,* 25 Jan. 1882, p. 1; U. S. Department of Labor, "Italians in Chicago," *Ninth Special Report* (1897), p. 727.

118. Illinois Free Employment Office, *Thirteenth Annual Report* (1911), p. 8.

119. Devine, *Report on Establishing an Employment Bureau,* pp. 183–184.

120. Pittsburgh *Commercial Gazette,* 11 Dec. 1883, quoted in *House Reports,* 48c., 1s., no. 444, II, 4. See also account by Harry W. Heichold, son of an Inspector of Customs, who had just returned to Erie from the Lake Superior Region, in *John Swinton's Paper,* 23 Dec. 1883, p. 1; *Labor Enquirer,* Denver, 13 Sept. 1884, p. 3. For another case of Italian and French workmen deceived about the work to which they were being taken, see *Iron Molders Journal,* 30 Sept. 1881, pp. 10–11.

121. *American Iron and Steel Bulletin,* XVII (1 Oct. 1884), 252; same story in *Interocean,* 11 Oct. 1884, p. 12.

122. U. S. Ind. Comm., *Immigration,* XV (1898), xli.

123. *John Swinton's Paper,* 20 Jan. 1884, p. 1. For similar hardships among Italian railroad workers in Denver, see *Labor Enquirer,* 14 June 1884, p. 3; 19 Jan. 1884, p. 2; 7 June 1884, p. 3.

124. Philadelphia *Times,* 25 June 1882, p. 1; New York *Tribune,* 24 June 1882, p. 2; *Iron Molders Journal,* 1 July 1882, p. 12.

125. U. S. Dept. of Labor, *Ninth Special Report* (1897), p. 726; U. S. Ind. Comm., *Immigration,* XV (1901), 433.

126. U. S. Secretary of Treasury, *Causes Inciting Immigration* (1892), I, 300.

6. REACTIONS IN THE MINES AND ON THE RAILROADS

1. *Railway Age,* 10 Feb. 1881, p. 73.

2. Norman J. Ware, *The Labor Movement in the United States, 1860–1885* (New York, 1929), pp. 50, 80–91.

3. *Census of 1870,* I, 713; the British- and American-born together accounted for three out of four of the nation's miners.

4. See Chapter 3.

5. ". . . the consensus of opinion among superintendents and foremen in the anthracite coal industry is that the mines could never be operated if they depended upon the native-born for the labor supply. . . . The labor, which has developed the anthracite coal fields has virtually been wholly supplied by emmigrants [*sic*] and their descendents of the first generation" (Peter Roberts, *Anthracite Coal Communities,* New York, 1904, p. 22).

6. *Census of 1870,* 1890, I, 369–370.

7. Jones, *Emigrants Friend* (1882 revision), p. 326.

8. Walter Coleman, *The Molly Maguire Riots* (Richmond, Va., 1936), p. 19.

9. Charles E. Killeen, "John Siney," Ph.D. Thesis (University of Wisconsin 1942), pp. 278–279; Peter Roberts, *The Anthracite Coal Industry* (New York, 1901), p. 174; Lehigh Coal Company, *Annual Report* (1870), p. 9.

10. Roberts, *Anthracite Coal Industry,* pp. 109–110; John R. Commons *et al., History of Labor in the United States,* vol. II, by J. B. Andrews and Selig Perlman (N. Y., 1935), p. 31.

11. Philadelphia and Reading Railroad, *Annual Report* (1868), p. 13; Lehigh Coal Company, *Annual Report* (1868), p. 10; (1869), pp. 5, 7; (1870), p. 5.

12. Lehigh Coal Company, *Annual Report* (1871), p. 7; Roberts, *Anthracite Coal Industry,* p. 174.

13. Roberts, *Anthracite Coal Industry,* pp. 105–106; Coleman, *Molly Maguires,* p. 11; Killeen, "John Siney," p. 75.

14. Coleman, *Molly Maguires,* p. 20.

15. J. F. Patterson, "Reminiscences of John Maguire," *Publications of the Historical Society of Schuylkill County,* IV (1914), 308; Coleman, *Molly Maguires,* p. 17; letter from Thomas Connelly, English mechanic, Pottsville, Penn., *Iron and Coal Trades Review,* London, 4 Jan. 1878, p. 10.

16. *Iron Age,* 3 Dec. 1874, p. 3.

17. *Railway World,* Philadelphia, 3 April 1875, p. 211.

18. Coleman suggests that one reason for the crimes of the Molly Maguires was that the English and Welsh, being more experienced miners, were given preference in promotions (Coleman, *Molly Maguires,* p. 19).

19. *Iron and Coal Trades Review,* 4 Jan. 1878, p. 10; Roberts, *Anthracite Coal Industry,* p. 110.

20. *Labor Enquirer,* 2 Feb. 1884, p. 3; *Irish World,* New York, 26 April 1884, p. 7.

21. Selig Perlman, *A History of Trade Unionism in the United States* (New York, 1922), p. 33; Twentieth Century Fund, Labor Committee, *How Collective Bargaining Works,* section by Waldo E. Fisher (New York, 1942), pp. 286–287.

22. U. S. *Reports of the Industrial Commission, Immigration*, XV (1901), 392. See also report of Jules Rosendale, special agent of the Pennsylvania Department of Agriculture, 11 Jan. 1900, *ibid.*, p. 189.

23. *Census of 1880*, I, 735; John Allan, Scranton, Osage County, Kansas, to T. V. Powderly, 15 Oct. 1881, Powderly Papers, Catholic University Library.

24. *How Collective Bargaining Works*, p. 231.

25. Commons *et al.*, *History of Labor*, II, 179; Christopher Evans, *History of the United Mine Workers* (Indianapolis, 1918), I, 85; Killeen, "John Siney," pp. 293–294.

26. In Braidwood, Illinois, Italian and Bohemian immigrants were used as strikebreakers in 1867–68 (George E. McNeill, *Labor Movement, Problem of Today*, New York, 1887, p. 258).

27. Andrew Roy, *The Coal Miners* (Cleveland, 1876), p. 104; *National Labor Tribune*, Pittsburgh, 5 June 1875, p. 2; 3 July 1875, p. 2; 10 July 1875, p. 1; 7 Aug. 1875, p. 2; McNeill, *Labor Movement*, p. 259.

28. *National Labor Tribune*, 1 May 1875, p. 1; 5 June 1875, p. 2; Pennsylvania, *Annual Report of Secretary of Internal Affairs*, X (1880–81), 313.

29. McNeill, *Labor Movement*, pp. 259, 260; Roy, *Coal Miners*, p. 34; *National Labor Tribune*, 5 June 1875, p. 2; Pennsylvania, *Annual Report of Secretary of Internal Affairs*, X, 310, 314, 315.

30. *Workingman's Advocate*, Chicago, 20 June 1874, p. 2; 6 March 1875, p. 2; *Equity*, Boston, July 1874, pp. 30–31; Evans, *History of the United Mine Workers*, I, 54.

31. *National Labor Tribune*, 17 July 1875, p. 1.

32. Roy, *Coal Miners*, p. 104.

33. *Iron Molders Journal*, 10 Nov. 1874, pp. 104–105.

34. *National Labor Tribune*, 22 May 1872, p. 2; Killeen, "John Siney," p. 316; Pennsylvania, *Annual Report of Secretary of Internal Affairs*, X, 210, 314–315.

35. McNeill, *Labor Movement*, p. 260; *National Labor Tribune*, 5 June 1875, p. 2.

36. Roy, *Coal Miners*, p. 104.

37. Killeen, "John Siney," p. 316; for other cases, see Roy, *Coal Miners*, p. 134, and *Iron Molders Journal*, 10 July 1875, p. 358.

38. Commons *et al.*, *History of Labor*, II, 180; Roy, *Coal Miners*, pp. 159, 162–163.

39. Commons *et al.*, *History of Labor*, II, 180n.

40. *National Labor Tribune*, 5 July 1875, p. 1; Killeen, "John Siney," p. 314. Several cases of successful persuasion of strikebreakers hired in Philadelphia to leave the mines are described in *National Labor Tribune*, 22 May 1875, p. 2.

41. Roy, *Coal Miners*, p. 165; Killeen, "John Siney," pp. 314–316; Pennsylvania, *Annual Report of Secretary of Internal Affairs*, X, 313–315; *National Labor Tribune*, 1 May 1875, p. 2; 5 June 1875, p. 2.

42. *National Labor Tribune*, 17 Aug. 1875, p. 2.

43. The mining companies held that they could not compete at the existing rate of wages (New York *Tribune*, 15 March 1882, p. 2; Philadelphia *Times*, 26 May 1882, p. 2; "Circular to Mining Companies of George's Creek, Cumberland Coal Region," pamphlet, n. d., received by Powderly, 7 April 1882, Powderly Papers).

44. New York *World,* 26 May 1882, p. 1.

45. "Circular to Mining Companies . . . Cumberland Coal Region," Powderly Papers.

46. Henry J. Browne, *The Catholic Church and the Knights of Labor* (Washington, D. C., 1949), p. 57.

47. Charles F. Mayer, Office of Consolidated Coal Company, to D. J. Foley, 6 June 1882, copy lent by Rev. Henry J. Browne from Church archives in Baltimore.

48. Philadelphia *Times,* 26 May 1882, p. 1; 27 May 1882, p. 1; New York *World,* 26 May 1882, p. 1; 27 May 1882, p. 1; New York *Sun,* 27 May 1882, p. 1; *Labor Enquirer,* 22 Sept. 1883, p. 3; Powderly's Testimony, *Ford Committee Report* (1889), p. 498.

49. *Iron Age,* 1 June 1882, p. 32.

50. New York *World,* 26 May 1882, p. 1.

51. *Iron Age,* 1 June 1882, p. 32; 27 July 1882, p. 19; Philadelphia *Times,* 1 June 1882, p. 2; New York *Tribune,* 3 June 1883, p. 5; 6 June 1882, p. 2; *Labor Standard,* Patterson, 10 June 1882, p. 1; 17 June 1882, p. 1; New York *World,* 1 June 1882, p. 1; 11 June 1882, p. 1; 13 July 1882, p. 5; V. F. Schmitt, Frostburg, to Archbishop Gibbons, 8 June 1882, copy of letter lent by Rev. Henry J. Browne. According to Powderly, many of the immigrants were engaged right at Castle Garden (*House Reports,* 48c., 1s., no. 444, II, 8).

52. New York *Sun,* 29 June 1882, p. 1. New York *World,* 24 June 1882, p. 1.

53. V. F. Schmitt, Frostburg, to Archbishop Gibbons, 8 June 1882, copy of letter lent by Rev. Henry J. Browne.

54. Charles F. Mayer to D. J. Foley, 6 June 1882, copy lent by Browne.

55. V. F. Schmitt, Frostburg, to Archbishop Gibbons, 8 June 1882, copy lent by Browne.

56. Myles McPadden, DuBoise, to T. V. Powderly, 10 Aug. 1882, Powderly Papers.

57. Schmitt to Gibbons, 8 June 1882.

58. The situation was described as "threatening" in the Laconing region, with strikers preparing to attack police guards (New York *World,* 4 Aug. 1882, p. 1).

59. New York *Tribune,* 13 June 1882, p. 5.

60. Philadelphia *Times,* 6 June 1882, p. 2; *Iron Age,* 27 July 1882, p. 19.

61. New York *World,* 13 July 1882, p. 5; New York *Sun,* 11 June 1882, p. 1.

62. New York *Sun,* 11 Aug. 1882, p. 1; 18 Aug. 1882, p. 1; 21 Aug. 1882, p. 1.

63. "Appeal for Aid," Executive Board of Knights of Labor, Pittsburgh, 6 Oct. 1882, Powderly Papers.

64. Pennsylvania, *Annual Report of Secretary of Internal Affairs, Industrial Statistics,* XI (1881–82), Pt. 3, pp. 147–156; McPadden, Osceola Mills, Clearfield County, Penn., to Powderly, 24 June 1882, Powderly Papers.

65. Pennsylvania, *Industrial Statistics,* vol. XI, Pt. 3, pp. 160–161; Philadelphia *Times,* 26 June 1882, p. 1; 7 July 1882, p. 1.

66. Pennsylvania, *Industrial Statistics,* vol. XI, Pt. 3, p. 163; Philadelphia *Times,* 16 July 1882, p. 1; Cornelius Cotter, Osceola Mills, Clearfield County, Penn., to Powderly, 4 July 1882, Powderly Papers.

67. Philadelphia *Times,* 13 June 1882, p. 1; Pennsylvania, *Industrial Statistics,* vol. XI, Pt. 3, pp. 168–169.

68. Roy, *Coal Miners,* pp. 216–217, 219; Report of Henry Lusky, Commissioner of Ohio Bureau of Labor, in Michigan, Bureau of Labor and Industrial Statistics, *Second Annual Report* (1885), p. 33; *Engineering and Mining Journal* XXXVIII, (29 Nov. 1884), 359–360.

69. Roy, *Coal Miners,* p. 219; *John Swinton's Paper,* 17 Aug. 1884, p. 1; 3 Aug. 1884, p. 2; Michigan Bureau of Labor Statistics (1885), p. 33.

70. *John Swinton's Paper,* 17 Aug. 1884, p. 1; *Irish World,* 17 May 1884, p. 7; Evans, *United Mine Workers,* I, 118, 120. The *Engineering and Mining Journal* admitted that 1,300 new men had been introduced, but claimed that they were all "practical miners" from other parts of the United States. The editor was indignant at the refusal of the governor of Ohio to provide an armed guard in advance of violence since it meant that the operators were having to pay for the "standing army" needed to get the mines operating at "half-capacity" during the strike (vol. XXXVIII, 29 Nov. 1884, p. 360, 19 July 1884, p. 33).

71. For other cases of strikebreaking in mines with English, Scandinavian, and Hungarian labor, see Pennsylvania, *Industrial Statistics,* vol. XI, Pt. 3, p. 147; Boston *Pilot,* 9 Feb. 1884, p. 8; *Irish World,* 26 April 1884, p. 7; testimony of John Costello and John Murray, *House Reports,* 48c., 1s., no. 444, II, 11.

72. Vol. XXIX (15 May 1880), p. 335.

73. James McGreddie, Arnot, Tioga County, Penn., to T. V. Powderly, 18 July 1880, Powderly Papers.

74. "An Appeal from D. A. no. 9, of the Knights of Labor," Pittsburgh, 15 July 1882, Powderly Papers; *Labor Standard,* 8 July 1882, p. 1. In a study which has appeared since this section was written, John Higham has emphasized strikebreaking in mines as contributing to nativist sentiment in the eighties (*Strangers in the Land,* Rutgers University Press, 1955, pp. 47–48).

75. Powderly Testimony, *Ford Committee Report,* pp. 500–501: See also New York, Bureau of Labor Statistics, *Report* (1885), p. 511. Pennsylvania, *Industrial Statistics,* vol. XI, Pt. 3, pp. 145–146a, 862; *Irish World,* 26 April 1884, p. 7; 2 Aug. 1884, p. 7. *National Labor Tribune,* 3 July 1875, p. 2.

76. *House Reports,* 48c., 1s., no. 444, II, 9–10; Boston *Pilot,* 16 Feb. 1884, p. 4; *Labor Enquirer,* 31 May 1884, p. 3.

77. *National Labor Tribune,* 1 May 1875, p. 2.

78. Barclay's testimony, *House Reports,* 48c., 1s., no. 444, II, 9.

79. Testimony of Barclay, Schoonmaker, and Powderly, *House Reports,* 48c.,1s., no. 444, II, 4, 8–10. Testimony of P. J. Maguire, Senate Committee on Education and Labor, *Report on Relations between Capital and Labor* (1885), I, 337; Pennsylvania, *Industrial Statistics,* vol. XII (1884), Pt. 3, pp. 65, 66, 69, 70; New York, Bureau of Labor Statistics, *Report* (1885), pp. 511–512; Knights of Labor, *Proceedings* (1884), pp. 576–577; T. V. Powderly, *The Path I Trod,* pp. 409–410; *Labor Enquirer,* 5 April 1884, p. 3; *Irish World,* 7 June 1884, p. 7; 26 April 1884, p. 7; *John Swinton's Paper,* 4 May 1884, p. 1; 18 May 1884, p. 1; 6 Jan. 1884, p. 3; 3 Aug. 1884, p. 1; 31 Aug. 1884, p. 1; *Labor Standard,* 23 Sept. 1882, p. 2.

80. Michigan, Bureau of Labor Statistics, *Annual Report* (1884), pp. 180–181;

Maguire, *Irish in America,* pp. 232–233; Handlin, *Boston's Immigrants,* pp. 106–120.

81. *Iron Age,* 7 Dec. 1882, p. 23; *Labor Enquirer,* 21 June 1884, p. 3; *Irish World,* 5 July 1884, p. 4.

82. *Irish World,* 3 May 1884, p. 7; 9 Aug. 1884, p. 8; 10 May 1884, p. 7. See also *John Swinton's Paper,* 18 May 1884, p. 1; *Labor Enquirer,* 5 Jan. 1884.

83. *Races and Immigrants in America* (New York, 1907), p. 151.

84. See Appendix II.

85. *Census of 1890,* vol. II, Table 109.

86. *John Swinton's Paper,* 23 Dec. 1883, p. 1; *The Trades,* Philadelphia, 24 April 1880, p. 1; *American Iron and Steel Bulletin,* 1 Oct. 1884, p. 252; *Labor Enquirer,* 27 Sept. 1884, p. 4; *Irish World,* 9 Aug. 1884, p. 8; *House Reports,* 48c., 1s., no. 444, II, 4.

87. Philadelphia *Times,* 19 July 1882, p. 1; *John Swinton's Paper,* 23 Dec. 1883, p. 1; *Labor Enquirer,* 17 May 1884, p. 3.

88. Philadelphia *Times,* 26 June 1882, p. 1; *Railway World,* 1 July 1882, p. 606; New York *Sun,* 15 June 1882, p. 1; 18 June 1882, p. 1.

89. New York *Tribune,* 23 June 1882, p. 5; New York *World,* 22 June 1882, p. 1; 24 June 1882, p. 2; 28 June 1882, p. 1.

90. New York *World,* 22 June 1892, p. 1.

91. Philadelphia *Times,* 24 June 1882, p. 1.

92. New York *Tribune,* 24 June 1882, p. 1; 23 June 1882, p. 5.

93. Philadelphia *Times,* 4 July 1882, p. 2.

94. New York *Tribune,* 29 June 1882, p. 5. Compare statement of the Freight-handlers Central Union, 5 July 1882: "The raw immigrants from European cities are brought here by padrones and others, and these poor creatures, unacquainted with our language or customs, are taken off the ships and put at work without being allowed to converse with anybody who could be likely to explain the real situation of affairs. We do not blame them. We pity them. . . . " Philadelphia *Times,* 6 July 1882, p. 2). The remainder of this account of the freighthandlers' strike is based upon the accounts in four newspapers, Philadelphia *Times,* New York *Tribune,* New York *Sun,* and New York *World* for June and July 1882. Detailed references may be found in the author's thesis at Cornell University Library.

95. New York *World,* 17 July 1882, p. 2; Senate Committee on Education and Labor (1885), I, 810.

96. In one of these incidents, it was admitted that the violence was the work of drunkards, not strikers (New York *Tribune,* 29 July 1882, p. 5); Philadelphia *Times,* 25 July 1882, p. 1; 9 July 1882, p. 2; New York *World,* 12 July 1882, p. 1.

97. New Jersey, Bureau of Industry and Labor, *Seventh Annual Report* (1884), p. 295.

98. *Report* (1885), p. 484. Compare statement in *American Iron and Steel Bulletin:* "Our immigrants, the Chinese excepted, soon fall in with the American idea of comfort. They are not content to live less handsomely than they see others live. They will take no lower wages . . ." (vol. XVI, 23 Aug. 1882, p. 225).

99. 20 May 1882, p. 1. See also George D. Albert, *History of the County of West-*

moreland, Pennsylvania (Philadelphia, 1882), p. 408. Note that although Polish immigrants were imposed upon when they first arrived, they soon demanded regularly paid wages, and would strike for them, in Pennsylvania, *Annual Report of Secretary of Internal Affairs, Industrial Statistics,* vol. XII, Pt. 3, p. 67. For other cases of immigrant workmen in mines striking or joining strikes, see *Iron Molders Journal,* 10 Dec. 1874, pp. 146–147; 10 Dec. 1874, p. 146; Detroit *Unionist,* 26 June 1882, p. 4; *Labor Standard,* 17 June 1882, p. 1.

100. Cases are listed in thesis, p. 522n.; *Workingman's Advocate,* 23 April 1870, p. 2; *The Exponent,* Cincinnati, 23 Oct. 1880, p. 1; *Labor Standard,* 10 Sept. 1881, p. 1; 30 April 1881, p. 1; 30 July 1881, p. 1; 29 April 1882, p. 1; *Irish World,* 24 Nov. 1883, p. 4; 31 May 1884, p. 7; 16 Aug. 1884.

101. *Irish World,* 9 Aug. 1884, p. 8.

102. *Labor Standard,* 28 April 1877, p. 1; Philadelphia *Times,* 9 July 1882, p. 2; *Labor Enquirer,* 10 March 1883, p. 8.

103. Philadelphia *Times,* 23 June 1882, p. 1; New York *Tribune,* 23 June 1882, p. 5.

7. MACHINERY AND IMMIGRATION

1. Letter from West Meriden, Conn., *Ryland's Iron Trade Circular,* Birmingham, 11 Feb. 1865, p. 16. See also letter from John Brown and Wm. B. Hatfield, South Meriden, Conn., 31 May 1869, *ibid.,* 3 July 1869, p. 7; Aaron Chambers, superintendent, American File Co., Pawtucket, R. I., 29 May 1866, Sheffield *Independent,* 30 June 1866, p. 6.

2. *Ryland's Iron Trade Circular,* 3 July 1869, p. 7.

3. Letter from Henry Walker, formerly manager of W. and S. Butcher, Sheffield, in an account of his experiences as manager of a steel manufacturing establishment in Pittsburgh, Sheffield *Independent,* 22 March 1865, p. 2.

4. *Amerika,* Gothenberg, 28 July 1870, p. 2; 4 Aug. 1870, p. 3; Axel Bruun, *Breve Fra Amerika* (Kristiana, 1870), pp. 37–38.

5. Brandenburg, *Imported Americans,* p. 244; G. La Piana, *Italians in Milwaukee* (Milwaukee, 1915), pp. 7, 8, 79; Kellor, *Out of Work,* p. 115.

6. *United Mine Workers Journal,* 21 Jan. 1904, p. 1; Harry Jerome, *Mechanization in Industry* (National Bureau of Economic Research, 1934), p. 130.

7. See summary of Part III by John R. Commons, U. S. *Reports of the Industrial Commission, Immigration,* XV (1898), xxiii. U. S. Immigration Commission, *Report,* vols. XL-XLI (1911); Jeremiah W. Jenks and W. Jett Lauck, *The Immigration Problem* (New York, 1922), fifth ed., chap. xii; Henry Pratt Fairchild, *Immigration, a World Movement* (New York, 1928), rev. ed., pp. 299, 309, 344.

8. Francis Walker, "Our Foreign Population, What They Are Doing," *The Advance,* VIII (10 Dec. 1874), 262.

9. The most important, although by no means definitive, criticism of the immigration commission's work in these terms was Isaac Hourwich, *Immigration and Labor* (New York, 1913).

10. See Chapter 3, pp. 62–63, and also Thomas Brassey, *On Work and Wages* (London, 1873), p. 25; National Association of Wool Manufacturers, *Bulletin,* VIII (July-Sept. 1878), 306–307; Melvin T. Copeland, *The Cotton Manufactur-*

ing Industry of the United States (Harvard University Press, 1912), Harvard Economic Studies, VIII, 3.

11. Hourwich, *Immigration and Labor,* pp. 424–425; Brinley Thomas, *Migration and Economic Growth* (Cambridge University Press, 1954), pp. 130–134. Much evidence on this point is to be found in the *Report* of the United States Immigration Commission issued in 1911.

12. Charles E. Kortright, Philadelphia, to Earl of Clarendon, 28 Sept. 1869, U. K. Consular Reports, Philadelphia, 1869, FO5/1167, P. R. O., London.

13. N. A. W. M., *Bulletin,* VIII (July–Sept. 1878), 307.

14. *Iron Age,* 14 April 1881, p. 26; 21 April 1881, p. 24; Commons, *Races and Immigrants,* pp. 149–150.

15. Blanche E. Hazard, *Organization of the Boot and Shoe Industry in Massachusetts* (Harvard University Press, 1921), p. 124.

16. Don D. Lescohier, "The Knights of St. Crispin, 1867–1874," *Bulletin of the University of Wisconsin,* Economic and Political Science Series, VII (May 1910), 24–25.

17. Lescohier, "The Knights of St. Crispin," pp. 36–37. The significance of this event was brilliantly discussed by Professor Frederick Rudolph in "Chinamen in Yankeedom," *American Historical Review,* LIII (Oct. 1947), 1–29.

18. Lescohier, "The Knights of St. Crispin," pp. 38–48.

19. John Andrews Fitch, *The Steel Workers* (New York, 1910), pp. 27, 29, 33–34, 78, 87; John Maguire, *Essay on the Advantages . . . of St. Louis as a Manufacturing City* (St. Louis, 1867), pp. 17–18; James Swank, *Twenty-One Years of Progress* (Philadelphia, 1886), p. 2.

20. Charles Reitell, *Machinery and Its Benefits to Labor in the Crude Iron and Steel Industries* (The Collegiate Press, Menasha, Wisconsin, 1917), pp. 23–33; Jerome, *Mechanization in Industry,* p. 63; Berthoff, *British Immigrants in Industrial America,* p. 66.

21. Reitell, *Machinery and Its Benefits,* pp. 9–17; Fitch, *Steel Makers,* pp. 27, 29; Jerome, *Mechanization in Industry,* pp. 59–60.

22. The prejudice of the skilled workers who dominated the Amalgamated Association against admitting unskilled workers was an important factor in the weakness of trade unionism in the new heavy steel industry. Not until the Knights of Labor threatened to organize mills on industrial lines did the president of Amalgamated suggest admitting "anybody and everybody working in and around rolling mills and steel mills." The membership qualifications were consequently broadened in 1889, but still excluded common laborers (Jesse S. Robinson, *Amalgamated Association of Iron, Steel, and Tin Workers* (Baltimore, 1920), pp. 43, 47–49, 56. Hourwich, *Immigration and Labor* pp. 411–412).

23. U. S. Industrial Commission, *Immigration,* XV (1901), 425; XV (1898), xxxviii.

24. Testimony of Abram Hewitt, U. K., *B. P. P.* (1867), XXXVII, 25ff.

25. *The Trades,* Philadelphia, 19 April 1879, p. 4.

26. *The Trades,* 19 April 1879, p. 4; 26 April 1879, p. 4. *Iron Age,* 29 March 1883, p. 14.

27. *Iron Molders Journal,* 10 May 1880, p. 6.

28. Robinson, *Amalgamated Association of Iron, Steel, and Tin Workers,* pp. 88–89.

29. New York *Tribune,* 16 March 1880, p. 2; 1 June 1880. p. 4. Jesse Robinson discussed in some detail Amalgamated's efforts to regulate wage differentials, but concluded: "Uniformity was brought about, however, by the refusal of employers in one district to pay a higher price than those in another, and not by the enforcement in lower-priced districts of prices paid in the districts enjoying a differential advantage" (*Amalgamated Association of Iron, Steel, and Tin Workers,* pp. 91–93).

30. See Chapter 3, pp. 57–58. Berthoff, *British Immigrants,* p. 65.

31. The acknowledgedly unreliable United States immigration figures for the immigration of iron molders, puddlers, iron workers, and founders from Britain and Ireland suggest such a decline: 1880, 425; 1881, 302; 1882, 276; 1883, 203; 1884, 188; 1885, 152 (U. S. Dept. of Treasury, Bureau of Statistics, *Arrivals of Alien Passengers and Immigrants,* 1880–1885).

32. London *Times,* 25 Aug. 1879, p. 6; 2 Sept. 1879, p. 4; *Capital and Labour,* London, 13 Aug. 1879, p. 472; 17 Sept. 1879, p. 519; *The Trades,* 27 Dec. 1879, p. 2.

33. *Iron Age,* 14 April 1881, p. 26; 21 April 1881, p. 24; *Iron Molders Journal,* 31 May 1881, p. 6.

34. James H. Bridge, *The Inside History of the Carnegie Steel Company* (New York, 1903), p. 154; Ware, *Labor Movement,* p. 299; Robinson, *Amalgamated,* p. 124. Compare New York *Sun,* 14 May 1882, p. 1. Hourwich quotes Fitch to the effect that of the 3,800 men at Homestead when the strike began in 1892, only 752 were members of Amalgamated (*Immigration and Labor,* p. 411).

35. Allan Nevins, *Abram S. Hewitt* (New York, 1935), p. 422.

36. *Iron Age,* 18 May 1882, p. 13. In 1882 these mills comprised 27 single puddling furnaces, 5 heating furnaces, and 4 trains of rolls (American Iron and Steel Association, *Directory to the Iron and Steel Works of the United States,* corrected to 25 July 1882, Philadelphia, 1882, p. 118).

37. *Iron Age,* 9 May 1882, p. 13; Pennsylvania, *Annual Report of Secretary of Internal Affairs, Industrial Statistics,* vol. XI (1881–82), Pt. 3, pp. 170–171. This firm was still employing 21 double puddling furnaces in 1882 (*Directory to the Iron and Steel Works of the United States,* 1882, p. 106).

38. Bridge, *Carnegie Steel,* p. 156.

39. Pennsylvania, *Annual Report of Secretary of Internal Affairs, Industrial Statistics,* vol. XI, Pt. 3, pp. 171–174. Bridge remarked that William Clark, who was in charge of the Homestead works, was not so clever as Carnegie's Captain Jones in handling the various immigrant workmen. Before he went to Homestead, Clark had a reputation with the Amalgamated Association for taking pride in strikebreaking (*Carnegie Steel,* p. 153).

40. New York *World,* 2 June 1882, p. 1.

41. Bridge, *Carnegie Steel,* pp. 157–158; New York *Tribune,* 17 June 1882, p. 2; 3 June 1882, p. 5; *Labor Standard,* 10 June 1882, p. 1. The New York *Sun* (1 June 1882, p. 1) said that Carnegie's Union Iron Mills signed in order to avoid a strike at the Edgar Thompson Steel Works which had hitherto been non-union. See also New York *World,* 2 June 1882, p. 1.

42. New York *Tribune,* 13 June 1882, p. 5; New York *World,* 1 June 1882, p. 1; *Engineering and Mining Journal,* XXXIII (3 June 1882), 287–288.

43. These firms are listed in Pennsylvania, *Annual Report of Secretary of Internal Affairs, Industrial Statistics,* vol. XI, Pt. 3, pp. 178, 189; *Labor Standard,* 15 July 1882, p. 1; *American Iron and Steel Bulletin,* 9 and 16 Aug. 1882, p. 221.

44. *Iron Age,* 22 June 1882, p. 20; Detroit *Unionist,* 2 Oct. 1882, p. 4.

45. *Directory of the Iron and Steel Works of the United States* (1882), p. 135.

46. Philadelphia *Times,* 15 June 1882, p. 1; 23 July 1882, p. 1; New York *World,* 10 June 1882, p. 2.

47. New York *Tribune,* 6 July 1882, p. 1.

48. Philadelphia *Times,* 19 July 1882, p. 1; *Labor Standard,* 15 July 1882, p. 1; Detroit *Unionist,* 24 July 1882, p. 4; New York *Tribune,* 22 June 1882, p. 5. For Scottish iron molders sent to Troy by the New York Labor Bureau only to find a strike in progress, police on duty, and their baggage held by the manufacturers as security, see *Iron Molders Journal,* 30 Sept. 1883, p. 3.

49. Bridge, *Carnegie Steel,* p. 158; *American Iron and Steel Bulletin,* 27 Sept. 1882, p. 261; New York *Tribune,* 14 Sept. 1882, p. 5; Robinson, *Amalgamated,* p. 19.

50. Testimony of John Jarrett, 6 Sept. 1883, Senate Committee on Education and Labor (1885), I, 1139; William Weihe, 7 Sept. 1883, *ibid.,* II, 8–9.

51. Copeland, *Cotton Manufacturing,* pp. 66–67.

52. Copeland, *Cotton Manufacturing,* p. 73; U. S. Industrial Commission, *Immigration,* XV (1901), 420.

53. Young, *American Cotton Industry,* p. 4.

54. Albert S. Bolles, "Apprentice and Technical Education in Pennsylvania." Pennsylvania, *Annual Report of Bureau of Industrial Statistics* (1893), p. 19.

55. Cole, *Wool Manufacture,* II, 95.

56. U. S. Industrial Commission, *Immigration,* XV (1901), 420; (1898), xxxvi. Testimony of Robert Howard, 25 Aug. 1883, Senate Committee on Education and Labor (1885), I, 636. Brassey, *Work and Wages,* p. 46.

57. U. S. Industrial Commission, *Immigration,* XV (1901), xxxvi. The following comparison of productivity in the textile industries of England, Germany, and the United States appeared in the London *Times* in 1884:

No. lbs. worked per worker per year	England	Germany	U. S.
Cotton	2,914	1,200–1,500	4,350
Wool	1,375	1,000	1,640
Silk	71	59	87

(Boston *Journal of Commerce,* 13 Dec. 1884, p. 90.)

58. Herbert J. Lahne, *The Cotton Mill Worker* (Twentieth Century Fund, New York, 1944), pp. 73–74. Testimony of Gilbert B. Whitman, 12 Oct. 1883, Senate Committee on Education and Labor (1885), III, 29; testimony of Rev. Joseph A. Chevalier, 15 Oct. 1883, *ibid.,* III, 197, 200.

59. *Labor Standard,* 15 Oct. 1881, p. 4; *Labor Enquirer,* 10 March 1883, p. 8.

60. Detroit *Unionist,* 30 April 1883, p. 4.

61. See also testimony of Stephen N. Bourne, agent of the Stark Corporation, Manchester, N. H., 13 Oct. 1883, Senate Committee on Education and Labor (1885), III, 125.

62. *John Swinton's Paper,* 23 Dec. 1883.

63. *Labor Enquirer,* 10 March 1883, p. 8.

64. New York *Tribune,* 18 July 1881, p. 2. New York, *Annual Report Commissioners of Immigration* (1881), p. 54; 1880, p. 51.

65. Broadus Mitchell, *The Rise of Cotton Mills in the South* (Baltimore, 1921), pp. 204–205.

66. Commons *et al.*, *History of the Labor Movement*, II, 304–305; Phillip S. Foner, *History of the Labor Movement in the United States* (New York, 1947), p. 503.

67. Testimony of Frank Porter, *House Reports*, 48c., 1s., no. 444, II, 12.

68. Testimony of Hugh T. Elmer, Boston trade unionist, 19 Oct. 1883, Senate Committee on Education and Labor (1885), III, 577–578.

69. *Labor Enquirer*, 16 Aug. 1884, p. 4.

70. Dexter to Howe, 25 June 1881, Pepperell Mfg. Co., *Letter Book*, vol. 647, p. 444; Dexter to Howe, 10 Dec. 1881, *Letter Book*, vol. 648, no. 164, Pepperell Papers.

71. *Labor Standard*, 16 Aug. 1879, p. 3.

72. Carroll D. Wright, "Strikes in Massachusetts, 1830–1880," Massachusetts Bureau of Statistics of Labor, *Eleventh Annual Report* (1879), p. 57; Lahne, *Cotton Mill Worker*, p. 73; New York *Tribune*, 28 June 1879, p. 1; *Labor Standard*, 1 Nov. 1879, p. 4.

73. *Labor Standard*, 8 Oct. 1881, p. 4.

74. New York *Tribune*, 3 Feb. 1884, pp. 1, 6; *John Swinton's Paper*, 27 April 1884, p. 4.

75. Foner, *History of the Labor Movement*, p. 503; *Labor Standard*, 27 March 1880, p. 5; *The Exponent*, Cincinnati, 3 April 1880, p. 1.

76. Philadelphia *Times*, 26 July 1882, p. 1. One estimate stated that when the strike was eight weeks old 2,000 of the 5,000 strikers had migrated elsewhere (New York *Sun*, 14 June 1882, p. 1). But in August a mass meeting of 4,000 strikers was held in Cohoes, which, if true, indicates that the majority of the strikers were forced by circumstances to remain on the scene (Detroit *Unionist*, 7 Aug. 1882, p. 1).

77. Philadelphia *Times*, 10 June 1882, p. 1; New York *World*, 10 June 1882, p. 1.

78. Philadelphia *Times*, 29 July 1882, p. 2; 26 July 1882, p. 1; New York *Tribune*, 29 June 1882, p. 5. The Harmony Mills were reported to have arranged with the Inman Line to import the first twenty-five Swedish families "as an experiment" (New York *Sun*, 26 July 1882, p. 1).

79. Philadelphia *Times*, 4 Aug. 1882, p. 2; 8 Aug. 1882 p. 2; 17 Aug. 1882, p. 2; Detroit *Unionist*, 7 Aug. 1882, p. 1; 2 Oct. 1882, p. 4; *John Swinton's Paper*, 6 Jan. 1884, p. 1.

80. Compare Carroll D. Wright, "Influence of Unions on Immigrants," U. S. Bureau of Labor, *Bulletin*, no. 56 (Jan. 1905), pp. 1, 4–7.

81. William M. Leiserson, *Adjusting Immigrant and Industry* (New York, 1925), p. 174. Contrast with Jenks and Lauck who maintained that the willingness of the "new immigrant" to work under any conditions weakened and destroyed trade unions (*Immigration Problem*, p. 202). Fairchild said that southern Europeans were "natural strikebreakers" (*Immigrant Backgrounds*, p. 309).

82. For further evidence on this point, see U. S. Industrial Commission, *Immigration*, XV (1898), xxvi, xxxiv-xxxv; (1901), pp. 310–311.

8. THE WINDOW GLASS WORKERS

1. Boris Stern, *Productivity of Labor in the Glass Industry* (Washington: G. P. O., 1927), p. 1.

2. Pearce Davis, *The Development of the American Glass Industry* (Harvard University Press, 1949), pp. 120–126, 180–191.

3. Warren C. Scoville, *Revolution in Glassmaking* (Harvard University Press, 1948), p. 31.

4. Davis, *The Development of the American Glass Industry,* Table 10, p. 124.

5. John R. Commons and John B. Andrews, editors, *A Documentary History of American Industrial Society* (Cleveland, 1910–11), IX, 334.

6. Joseph Slight, "A History of the Handblown Window Glass Trade in the United States," p. 6, manuscript, Labadie Collection, University of Michigan; Ware, *Labor Movement,* pp. 191–192; Davis, *American Glass Industry,* p. 127.

7. John Fetter, Pittsburgh, to T. V. Powderly, 7 March 1880, Powderly Papers.

8. Davis, *American Glass Industry,* p. 126.

9. Joseph Button, Baltimore, to Powderly, 28 Oct. 1879, Powderly Papers.

10. A "Gatherers' Temporary Organization" threatened to withdraw from Local 300 in 1881 on the grounds that the latter was permitting too many apprentices, and that foreign workmen were being admitted to the Assembly (Printed resolution headed "Gatherers Temporary Organization," Pittsburgh, 18 Oct. 1881, Powderly Papers).

11. Davis, *American Glass Industry,* Table 10, pp. 124, 125.

12. Slight, "History of the Handblown Window Glass Trade," p. 5; testimony of E. Bouillet, William Ashton, Van Haas, *House Reports,* 48c., 1s., no. 444, II, 8, 10; *The Exponent,* 17 April 1880, p. 1.

13. One of the immigrants, Bouillet, who later joined the union, claimed that the rate of the contracts was 25 per cent lower than Ohio prices (*House Reports,* 48c., 1s., no. 444, II, 10).

14. "Agreement made by and between the firm of Day, Williams and Co., of Kent, Ohio, of the first part, and each of the signers hereto of the second part . . . ," 2 Dec. 1879, *House Reports,* 48c., 1s., no. 444, II, 10.

15. Testimony of Ashton and Van Haas, *House Reports,* 48c., 1s., No. 444, II, 10.

16. *Iron Age,* 13 Jan. 1881, p. 15.

17. *Iron Age,* 9 Feb. 1882, p. 26.

18. Michigan, Bureau of Labor and Industrial Statistics, *Annual Report* (1885), p. 273; *House Reports,* 48c., 1s., no. 444, II, 12.

19. New York *Tribune,* 22 June 1882, p. 5.

20. Slight, "History of the Handblown Window Glass Trade," p. 6; Ware, *Labor Movement,* p. 196.

21. Edgar Gillot, "Window Glass Cutters League of America," p. 1, manuscript in Labadie Collection, University of Michigan. Davis states (p. 132) that the western strike began in 1883, but my evidence indicates that western manufacturers began a fight against the differentials on two fronts during the summer of 1882 by encouraging the union to get eastern wages raised and by declaring a reduction in their own factories.

22. John Van Zant, Malaga, N. J., to Powderly, 29 Nov. 1882, Powderly Papers.

23. *Iron Age,* 28 Sept. 1882, p. 26; *Labor Enquirer,* 17 Feb. 1883, p. 8; D. Van Hook, Recording Secretary, Local Assembly 872, Malaga, N. J., to Powderly, 21 Jan. 1883, Powderly Papers.

24. Knights of Labor, *Proceedings* (1883), p. 427.

25. Slight, "History of the Handblown Window Glass Trade," p. 6; Davis, *American Glass Industry*, p. 132.

26. *Labor Enquirer*, 17 Feb. 1883, p. 8.

27. *Iron Molders Journal*, 1 Jan. 1883, p. 4; *Labor Enquirer*, 3 Feb. 1883, p. 8; 6 Jan. 1883, p. 6; Detroit *Unionist*, 8 Jan. 1883, p. 4.

28. John Van Zant, Malaga, N. J., to Powderly, 29 Nov. 1882, Powderly Papers.

29. Van Zant to Powderly, 29 Nov. 1882.

30. Van Zant to Powderly, 29 Nov. 1882; D. Van Hook, Recording Secretary, Local 872, Malaga, N. J., to Powderly, 21 Jan. 1883; D. Van Hook to Powderly, 28 Jan. 1883; D. Van Hook to Powderly, 4 Feb. 1883, Powderly Papers. The situation was complicated by rivalries within Local 872. Van Zant was prejudiced against the skilled workers of 300, while Van Hook accused Van Zant of coming to meetings drunk, a charge which he undoubtedly knew would appeal to Powderly's own prejudices, and, indirectly, of being a spy for management.

31. *House Reports*, 48c., 1s., no. 444, II, 7; Michigan, Bureau of Labor and Industrial Statistics, *Annual Report* (1885), p. 275.

32. *Labor Enquirer*, 10 Nov. 1883, p. 3; Boston *Pilot*, 29 March 1884, p. 8.

33. A. C. Robertson, of Pittsburgh, stated that eighty foreign glass blowers had been brought to the western states: 36 to La Salle, Illinois; 13 to Covington, Kentucky; 14 to Louisville, Kentucky; and others to Streater, Illinois, and New Albany, Indiana (*House Reports*, 48c., 1s., no. 444, II, 8, 11, 12); *Iron Age*, 28 Sept. 1882, p. 26; *Labor Enquirer*, 17 Feb. 1883, p. 8; "Report of the Second National Convention of Window Glass Workers," Assembly Number 300, Knights of Labor, p. 27.

34. Agreement between Swindell Brothers and John Schmidt, gatherer, and Carl Wagner, blower, Antwerp, 15 Dec. 1882. A. C. Robertson maintained that imported workmen in the western states made 40 per cent less than American glass blowers (*House Report*, 48c., 1s., no. 444, II, 11, 12, 10).

35. Window Glass Workers of America no. 300, "Official Bulletin," 19 Nov. 1883, Powderly Papers.

36. James Campbell, Pittsburgh, to Powderly, 22 Oct. 1883; Powderly to Campbell, 5 Nov. 1883, Powderly Papers.

37. Robert Layton, Secretary, Knights of Labor, Pittsburgh, to Powderly, 11 Oct. 1883; Layton, Sewickly, to Powderly, 28 Oct. 1883, Powderly Papers.

38. *Labor Enquirer*, 7 April 1883, p. 8; 24 May 1884, p. 3. Testimony of John Schlicker, Window Glass Workers of America, Pittsburgh, *House Reports*, 48c., 1s., no. 444, II, 10; Michigan, Bureau of Labor and Industrial Statistics, *Second Annual Report* (1885), p. 276.

39. "Report of the Second National Convention of Window Glass Workers, Assembly Number 300, Knights of Labor," p. 12.

40. "Report of the Second National Convention of Window Glass Workers," p. 27.

41. The following estimates of skilled workmen in the window glass industry were compiled by the union: Belgium, 5,000; England, 1,500; France, 1,500; Germany & other, 1,500; U.S.A., 2,800; total, 12,300 (Window Glass Workers of America, Assembly no. 300, "Report of the Third National Convention," 8–12 July 1884, p. 11).

42. *Labor Enquirer*, 19 Jan. 1883, p. 3; 15 March 1884, p. 3; *Irish World*, 5 April

1884, p. 7; New York *Times*, 24 April 1884, p. 5; W. G. W. A., "Report of Third National Convention," 8–12 July 1884, p. 6.

43. *Labor Enquirer*, 28 June 1884, p. 3; 5 July 1884, p. 3; 26 July 1884, p. 3; 23 Aug. 1884, p. 3; *John Swinton's Paper*, 27 July 1884, p. 1. The permanent organizer was John Malcohn, an immigrant from Bradford, England. See also W. G. W. A., "Report of Third National Convention," 8–12 July 1884, p. 11.

44. Davis, *American Glass Industry*, p. 132.

45. "Constitution and Articles of Confederation of the Universal Federation of Window Glass Workers" (1885), Article 6, section 1, p. 12.

9. THE FORAN ACT

1. See, for example, Massachusetts, *Thirteenth Annual Report of the State Board of Charities* (1876–77).

2. *The Railroad Gazette*, New York, 6 May 1881, p. 25. See also 10 Oct. 1879; 26 Aug. 1881, p. 470; 23 Sept. 1881, p. 526.

3. *Railroad Gazette*, 1 Dec. 1882, p. 74. See also 23 Feb. 1883, p. 122.

4. Brandenburg, *Imported Americans*, p. 200.

5. Commons *et al.*, *History of Labor*, II, 373.

6. Statements by a Milwaukee tanner, a Marinette carpenter, a laborer in the lumbering industry, Peshtigo, and a laborer from Marinette, Wisconsin, in Wisconsin, Bureau of Labor Statistics, *Biennial Report* (1885–86), p. 437; New Jersey, Bureau of Industry and Labor, *Seventh Annual Report* (1884), pp. 242–243.

7. See account of huge labor demonstration held in Pittsburgh, 17 June 1882, in Philadelphia *Times*, 18 June 1882, p. 1; letter from "Molder," Ohio Bureau of Labor Statistics, *Report* (1884), Appendix, p. 287.

8. 13 Jan. 1881, p. 15.

9. Knights of Labor, *Proceedings* (1883), p. 459; (1884), pp. 575–576. See also *Journal of United Labor*, 15 Jan. 1881, p. 82.

10. Knights of Labor, *Proceedings* (1880), pp. 175, 178.

11. Federation of Organized Trade and Labor Unions, Second Annual Session, *Report of Proceedings* (1882), p. 19. At its first annual convention this organization had sent fraternal greetings to Henry Broadhurst and the Parliamentary Committee of the British Trade Union Congress (*Report of Proceedings*, 15–18 Dec. 1881, p. 15).

12. Quoted in *John Swinton's Paper*, 8 Feb. 1885, p. 1. The *Labor Standard* carried weekly summaries of trade conditions and the location of strikes throughout the years 1876–1881.

13. *John Swinton's Paper*, 23 Dec. 1883, p. 1; *Labor Enquirer*, 29 Dec. 1883, p. 3.

14. *Labor Enquirer*, 22 Nov. 1884, p. 3; *John Swinton's Paper*, 30 Dec. 1883, p. 1.

15. Pennsylvania, *Annual Report of Secretary of Internal Affairs, Industrial Statistics*, vol. XI (1881–82), Pt. 3, pp. 168–169; *Labor Standard*, 17 June 1882, p. 1; *Iron Age*, 17 Aug. 1882, p. 26; *John Swinton's Paper*, 17 Aug. 1884, p. 1; 3 Aug. 1884, p. 2; 17 Aug. 1884, p. 1; Michigan, Bureau of Industrial and Labor Statistics, *Second Annual Report* (1885), p. 33.

16. *Labor Enquirer,* 1 Nov. 1884, p. 1; 11 Oct. 1884, p. 3.

17. *Report of Proceedings,* Fourth Annual Session (Oct. 1884), p. 14. Compare to suggestion of Piano Makers Union that a labor exchange be incorporated in the proposed Labor Union Hall in New York City (*John Swinton's Paper,* 5 Oct. 1884, p. 4).

18. Senate Committee on Education and Labor, *Relations Between Capital and Labor* (1885), III, 399–400, 406. New Jersey, *Annual Report Bureau of Industry and Labor* (1884), p. 254.

19. Testimony of T. V. Powderly, *Ford Committee Report* (1889), p. 501. At a demonstration of the Amalgamated Trades and Labor Union in Chicago in 1878, George McNeill had spoken, "demanding" that no one should be allowed to come to America on a contract made on foreign soil. He, too, referred to Chinese labor (*Labor Standard,* 14 July 1878, p. 1).

20. Federation of Organized Trades and Labor Unions, First Annual Session, 15–18 Dec. 1881, "Declaration of Principles."

21. Foner, *History of the Labor Movement,* p. 520.

22. Foner, *Labor Movement,* p. 519; Commons *et al., History of Labor,* II, 321; Federation of Organized Trades and Labor Unions, First Annual Session, *Report,* 15–18 Dec. 1881, pp. 8-9.

23. Amalgamated Association of Iron and Steel Workers, *Journal of Proceedings,* 1–10 Aug. 1882, Chicago, pp. 834–835.

24. F. O. T. L. U., Third Annual Session, *Report of Proceedings,* 21–24 Aug. 1883; Senate Committee on Education and Labor (1885), I, 334–336, 578, 583, 791–792, 859; II, 5–6.

25. Samuel Gompers, *Seventy Years of Life and Labour* (New York, 1925), I, 154.

26. *Labor Standard,* 20 May 1882, p. 1; 8 July 1882, p. 1; Wisconsin, Bureau of Labor Statistics, *Biennial Report,* I (1883–84), 140–141; *Irish World,* 7 June 1884, p. 7; Gompers' testimony, 8 Aug. 1888, *Ford Committee Report* (1889), pp. 292–293.

27. Amalgamated Association of Iron and Steel Workers, *Journal of Proceedings,* 7–16 Aug. 1883, Philadelphia, pp. 1109–1111.

28. *Labor Enquirer,* 17 March 1883, p. 8.

29. Report of William Martin, Secretary of Amalgamated Association of Iron and Steel Workers, *Journal of Proceedings,* 5–13 Aug. 1884, Pittsburgh, p. 1390.

30. *Ford Committee Report* (1889), p. 501.

31. Knights of Labor, *Proceedings* (1883), p. 459. See also vague resolution presented by Dodd "that Congress speedily pass such laws as shall protect American labor from unjust and degrading competition" (*Ibid.,* pp. 432, 500).

32. *John Swinton's Paper,* 9 Dec. 1883, p. 4; 23 Dec. 1883, p. 1; 30 Dec. 1883, p. 1; 13 Jan. 1884, p. 2; *Labor Enquirer,* 19 Jan. 1884, p. 2.

33. *Iron Molders Journal,* 1 Jan. 1884, p. 11. Bricklayers International Union voted to urge passage of Foran Act at convention reported in *Labor Enquirer,* 26 Jan. 1884, p. 3. Petitions sent to House of Representatives by Bricklayers and Masons' International Union branches, *Congressional Record,* 48c., 1s., vol. XV, Pt. 2, pp. 1234, 1374, 1477, 1574, 1771, 1788, 1233, 1639, 1335, 1548; by Topographers, *ibid.,* pp. 1109, 1176.

34. Amalgamated Association of Iron and Steel Workers, *Journal of Proceedings,* 5–13 Aug. 1884, Pittsburgh, p. 1390.

35. Martin Foran, born Susquehanna County, Penn., 11 Nov. 1844, son of a farmer; worked on his father's farm where he learned the trade of cooper, after being educated in public schools of Susquehanna County; at 18, entered St. Joseph's College, near Montrose, Penn.; taught school for two years; then went to Cleveland where he practiced his trade of cooper; admitted to Ohio Bar 11 May 1874; elected prosecuting attorney for Cleveland in 1875; served two years; elected Democratic Representative from twentieth and twenty-first districts of Ohio, 1882; re-elected 1884 and 1886; private law practice in Ohio, 1889–1910; Judge of Court of Common Pleas, 1910 to death in 1921 (*National Cyclopedia of American Biography*, XIX, 156. *The Bench and Bar of Northern Ohio*, pp. 396–397).

36. *Coopers Journal*, vol. III, no. 10 (Oct. 1872), pp. 598–599; 609; vol. II, no. 11 (Dec. 1871), p. 505; vol. III, no. 3 (March 1872), p. 155.

37. *Coopers Journal*, vol. IV, no. 1 (Jan. 1873), p. 13.

38. Speech of Richard Powers of Lake Seaman's Union, F. O. T. L. U., *Report of Proceedings*, Second Annual Session, 1882. See also speech of Hon. Martin A. Foran to Congress.

39. Martin A. Foran, House of Representatives, to Powderly, 22 Jan. 1884, Powderly Papers.

40. T. V. Powderly, Scranton, to Foran, 24 Jan. 1884, Powderly Papers.

41. Foran, Washington, to Powderly, 28 Jan. 1884, Powderly Papers.

42. Frederick Turner, Grand Secretary, Philadelphia, to Powderly, 27 Jan. 1884; telegram dated 31 Jan. 1884, Turner to Powderly, Powderly Papers.

43. *House Reports*, 48c., 1s., no. 444, II, 8, 9, 11, 12.

44. *House Reports*, 48c., 1s., no. 444, II, 8, 10, 11, 12–13.

45. New York *Tribune*, 2 Feb. 1884, p. 2.

46. Amalgamated Association of Iron and Steel Workers, *Journal of Proceedings*, 5–13 Aug. 1884, Pittsburgh, pp. 1390–1391, 1398.

47. F. O. T. L. U., Fourth Annual Session, *Report of Proceedings*, Oct. 1884.

48. *Congressional Record*, vol. XV, 48c., 1s. Pt. 1, p. 875.

49. Knights of Labor, *Proceedings* (1884), pp. 623–624, 726, 787.

50. *Irish World*, 5 April 1884, p. 7.

51. *Irish World*, 20 April 1884, p. 1; *John Swinton's Paper*, 20 April 1884, p. 1.

52. *Irish World*, 10 May 1884, p. 7. For report of another demonstration, see *Labor Enquirer*, 5 April 1884, p. 3.

53. See, for example, *Congressional Record*, vol. XV, 48c., 1s., Pt. 2, pp. 5358, 5367, 5357, 5356, 5354–5355.

54. *Congressional Record*, vol. XV, 48c., 1s., Pt. 2, pp. 5349–5352.

55. *Congressional Record*, vol. XV, 48c., 1s., Pt. 5, pp. 5370–5371.

56. *Congressional Record*, vol. XV, 48c., 1s., Pt. 6, pp. 6057, 6058, 6059, 6065; *Senate Reports*, 48c., 1s., Report no. 820.

57. See, for example, remarks of Senator Miller of New York, *Congressional Record*, vol. XVI, 48c., 2s., Pt. 2, p. 1778; or Senator Sherman, *ibid.*, p. 1636.

58. *The Trades*, 19 April 1879, p. 2.

59. Quoted in *Labor Standard,* 17 July 1882, p. 4.

60. *Iron and Coal Trades Review,* 19 April 1878, p. 434. For other labor discussions of the tariff and immigration, see *Labor Standard,* 5 Nov. 1880, p. 1; 20 May 1882, p. 1; 8 July 1882, p. 4; Detroit *Unionist,* 18 Dec. 1882, p. 1; 8 Jan. 1883, p. 1; *Labor Tribune,* 23 Dec. 1882.

61. Frederick J. Harris, *Welshmen and the United States* (Pontypridd, 1927), p. 65; *Iron and Coal Trades Review,* 4 Jan. 1878, p. 5.

62. F. O. T. L. U., First Annual Session, *Report of Proceedings,* 15–18 Dec. 1881, p. 19.

63. F. O. T. L. U., Second Annual Session, "Declaration of Principles," 1882, p. 4.

64. Testimony of William McClelland, 27 Aug. 1883, Senate Committee on Education and Labor (1885), I, 680; testimony of Robert Howard, 25 Aug. 1883, *ibid.,* p. 656; letter from a "Boston Workingman," 23 Aug. 1883, *ibid.,* II, 388. See also New Jersey, Bureau of Industry and Labor, *Seventh Annual Report* (1884), p. 279.

65. *Interocean,* 11 Oct. 1884, p. 12; N. A. W. M., *Bulletin* (1882), p. 98; *Engineering and Mining Journal,* XXXIII (29 April 1882), 217.

66. Philadelphia *Times,* 8 June 1882, p. 2.

67. President's report, Amalgamated Association of Iron and Steel Workers, *Journal of Proceedings,* 7–16 Aug. 1883, Philadelphia, p. 1105.

68. *American Iron and Steel Bulletin,* 12 Sept. 1883, p. 252.

69. *American Iron and Steel Bulletin,* 1 Oct. 1884, p. 252; 29 Oct. 1884, p. 27; *Interocean,* 11 Oct. 1884, p. 12.

70. Compare Morris Heald, "Business Attitudes Toward Immigration," *Journal of Economic History,* XIII (Summer 1953), 295.

71. *Selected Writings of Abram S. Hewitt,* ed. Allan Nevins (New York, 1937), pp. 234–235.

72. Heald, *J. E. H.,* XIII, 293.

73. James Swank, Philadelphia, to Senator William Chandler, 5 Dec. 1892, L. C. Chandler Papers, Historical Society of Pennsylvania. Reference pointed out to me by Harry J. Brown.

74. *John Swinton's Paper,* 20 July 1884, p. 1; *American Iron and Steel Bulletin,* 29 Oct. 1884, p. 276.

75. *Congressional Record,* vol. XV, 48c., 1s., Pt. 5, pp. 5356, 5369, 5370; vol. XVI, 48c., 2s., Pt. 2, p. 1778.

76. *Congressional Record,* vol. XV, 48c., 1s., Pt. 5, pp. 5357, 5358, 5364, 5367; vol. XVI, Pt. 2, pp. 1632, 1781, 1833.

77. *Congressional Record,* vol. XVI, 48c., 1s., Pt. 2, pp. 1835–1836.

78. *Congressional Record,* vol. XVI, 48c., 1s., Pt. 2, pp. 1625, 1627.

79. Saulsbury of Delaware and McPherson of New Jersey joined this group.

80. *Congressional Record,* vol. XVI, 48c., 2s., Pt. 2, pp. 1787–1788, 1791, 1797, 1833, 1837.

81. *Congressional Record,* vol. XVI, 48c., 2s., Pt. 2, pp. 1631, 1632, 1793.

82. *Congressional Record,* vol. XVI, 48c., 2s., Pt. 2, pp. 1626, 1625.

83. *Biographical Encyclopedia of Connecticut and Rhode Island of the Nineteenth Century* (New York, 1881), p. 92.

84. W. S. Waudby, Knights of Labor, Assembly no. 66, Washington, D. C., to Senator Congar, 17 Jan. 1885, *Congressional Record*, vol. XVI, 48c., 2s., Pt. 2, p. 1633.

85. *Congressional Record*, vol. XVI, 48c., 2s., Pt. 2, p. 1786. See also *John Swinton's Paper*, 17 Aug. 1884, p. 2. For further direct pleas to Senator Blair from Powderly, see *Journal of United Labor*, 25 Jan. 1885, pp. 896–897.

86. *Congressional Record*, vol. XVI, 48c., 2s., Pt. 2, p. 1834.

87. See, for example, remarks of Senator Vest, *Congressional Record*, vol. XVI, 48c., 2s., Pt. 2, p. 1781.

88. *Congressional Record*, vol. XVI, 48c., 2s., Pt. 2, pp. 1628, 1785.

89. *United States Statutes at Large*, 48c., XXIII (1883–1885), 332–333.

90. F. O. T. L. U., Fifth Annual Session, *Report of Proceedings*, 8–11 Dec. 1885, p. 4.

91. U. S. Commissioner General of Immigration, *Annual Report* (1905), p. 44; (1904), p. 38.

92. *House Reports*, 48c., 1s., no. 444, II, 2, 9. For "citizens'" petitions, see *Congressional Record*, vol. XV, 48c., 1s., Pt. 1, pp. 906, 875, 974, 423; Pt. 2, pp. 1771, 1788, 1741, 1604, 1770, 1995, 1041, 1140, 1742. For pressure from state bureaus, see *Senate Miscellaneous Documents*, 44c., 1s., no. 96, 1876; *House Miscellaneous Documents*, 45c., 2s., no. 22, 4 March 1878; Library of Congress, *Miscellaneous Lists*, 1906–07, *Immigration*, p. 100; New Jersey, Bureau of Industry and Labor, *Seventh Annual Report* (1884), p. 278; Michigan, Bureau of Labor Statistics (1884), pp. 92–99; New York, Bureau of Labor Statistics, *Seventh Annual Report* (1884), pp. 279, 290, 292–293, 274–279, 199; *Eighth Annual Report* (1885), pp. 481–484, 485, 614, 487.

93. Knights of Labor, *Proceedings* (1885), p. 10.

94. Knights of Labor, *Proceedings* (1885), p. 16.

10. EXPERIMENTS WHICH FAILED

1. Testimony of Henry J. Jackson, Superintendent of the Immigrants' Landing Depot at Castle Garden, and Daniel Magone, Collector of the Port of New York, *Testimony Taken by the Ford Committee on Violations of the Contract Labor Prohibition Laws, House Miscellaneous Documents*, 50c., 1s., no. 572 (1889), pp. 419–420, 491–494, 548–549.

2. Testimony of Dr. Lorenzo Ullo, Legal Counsel, Immigration Bureau, U. S. *Reports of the Industrial Commission, Immigration*, XV (1901), 138–141.

3. Ruth Krouse, "Attitude of the American Federation of Labor Toward Immigration," M. A. Thesis (Columbia University, 1931), p. 4; U. S. *Statutes at Large*, 49c. (1885–1887), XXIV, 414–418.

4. U. S. *Statutes at Large*, 50c. (1887–1889), XV, 566–567.

5. Krouse, "Attitude of the A. F. of L. Toward Immigration," p. 6. U. S. *Statutes at Large*, vol. XXXIV, Pt. 1, p. 898.

6. U. S. Industrial Commission, XV (1898), lxi–lxii.

7. U. S. Commissioner General of Immigration, *Annual Report* (1910), 122.

8. Testimony submitted 16 Aug. 1888, *Ford Committee Report* (1889), p. 401.

9. Krouse, "Attitude of the A. F. of L.," p. 5.

10. *Report of the Immigration Investigating Commission to the Secretary of the Treasury* (Washington, 1895), pp. 20–21.

11. See Appendix IV.

12. See Appendix IV. Both Prescott Hall, Secretary of the Immigration Restriction League, and John R. Commons maintained that the law had been enforced chiefly against skilled labor from northwestern Europe. (See Hall's testimony, 8 April 1899, U. S. Industrial Commission, XV, 1901, p. 65. John R. Commons, *Races and Immigrants*, 1907, p. 118).

13. Testimony of William Weihe, 26 July 1899, U. S. Industrial Commission, XV (1901), 152; testimony of Edward Holman, Immigration Inspector, *ibid.*, p. 135; Report by Marcus Braun, Special Immigration Inspector, Commissioner General of Immigration, *Annual Report* (1903), pp. 91–92. See also *Reports* for 1905, pp. 44–46; 1908, pp. 122–123; 129–130; 1912, pp. 12–13; 1913, p. 204. Gompers held that such coaching should be made a misdemeanor (*Report of the Immigration Investigating Commission*, 1895, p. 36).

14. Testimony of T. J. Schaeffer, Amalgamated Association of Iron, Steel and Tin Workers, 23 Sept. 1899, U. S. *Reports of the Industrial Commission*, VII, *Capital and Labor* (1901), 394. Testimony of Romlan Doblar, Inspector of First and Second Class Passengers, 26 July 1899, U. S. Industrial Commission, XV (1901), 149.

15. Testimony of S. C. Wrightington, *Ford Committee Report* (1889), 548–549, 551; testimony of Jonas Denby, *ibid.*, p. 582.

16. Commissioner General of Immigration, *Annual Report* (1903), pp. 51–52; (1908), p. 133; (1909), p. 119.

17. U. S. Industrial Commission, XV (1901), 124–125.

18. Krouse, "Attitude of the A. F. of L.," p. 5; Robert Bandlow, Manager of Cleveland *Citizen*, organ of the Cleveland Central Labor Union, to Hon. Edward F. McSweeney, 21 July 1894, *Report of the Immigration Investigating. Commission* (1895), pp. 59–60. For example of a case delayed until all the witnesses had dispersed, see Ellsworth Coal Company case, begun Oct. 1903 and discontinued in Aug. 1905, Commissioner General of Immigration, *Annual Report* (1906), pp. 65–66.

19. Testimony of Dr. Lorenzo Ullo, U. S. Industrial Commission, XV (1901), 138.

20. Commissioner General of Immigration, *Annual Report* (1904), p. 39. For cases not prosecuted because of loopholes in contracts which were not expected to stand up in the courts, see U. S. Industrial Commission, XV, 669–670; Commissioner General of Immigration, *Annual Report* (1909), pp. 118–119. See also opinions in *U. S.* v. *Craig*, 28 F 795, 11 Oct. 1886; *U. S.* v. *Edgar*, 45 F 44, 29 Jan. 1891.

21. U. S. Industrial Commission, XV (1898), lix; *Report of the Immigration Investigating Commission* (1895), p. 41.

22. *Senate Executive Documents*, 53c., 2s. (1893–94), vol. IV, no. 102, pp. 3–8.

23. Commissioner General of Immigration, *Annual Report* (1904), p. 38.

24. Testimony of T. V. Powderly, U. S. Industrial Commission, XV (1901), 33, 44; Commissioner General of Immigration, *Annual Report* (1911), p. 131.

25. U. S. Industrial Commission, XV, 152–153.

26. U. S. *Statutes at Large*, 51C. (1889–1891), XVI, 1084–1087.

27. U. S. Industrial Commission, XV (1898), lix.

28. U. S. Industrial Commission, XV (1901), 138–141; Commissioner General of Immigration, *Annual Report* (1906), p. 66.

29. Testimony of William Weihe, U. S. Industrial Commission, XV, 152–153; Quinlan's testimony, *ibid.*, pp. 123–124; Commissioner General of Immigration, *Annual Report* (1907), pp. 125–126; 1910, pp. 122–123.

30. U. S. *Statutes at Large*, 51C. (1889–1891), XVI, 1084–1087.

31. Krouse, "Attitude of the A. F. of L.," p. 6.

32. U. S. *Statutes at Large*, vol. XXXIV, Pt. 1, p. 898.

33. "The Immigration Law and Its Violations," *American Federationist*, XIV (April 1907), 259–262.

34. Testimony of Samuel Gompers, 16 Aug. 1888, *Ford Committee Report* (1889), p. 402.

35. *U. S.* v. *Gay*, 95 G 226, 6 June 1899. See also *U. S.* v. *Laws*, 163 U. S. 258 and 16 Sup. Ct. 998. See also for discussion, U. S. Industrial Commission, XV, 652, 654; Commissioner General of Immigration, *Annual Report* (1903), pp. 40–41.

36. U. S. Industrial Commission, XV (1898), lx–lxi.

37. *U. S.* v. *Bromily*, 58 F 554, 23 Nov. 1893.

38. U. S. Industrial Commission, XV (1901), 668–669.

39. U. S. *Statutes at Large*, vol. XXXII, Pt. 1, p. 1213.

40. Commissioner General of Immigration, *Annual Report* (1905), p. 46; (1908), p. 133; (1909), pp. 119–120; (1910), pp. 123–124; (1911), pp. 128–129, 132.

41. *Annual Report* (1907), p. 70; "Protest Against Alien Contract Labor Decision," *American Federationist*, XIV (Aug. 1907), 550–555.

42. U. S. Industrial Commission, XV (1898), lviii.

43. Report of Commissioner Judson N. Cross, 20 Jan. 1892, U. S. *Letters from the Secretary of the Treasury Transmitting a Report of the Commissioners of Immigration upon the Causes which Incite Immigration into the United States* (Washington, 1892), I, 182–183.

44. Testimony of Matthes Wolfensperk, 8 Aug. 1888, *Ford Committee Report* (1889), pp. 229–231; Testimony of William Martin, *ibid.*, p. 511; Report from Consul F. B. Loomis, St. Etienne, U. S. Dept. of Treasury, *Causes Inciting Immigration*, I, 124; Report from Consul George Gifford, Basle, Switzerland, *ibid.*, p. 124.

45. Testimony of Paul Joseph F. Glinton, 8 Aug. 1888, *Ford Committee Report*, pp. 231–235; *U. S.* v. *McCallum*, 44 F 745, 16 Jan. 1891; U. S. Industrial Commission, XV (1901), 654.

46. *U. S.* v. *Bromily*, 58 F 554, 23 Nov. 1893. See also U. S. Industrial Commission, XV (1901), 668–669; U. S. Commissioner General of Immigration, *Annual Report* (1904), p. 4; (1910), pp. 123–124; (1909), p. 119; (1911), p. 132.

47. Of 231 cases instituted or pending during the five years from March 1889 to May 1894 only nine attempted to recover fines from railroad companies. All but one case, that of the Northern Pacific which paid a fine of $43, were dismissed for insufficient evidence (*Senate Executive Documents*, 53C., 2s., 1893–94, vol. IV, no. 102, pp. 3–8).

48. For example, see U. S. Commissioner General of Immigration, *Annual Report* (1908), pp. 131, 132; (1911), pp. 126–127, 128.

49. J. E. Conner, "Free Employment Offices in the United States," U. S. Bureau of Labor, *Bulletin*, vol. XIV (Jan. 1907), no. 68, p. 88.

50. T. V. Powderly, Scranton, to the Commission, 23 Aug. 1894, *Report of the Immigration Investigating Commission* (1895), p. 35.

51. Testimony of Powderly as Commissioner General of Immigration, 10 Feb. 1899, U. S. Industrial Commission, XV (1901), 39.

52. Conner, U. S. Bureau of Labor, *Bulletin*, XIV, 88–90.

53. Frances A. Kellor, *Out of Work* (New York, 1915), pp. 238–239; Edward T. Devine, *Report on the Desirability of Establishing an Employment Bureau in the City of New York* (New York, 1909), Russell Sage Foundation, pp. 159–160; Edwin H. Sutherland, *Unemployed and Public Employment Agencies* (University of Chicago Press, 1914), pp. 150–153, 162; Illinois, Bureau of Labor Statistics, *Tenth Annual Report* (1898), Pt. 2, pp. 46–47.

54. Grace Abbott, "The Chicago Unemployment Agency and the Immigrant Worker," *American Journal of Sociology*, XIV (Nov. 1908), 295; Illinois, Bureau of Labor Statistics, *Tenth Annual Report* (1898), Pt. 2, pp. 48–50.

55. Kellor, *Out of Work*, p. 157.

56. Sutherland, *Public Employment Agencies*, p. 111.

57. Abbott, *American Journal of Sociology*, XIV, 293. Compare Frank J. Sheridan, "Italian, Slavic and Hungarian Unskilled Immigrant Laborers in the United States," U. S. Bureau of Labor, *Bulletin*, vol. XV (Sept. 1907), no. 72, pp. 416–418.

58. Illinois, Free Employment Offices, *Thirteenth Annual Report* (1911), p. 8.

59. Sutherland, *Public Employment Agencies*, p. 150; Conner, U. S. Bureau of Labor, *Bulletin*, vol. XIV, no. 68, p. 57; Illinois, Bureau of Labor Statistics, *Tenth Annual Report* (1898), Pt. 2, p. 96.

60. Sutherland, *Public Employment Agencies*, p. 161.

61 Conner, U. S. Bureau of Labor, *Bulletin*, XIV, 88–90; Illinois, Free Employment Offices, *Sixth Annual Report* (1904), p. 4.

62. Conner, pp. 90–94; Sutherland, p. 154.

63. Sutherland, p. 125.

64. Kellor, *Out of Work*, p. 154; E. L. Bogart, "Public Employment Offices," *Quarterly Journal of Economics*, XIX (May 1900), 364–365.

65. New York Commissioner of Labor, *Fifth Annual Report* (1905), Pt. 1, pp. 14–17; Bogart, *Quarterly Journal of Economics*, XIX, 351, 353, 364–365.

66. Illinois, Free Employment Offices, *Thirteenth Annual Report* (1911), pp. 8, 109–110.

67. *Thirteenth Annual Report*, p. 8; *Fourteenth Annual Report* (1912), p. 5. New York Commissioner of Labor, *First Annual Report* (1901), p. 25; Abbott, *American Journal of Sociology*, XIV, 294.

68. Illinois, Free Employment Offices, *Seventh Annual Report* (1905), p. 71.

69. Devine, *Report on Establishing an Employment Bureau in New York*, p. 183.

70. Bogart, *Quarterly Journal of Economics,* XIX, 355; Conner, U. S. Bureau of Labor, *Bulletin,* vol. XIV, no. 68, p. 76; Lindley L. Clark, "Legal Status of Organized Labor," *Journal of Political Economy,* XIII (March 1905), 175–176; Illinois, Free Employment Offices, *Sixth Annual Report* (1904), p. 3.

71. *Matthews* v. *People.* 67 N. E. Rep. 28.

72. Kellor, *Out of Work,* p. 333.

73. Kellor, p. 333; Sutherland, *Public Employment Agencies,* pp. 151, 168; Conner, U. S. Bureau of Labor, *Bulletin,* XIV, 13, 37, 47.

74. Conner, pp. 73–74.

75. Conner, pp. 90–94; Devine, *Report on Employment Bureau,* p. 161; Sutherland, *Public Employment Agencies,* p. 153; Kellor, *Out of Work,* pp. 241–242.

76. Frances Kellor maintained that the greatest single element delaying the extension of public employment offices was the fear of their partisan use in strikes (*Out of Work,* p. 333).

77. Sheridan, U. S. Bureau of Labor, *Bulletin,* vol. XV, no. 72, p. 423.

78. Sheridan, *Bulletin* XV, no. 72, pp. 423–424. Testimony of Theodor Ritter, Manager, Austro-Hungarian Home of New York, 21 May 1901, U. S. Industrial Commission, XV (1901), 219–221.

79. Conner, U. S. Bureau of Labor, *Bulletin,* XIV, 104–105; Devine, p. 14.

80. Devine, p. 117. Kellor, *Out of Work,* p. 272. Sutherland, *Public Employment Agencies,* pp. 109–110.

81. Devine, pp. 113–114.

82. Commissioner General of Immigration, *Annual Report* (1912), pp. 209–210; (1913), pp. 160–164; (1914), pp. 16–20.

83. Immigration Law of 1907, Section 40, U. S. *Statutes at Large,* vol. XXXIV, Pt. 1, p. 898.

84. See Appendix V.

85. Commissioner General of Immigration, *Annual Report* (1909), p. 219; (1913), p. 160; (1914), pp. 169–186.

86. *Annual Report* (1910), pp. 229–241.

87. See Appendix V.

88. Commissioner General of Immigration, *Annual Report* (1909), p. 234; (1911), pp. 247–248.

89. *Annual Report* (1912), p. 219.

90. *Annual Report* (1914), p. 20.

91. *Annual Report* (1908), pp. 175, 179, 180–181, 241.

92. *Annual Report,* p. 173; T. V. Powderly, Washington, to Samuel Gompers, 9 July 1907; T. V. Powderly to John Roach, Secretary, Amalgamated Leather Workers Union of North America, 8 July 1907, both letters printed in "For Better Distribution of Immigrants," *American Federationist,* XIV (August 1907), 556–557.

93. Samuel Gompers to T. V. Powderly, 10 July 1907, *American Federationist,* XIV, 558.

94. Commissioner General of Immigration, *Annual Report* (1909), p. 234.

95. Devine, *Report on Employment Bureau,* pp. 16–17.

96. Commons, *Races and Immigrants,* pp. 115–116n.

97. Resolution no. 77 at Annual Convention, Toronto, Nov. 1909, *American Federationist,* XVIII (Jan. 1911), 17.

98. "Schemes to Distribute Immigrants," *American Federationist,* XVIII (July 1911), 513–558; Sutherland, *Public Employment Agencies,* p. 152; Krouse, "Attitude of the A. F. of L.," p. 18.

99. Kellor, *Out of Work,* pp. 238–239.

100. Compare Sutherland, *Public Employment Agencies,* p. 153.

101. See testimony of G. W. Perkins, President of the Cigar Makers International Union, 5 May 1899, U. S. *Reports of the Industrial Commission,* VII, *Capital and Labor* (Washington, 1900), 179–180.

102. Krouse, "Attitude of the A. F. of L.," pp. 8–10.

INDEX

257